U.S.-China Relations and the Changing Security Dynamics in East Asia

Editor

Da-Jung Li

Tamkang University Press

U.S.-China Relations and the Changing Security Dynamics in East Asia

Editor

Da-Jung Li

ISBN: 978-986-5608-68-2

Published in Taiwan by
Tamkang University Press
151, Yingzhuan Rd., Tamsui Dist., New Taipei City 25137, R.O.C.
Tel: 886-2-8631-8661; Fax: 886-2-8631-8660
http://www.tkupress.tku.edu.tw/
E-mail: tkupress@www2.tku.edu.tw

Preface

The Graduate Institute of International Affairs and Strategic Studies (GIIASS) was established on March 23, 1982. Thereafter directors and dedicated professors have enriched teaching towards academic success. In 2004, GIIASS established "Memorial Conference for Professor Niu Sien-Chong" to advance domestic strategic studies. In 2010, former Director Dr. Wong Ming-Hsien explored the prospect of creating Tamkang School of Strategic Studies, and to broaden the establishment of academic conference. When I recall my predecessors' endeavors, it motivates me to carry forward our achievements.

Tamkang School of Strategic Studies 2016 Annual Events include topics , such as "U.S.-China Relations and the Changing Security Dynamics in East Asia" and "Rethinking the National Security of Taiwan: Theoretical Dialectics, Opportunities and Challenges". These topics focus on the competition between China and the US, and National Security of Taiwan in the 21 century. Since China raised "One Belt, One Road" in 2013, Beijing is better equipped to influence not only Asia's development but also global affairs. For Taiwan, national security is of utmost importance. Hence, we have to assess the U.S.-China competition carefully and comprehensively.

For aforementioned reasons, this book collects 9 papers which were presented at the annual conference. The papers' areas of investigation are U.S.-China relations, Asia Pacific Security, etc. Our goal is not only to describe and explain developments in international affairs, but also to find an alternative way to accomplish peace in the changing world.

As the editor in chief, I want to thank those who have helped to realize this publication of Tamkang School of Strategic Studies: U.S.-China Relations and the Changing Security Dynamics in East Asia. Firstly, we appreciate all local and foreign panelists' contributions. In addition, we are grateful to Dr. Flora Chang, President of TKU who has encouraged the publication. Furthermore, Dr. Lin Sinn-Cheng, Director of Center for Publication of TKU and his staff, Ms. Wu Chiu-Shya, Ms. Chang Yu-Lun and Ms. Chen Hui-Chi, helped smooth the publishing process. Also, I appreciate Assistant Professor York Chen's support, who has helped to articulate and advance our institute's academic achievements. Last but not least, thanks go to our assistant of the GIIASS Jasmine Chen, Ph.D. candidate Jiang Yu-Jen, Ph.D. student Cheng Chih-Huai, and graduate student Chao Shih-Chun took on arduous administrative responsibility with blithesome success.

This year, GIIASS celebrates 35th anniversary. I would like to dedicate this book to those who have been contributing to GIIASS. Furthermore, I expect that we not only maintain the key position in Taiwan's academia, but also create higher value for Taiwan's education, politics and environment.

Dr. Da-Jung Li

Director, Graduate Institute of International Affairs and Strategic Studies, Tamkang University

Contents

Crossing the Divide?
Challenges to a "New Type" of U.S.-China Relationship

Ming-Yen Tsai[*]

I. Introduction

The U.S.-China bilateral relationship is currently lying in a sensitive and shifting period. When both countries share common concerns on the maintenance of stable and predictable bilateral relations, strategic distrust between them has reached a historical new height. In 2012, then Chinese Vice President Xi Jinping proposed that the U.S. and China should build a "new type of great power relations." From Beijing's perspective, it is reasonable to demand U.S. acceptance of a rising China as a prime power in the Asia-Pacific region without excessive responsibilities, power competitions and potential conflicts. But Washington has no interest in following China's proposal unless Beijing can demonstrate its strong commitments to abide by global norms and shoulder international responsibilities.[1]

This development has highlighted several important questions to answer. Why is China so enthusiastic about a "new type of great power relations"? Why is the U.S. reluctant to adopt Beijing's idea? What are the major challenges to the proposal for a "new type of great power relations"? And what will be the characteristics of the U.S.-China relationship in the near future? To answer these questions, this paper will start with examining the rationale behind China's proposal for a "new type of great power

---

*   Professor, Graduate Institute of International Politics, National Chung Hsing University, Taiwan.

1   Daniel Blumenthal, "Old Type Great Power Relations," *Foreign Policy*, February 11, 2015, <http://foreignpolicy.com/2015/02/11/old-type-great-power-relations/>.

relations". It then moves to explore the strategic distrust, economic contests, and military competitions between these two giants. Lastly, this paper will conclude by arguing that Washington and Beijing retain the important consensus on a stable American-Sino relationship; however, the logic of "power transition" between declining and rising powers appears to prevent Washington and Beijing from moving closer with mutual trust.

II. Divergent Concerns and Interpretations about the "New Type"

It is no surprise that the United States and China which have different political systems, cultural traditions, security concerns and economic interests may have disagreements and misunderstandings. Washington and Beijing regard it as important to prevent a single issue or any specific dispute from undermining the overall bilateral relationship between them. How to explore new methods to control and manage divergences has become a crucial concern to political leaders in Washington and China.[2]

During a 2012 meeting with U.S. President Barack Obama, then Chinese Vice President Xi Jinping proposed building a "new type of great power relations" between China and the United States. A big push for the United States to agree to this concept came in 2013 when Xi Jinping came to power and met with Obama at Sunnylands. At this meeting, Xi Jinping defined "new type of great power relations" in three points: (1) no conflict or confrontation, through emphasizing dialogue and treating each other's strategic intentions objectively; (2) mutual respect, including for each other's core interests and major concerns; and (3) mutually beneficial cooperation, by abandoning the zero-sum game mentality and advancing areas of mutual

---

2   Su Ge, "A New Relationship Model: Xi's Upcoming U.S. Trip is Vital for Bilateral Ties," *Beijing Review*, September 17, 2015, <http://www.bjreview.com/World/201509/t20150917_800038580.html>.

interest.[3]

Several key implications can be found from the definitions offered by Xi Jinping. First, Xi Jinping's interpretation of "new type of great power relations" reflects that China wants equal status with the United States as superpower. The term "great power relations" is designed to win Washington's recognition of China's rising power status, with the aim to achieve "parity" and "mutual respect" between the two countries.[4]

Second, Beijing wants the U.S. recognize its "core interests" so as to build a new code of conduct in line with China's interests. By stressing the mutual respect of "core interests," China put great emphasis on the importance of protecting its territorial and sovereign claims. Washington's acceptance of this idea will imply that the United States adopts China's "core interests" and will not interfere in China's sovereign disputes with its neighbors.[5]

Third, China's proposal for a "new type of great power relations" can help to achieve domestic political goals. The Chinese media extensively reporting on the concept of "new type of great power relations" is to strengthen Beijing's view of itself as a respected "great power." As such, Beijing will be able to foster stronger nationalistic pride under the Xi Jinping leadership and gain political capital to consolidate his power base at home.[6]

---

3   The White House Office of the Press Secretary, "Remarks by President Obama and President Xi Jinping of the People's Republic of China After Bilateral Meeting," June 8, 2013, <https://www.whitehouse.gov/the-press-office/2013/06/08/remarks-president-obama-and-president-xi-jinping-peoples-republic-china->.

4   Cheng Li and Lucy Xu, "Chinese Enthusiasm and American Cynicism over the 'New Type of Great Power Relations,'" *The Brookings Institution*, December 4, 2014, <http://www.brookings.edu/research/opinions/2014/12/05-chinese-pessimism-american-cynicism-great-power-li-xu>.

5   Ibid.

6   Jimin Chen, "China-US: Obstacles to a 'New Type of Major Power Relations,'" *The Diplomat*, April 9, 2015, <http://thediplomat.com/2015/04/china-us-obstacles-to-a-new-type-of-major-power-relations/>.

On its part, Washington views Beijing's proposal with suspicions and has different views on the concept of "new type of great power relations."

Washington's first concern is that China's expectations for an "equal status" with the U.S. may hurt the American leadership in Asia. Xi Jinping has issued public statements to dismiss the U.S. role in Asia by arguing that the United States is not an Asian country and thus has no right to interfere in regional affairs. Xi Jinping also criticizes the U.S. dominated alliance system as "destabilizing" for Asian security environment and asks the U.S. alliance network to make more rooms for China's rise.[7] Meanwhile, Xi proposes that "the Pacific Ocean is big enough to accommodate both the United States and China."[8] It implies that the United States should content itself with the eastern half of the Pacific and stop competing with China in the western half.

Meanwhile, the U.S. believes "mutual respect" actually means that the U.S. has to recognize China's "core interests." By highlighting the mutual respect of core interests, Beijing wants to gain official American recognition of Chinese disputed territorial claims in both East and South China Seas. Japan and ASEAN countries like the Philippines and Vietnam worry that Washington's acceptance of China's "core interests" will encourage Beijing to take military adventurism in the East and South China Seas. Once Washington agrees with China's "core interests," the U.S. security commitments to its regional allies and alliance cooperative networks in Asia will be badly shaken.[9]

Accordingly, Washington regards China's "core interests" as

7　Yun Sun, "China's Preferred World Order: What Does China Want?" PacNet, No.62, September 21, 2015, pp.1-2.

8　The White House Office of the Press Secretary, "Remarks by President Obama and President Xi Jinping in Joint Press Conference," November 12, 2014, <https://www. whitehouse.gov/the-press-office/2014/11/12/remarks-president-obama-and-president-xi-jinping-joint-press-conference>.

9　Li and Xu, "Chinese Enthusiasm and American Cynicism over the 'New Type of Great Power Relations.'"

controversial. In 2014, Evan Medeiros, Senior Director of U.S. National Security Council, pointed out that "Some in China say that in order to build this new model, the United States must accept and accommodate China's core interests. That's their definition. We simply have a different view. We think there's too much of a focus in the U.S.-China relationship on China's core interests. We spent far too much time talking about this issue. We need to focus less on core interests and we need to focus more on common interests and ways in which we are acting together to solve those critical regional and global challenges that are consistent with all of our interests."[10]

Furthermore, Washington cast doubts over Beijing's long-term strategic intentions. After Xi Jinping took office, China's revisionist tendency has accelerated. By lifting the banner of "the great rejuvenation of the Chinese nation" (中華民族偉大復興) and "China dream" (中國夢), Xi has shifted China's foreign policy line from the old formula of "keeping a low profile" (韜光養晦) to a new one of "progressively making achievements" (奮發有為). In order to search for "more influence," "more respect" and "more space, China has become more and more active to take assertive policies toward the outside world.[11]

It is true that Washington and Beijing have a consensus on the stability of their bilateral relations. Nevertheless, they have different expectations for how to achieve this goal. By proposing a "new type of great power relations," China expects to outline the basic principles for the direction of U.S.-China bilateral relations - "no conflict or confrontation," "mutual respect," and "beneficial cooperation." By contrast, the United States prefers to start with reviewing the priority concerns and issues, then reaches a consensus to resolve the existing disputes over such key issues as Asian maritime disputes, cyber security, human rights, and China's military transparency. In other words, Beijing pays attentions to the macro principles

---

10   Chen, "China-US: Obstacles to a 'New Type of Major Power Relations.'"
11   Sun, "China's Preferred World Order: What Does China Want?"

for the U.S.-China relationship, while Washington focuses more on concrete cooperation on specific issues.[12]

It is clear that Washington and Beijing have different interpretations about the concept of "new type of great power relations." These divergences result from their opposite concerns about what a "new type" of bilateral relations should be developed. When China put great emphasis on "equal status" and "mutual respect of core interests," the United States pays concerns to China's potential intentions to challenge the status quo and dismiss the American leading role in Asia.

III. American-Sino Strategic Distrust

In spite of their expectations for a stable relationship, the U.S. and China are suspicious of the other side's political and strategic intentions. Three aspects of China's suspicions can be summarized as the followings:[13]

In the first place, China is one of the few surviving communist states and the Chinese Communist Party regards it as crucial to prevent any ideological threats to its survival. From the Chinese perspective, the U.S. proposals to promote liberal democracy, respect for human rights, and abide by the rule of law are designed to destabilize the Communist China. In particular, China has successfully created a successful development model that provides an alternative to Western democracy and experiences for the developing countries to copy. It is believed in China that United States attempts to prevent China from becoming an emerging power in order to maintain the U.S. political and economic dominance in the world platform.

In the second place, the U.S. military primacy in the Asia-Pacific region

---

12   Chen, "China-US: Obstacles to a 'New Type of Major Power Relations.'"

13   Kenneth Lieberthal and Wang Jisi, "Addressing U.S.-China Strategic Distrust," *John L. Thornton China Center Monograph Series*, No.4 (March 2012), pp.7-19.

has constrained China's freedom of action in dealing with issues that is regarded as crucial for China's sovereignty, such as Taiwan and the disputes in the East and South China Seas. The U.S. Navy and Air Force have intensified their close-in surveillance activities against China. Beijing views these military activities as provocative actions to constrain China's efforts to project its air and naval forces into the surrounding areas.

In the third place, there are strong voices in China, arguing that the United States is trying to carry out diplomatic and military containment against China. Guided by the strategy of "rebalancing," the United States has strengthened security and defense cooperation with China's neighboring countries, such as Japan, India, the Philippines, and Vietnam. Washington's latest actions to implement joint naval exercises, regular maritime patrols, and intensified military deployments in Asia are mainly targeted at China. The U.S. decisions to step into the South China Sea territorial disputes by asserting "freedom of navigation" is to weaken Beijing's sovereign claims which are important part of China's "core interests."

On its part, the United States has similar apprehensions about China. Washington fears that the balance of military power in Asia is now shifting and China may use military muscle to protect its sovereignty and maritime rights in the Asia-Pacific region. China's has invested more and more resources to improve its air and naval projection capabilities in the Western Pacific by acquiring new types of ballistic missiles, stealth fighters, and aircraft carriers. These weapon systems can serve to constrict U.S. military flexibility and deny U.S. forces access to the maritime area beyond China's territorial waters.[14]

Washington is also concerned about China's intentions to challenge the leading role of the United States in world affairs. China currently views itself as Number Two great power in the world and believes that the U.S. is a

---

14　The U.S. DoD, *Annual Report to Congress: Military and Security Developments Involving the People's Republic of China 2015*, April 2015, p.33.

declining superpower. As China's economic and military power continues to grow, Beijing will challenge the U.S. dominant security and economic orders in Asia step by step.[15] So far China has not only competed with the United States in international financial norms, but also created a different economic and political system to lure the supports from the developing countries around the world.[16]

Moreover, the United States worries that China will continue to conduct economic and technological competition on an unfair basis. China-based cyber operations have targeted against sensitive American capabilities and copy highly important military, diplomatic, and commercial data. The growing cyber threats from China have warranted strategic distrust on the U.S. side. In the National Security Strategy of 2015, the Obama administration voices its concerns over this issue by stating that "On cybersecurity, we will take necessary actions to protect our businesses and defend our networks against cyber-theft of trade secrets for commercial gain whether by private actors or the Chinese government."[17] It is the very first time that the U.S. government publically views China as a country that create serious cyber threats to the U.S. in such important official document.

To be sure, the U.S.-China relationship is changing rapidly in the aftermath of China's rise. In the absence of a vision of a shared values and interests, there will be uncertainties for the management of American-Sino relations, providing the grounds for fear and mistrust. Kenneth Lieberthal and Wang Jisi are rightly to highlight the problems with "strategic distrust" between the United States and China: "Strategic distrust... means a perception that the other side will seek to achieve its key long-term goals at concerted cost to your own side's core prospects and interests. The major

---

15 Lieberthal and Wang, "Addressing U.S.-China Strategic Distrust," p.22.

16 David Hollowaya and Cui Leib, "U.S.-China Relations in the Shadow of the Future," *Dynamics of Asymmetric Conflict*, Vol.7, Issue 4 (November 2014), pp.1-13.

17 The White House, *National Security Strategy*, February 2015, p.24.

concern is that it appears as of 2012 that strategic distrust is growing on both sides and that this perception can, if it festers, create a self-fulfilling prophecy of overall mutual antagonism."[18]

Strategic distrust has become an obstacle for the U.S. and China to set up policy agendas for managing their bilateral relations. The U.S. concerns focus mainly on such issues as climate change, nonproliferation, global growth, cyber security, and maritime security. Yet, the major task of China's foreign policy is to promote its international influence and safeguard this country's "core interests." The U.S. concerns over the global and regional challenges may be important for China; however, many of them are not the most pressing issues for China to handle. The Chinese side has argued that "to set the agenda solely from the perspective of the United States is not in China's interest, nor is it conducive to the development of bilateral relations."[19]

After the Obama-Xi summit of September 2015, China's "outcomes document" highlights the importance of "new type of great power relations," which is regarded by Xi Jinping as the priority of China's policy towards the United States. Nevertheless, the American side mentions nothing related to "major power relations" or any sort of "new model" in the "fact sheet" of this summit.[20] Clearly, Chinese concept of "new type of great power relations" got a quite cold response from the United States. The Obama administration has consistently refused to use "new type of great power relations" in official documents with the aim not to endorse China's assertiveness.

---

18   Lieberthal and Wang, "Addressing U.S.-China Strategic Distrust," p.5.

19   Chen, "China-US: Obstacles to a 'New Type of Major Power Relations.'"

20   Bonnie S. Glaser and Hannah Hindel, "A Tale of Two Documents: US and Chinese Summit Readouts," *China Brief*, Vol.15, Issue 20 (2015), pp.3-6.

IV. China's Challenges to Global Financial Institutions

Conflicting interests exist between the U.S. and China reflected not only in political ideology and strategic concerns, but also in international finance and economics. Although China has become increasingly integrated into the world market, Beijing is not entirely pleased with its position in the existing system. As a result, China has decided to develop alternative institutions for global financial governance by pushing for the creation of a BRICS Development Bank and Asian Infrastructure Investment Bank (AIIB).

In last decades, China has accumulated vast foreign exchange reserves and is becoming a major supplier of capital. China believes that its growing economic power will help to improve its political and economic status around the world, particularly in Asia. The AIIB is the realization of a long push by China to rewrite the rules of global economic and financial governance. Beijing has promised to provide half of the AIIB's $50 billion start-up capital to build more ports, roads, and other infrastructure across the region. The establishment of AIIB is to support the Chinese "One Belt, One Road Initiative" that aims to strengthen infrastructure both on the westward land route from China through Central Asia and on the southern maritime routes from China through Southeast Asia, South Asia, Africa, and Europe. If the AIIB can operate successfully, it will lend $20 billion per year. In five years, the AIIB will be able to reach the same scale compared to the World Bank's lending.[21]

A successful AIIB could pose a direct challenge to the traditional primacy of U.S.-dominated financial institutions, including the International Monetary Fund (IMF), World Bank (WB) and Asian Development Bank (ADB). Thus, Washington sought to discourage its allies from joining the AIIB. Even so, major American allies, such as the United Kingdom,

---

21   David Dollar, "China's Rise as A Regional and Global Power: The AIIB and the 'One Belt, One Road,'" *The Brookings Institution*, Summer 2015, <http://www.brookings.edu/research/papers/2015/07/china-regional-global-power-dollar>.

Australia, and South Korea, still announced to join the Chinese initiative.[22] The United States has voiced its concerns about governance standards at Beijing-proposed new institutions. Washington fears that the large share of the voting rights in the new institutions will be controlled by Beijing and the new institutions' decisions to lend for projects will not meet the social and environmental criteria currently employed by the U.S.-led multilateral development banks.[23]

Another fear is that the new institutions will be used to enhance China's leadership at the expense of the United States and its partners in Asia including Japan, India and Australia. As a result, Washington has sought to promote its initiative on the Trans-Pacific Partnership (TPP). After five years of tough negotiations between 12 countries that represent 40 percent of global trade, the TPP was finally signed on October 5, 2015. The TPP's 12 signatory countries include the U.S., Canada, Japan, Chile, Peru, New Zealand, Australia, Brunei, Malaysia, Vietnam, and Singapore. The deal will expedite economic integration in Asia, but it will also intensify the competition between the U.S. and China. On commenting the completion of the TPP talks, President Obama made it clear by saying: "we can't let countries like China write the rules of the global economy. We should write those rules, opening new markets to American products while setting high standards for protecting workers and preserving our environment."[24]

The establishment of the AIIB symbolizes Beijing's growing influence and ability to shape the rules of the investment and financial operations

---

22　John Kemp, "China's Silk Road Challenges U.S. Dominance in Asia," *Reuters*, November 10, 2014, via < http://www.reuters.com/article/china-apec-silkroad-idUSL6N0T03CY20141110>; Policy Department of Directorate General for External Policies, China's Foreign Policy and external Relations, European Parliament, July 2015, pp.18-19.

23　Kemp, "China's Silk Road Challenges U.S. Dominance in Asia."

24　The White House Office of the Press Secretary, "Statement by the President on the Trans-Pacific Partnership," October 05, 2015, < https://www.whitehouse.gov/the-press-office/2015/10/05/statement-president-trans-pacific-partnership >.

in Asia. One the other hand, the TPP also marks a diplomatic victory for the United States by creating a substantial economic bloc that helps to counter China's economic dominance in Asia. As a pillar of Washington's "rebalancing" towards Asia, the TPP is expected to enlarge its participating countries by US $285 billion benefits by 2025. It is estimated that the TPP's signatories such as Vietnam, Malaysia and New Zealand will be able to create big increases for their GDP growth, while Japan, Malaysia and Vietnam are going to achieve increased exports.[25]

A trade bloc in Asia promoted by the U.S. that excludes China makes Beijing feeling insecure. Therefore, during the years of TPP negotiations, Beijing has been pursuing its own trade architectures in Asia. These include the less ambitious Regional Comprehensive Economic Partnership (RCEP), which will exclude the U.S. but include ASEAN states, India, Japan, Australia, New Zealand, and South Korea. Chinese leaders have expressed their hope to conclude RCEP negotiations by the end of 2016 so as to reduce some of TPP's negative impact on China's economic development, estimated a big income loss between US $47 to $89 billion.[26]

In the aftermath of globalization, the existing institutions that manage the international economy and finance such as IMF, WB and ADB are now under strain. In China, many believe that globalization has entered into a third phase. The first phase was dominated by Great Britain and the second one by the United States. This current third phase is complicated and will be dominated by both established economies and newly emerging economics.[27]

This argument offers a reasonable position for China to establish

---

25   Michal Meidan, "The TPP and China: The Elephant That Wasn't in the Room," The Diplomat, October 15, 2015, <http://thediplomat.com/2015/10/the-tpp-and-china-the-elephant-that-wasnt-in-the-room/>.

26   Ibid.

27   Amy Studdart and Ye Yu, "The United States and China in the Global Economic Order," Center for Strategic and International Studies, September 2015, < http://csis.org/files/publication/150928_Studdart_USChinaGlobalEconOrder_Web.pdf >.

alternative institutions for the U.S.-led global financial governance system. It should be noted that there are three pillars of the existing global economic order - trade, international finance, and development. In terms of trade, the United States and China are pursuing separate regional agreements for free trade cooperation in Asia. In the field of international finance, Beijing's establishment of the AIIB has become a source of tension between the U.S. and China for competing financial norms and rules. As for development, China provides the developing countries with an alternative model that focuses on infrastructural building and economic growth, while the U.S. emphasizes the importance of good governance on human rights and environmental protection.[28]

As the balance of power within the global economy shifts, it is inevitable that established economic power and newly emerging economic power will compete for the dominance of international economic and financial orders. Obviously, Washington and Beijing have structural and perceived differences in their economic and strategic calculations. And the contests for trade and financial architectures have become crucial parts of mounting economic, political and military competitions between the United States and China across the region.

V. Competitions for Asia's Military Primacy

The military competitions between the United States and China are now rising up when the gap of their power relations is continuing to narrow down. The emerging pattern of Sino-US military interactions can be symbolized as "cold confrontation" between an existing superpower and a rising great power.[29]

---

28 Ibid.
29 Chintamani Mahapatra, "China and Air Defence Identification Zone (ADIZ): Cold Confrontation with the US?" *Institute of Peace and Conflict Studies*, December 10, 2013.

In the last decade, the U.S. strategic and defense planners have been carefully watching China's military modernization programs, particularly its capacity to project air and naval forces into the periphery areas. The United States worries that the PLA has been striving hard to acquire "anti-access/area denial" (A2/AD) capabilities that seek to counter against the rapid mobility of the U.S. navy and air force in the Asia Pacific region. Key systems that have been deployed or are under development include ballistic missiles, anti-ship and land-attack cruise missiles, nuclear submarines, modern surface ships, and aircraft carriers.[30]

Military competitions between the United States and China have further complicated due to the deterioration of China's maritime territorial disputes with the neighboring states. In a search for securing its position in Asia, China has become increasingly assertive to defend its sovereignty claims and maritime rights over the East and South China Seas.

In the East China Sea, the Senkaku/Diaoyu Islands are vital for China's territorial integrity. Also, the disputes of the Senkaku/Diaoyu Islands overlap with historical controversies between China and Japan that involve in a nationalistic and anti-Japanese discourse.[31]

On November 23, 2013, China declared to establish the air defense identification zone (ADIZ) over the East China Sea. The first ADIZ of China has shocked the surrounding countries as it covers the disputed Senkaku/Diaoyu Islands and overlaps with the existing ADIZs already established by Japan, South Korea and Taiwan. According to China's Ministry of National Defense, the establishment of the East China Sea ADIZ is "necessary measures for China to protect its state sovereignty and territory and airspace security." Beijing also warned that "China's armed forces will adopt

---

30 The U.S. DoD, *Annual Report to Congress: Military and Security Developments Involving the People's Republic of China 2015*, p.31.

31 Che-po Chan and Brian Bridges, "China, Japan, and the Clash of Nationalsims," *Asian Perspective*, Vol.30, No.1 (2006), pp.127-156.

defensive emergency measures to respond to aircraft that do not cooperate in the identification."[32]

China's East China Sea ADIZ suggests that China is seeking to show its military muscle to coerce the Japanese government into making concessions on territorial disputes. There are reasons to argue the Chinese ADIZ establishment is one part of a deliberate strategy to bolster Beijing's sovereignty claims, promote Chinese air and maritime control over the East China Sea and the surrounding airspace, and consolidate Xi Jinping's power base at home.[33]

China's increasing intentions and capabilities to pursue domination over its near-seas region have created significant impacts on the security environment of the Asia-Pacific region. In the face of China's assertiveness, U.S. Defense Secretary Chuck Hagel stressed that "we view this development as a destabilizing attempt to alter the status quo in the region. This unilateral action increases the risk of misunderstanding and miscalculations." Meanwhile, Hagel reaffirmed U.S. policy that Article V of the U.S.-Japan Mutual Defense Treaty applies to the Senkaku/Diaoyu Islands.[34]

Meanwhile, Washington has decided to respond to China's assertiveness by moving advanced weapon systems into Asia. Many of these capabilities will be placed in Japan and will be integrated into a strengthened and deepened U.S.-Japan alliance networks. The first F-35s are deployed into

---

32   Xinhua, "China Justifies Its Air Defense Identification Zone," *Chinadaily* USA, December 3, 2013, < http://usa.chinadaily.com.cn/china/2013-12/03/content_17149589.htm >

33   Nicholas Szechenyi, Victor Cha, Bonnie S. Glaser, Michael J. Green, Christopher K. Johnson, "China's Air Defense Identification Zone: Impact on Regional Security," *Center for Strategic and International Studies*, November 26, 2013.

34   U.S. Department of Defense, "Hagel Issues Statement on East China Sea Air Defense Identification Zone," November 23, 2013, *DoD News*, < http://archive.defense.gov/news/newsarticle.aspx?id=121223>.

Japan to improve Japan's capabilities of air force. The United States has also deployed V-22 Ospreys and the new P-8 Poseidon anti-submarine warfare aircraft to Okinawa in Japan.[35]

Apart from the East China Sea disputes, the South China Sea is another hot spot of China's sovereignty claims and maritime power expansion. China claims sovereignty over islands and exclusive control over maritime zones that are also vindicated by other states in the region. Beijing has taken a number of disturbing actions to protect its sovereignty over the South China Sea. These have included: the expulsion of Philippine vessels from the surrounding waters of Scarborough Shoal in 2011 and Second Thomas Shoal in 2013; the deployment of a deep-water oil exploration rig into the disputed waters with Vietnam in May 2014; and the periodical harassments of U.S. Navy ships exercising "freedom of navigation" deployments outside of Chinese territorial waters.[36]

In early 2015, China's land reclamation activities in the South China Sea attracted increasing concerns from neighboring countries. According to estimates, China's rapidly expanding land reclamation totals more than 2,000 acres in the South China Sea. China's island building activities are designed to boost claims and enhance power projection, with forward airfields and supply bases for patrol vessels and warships. It is reported that China has started to deploy advanced radars and HQ-9 air defense systems on its artificial islands.[37] In May 2015, two large artillery vehicles were detected on one of the artificial islands China is creating in the South China Sea. Many analysts have voiced their concerns on China's "salami-slicing"

---

35   Ida Torres, "Osprey Training To Be Relocated Outside Okinawa," *The Japan Daily Press*, April 17, 2014, < http://japandailypress.com/osprey-training-to-be-relocated-outside-okinawa-1747382/>.

36   Patrick M. Cronin et al., *Tailored Coercion: Competition and Risk in Maritime Asia* (Washington, DC: Center for New American Security, 2014), p.11.

37   "Asia Maritime Transparency Initiative," *Center for Strategic and International Studies*, < http://amti.csis.org/another-piece-of-the-puzzle/>.

strategy which employs a series of incremental actions to gradually change the status quo in China's favor.[38]

Although it is not a party to the sovereign disputes in the South China Sea, Washington has repeatedly emphasized that the South China Sea issues are related to its national vital interests. To prevent the situation in the area from getting worse, the United States has proposed that all relevant parties should seek a peaceful and multilateral resolution to the disputes based on international law. Washington has also encourages related states to reach consensus on the establishment of "code of conduct" in the South China Sea. To deter China from moving towards coercive diplomacy, the United States has promised to honor its mutual defense pact with Manila and increase its defense presence by conducting joint military exercises with the Philippines and Vietnam. Moreover, Washington has announced the plans for an expanded U.S. Marine presence in Australia to promote the U.S. capabilities and cope with any contingencies in the South China Sea.[39]

On its part, Beijing has expressed concerns over the United States' increasing engagement in the South China Sea, stressing that China opposes the "internationalization" of the maritime disputes.[40] Beijing insists that the South China Sea issue is a dispute over sovereignty about territory and maritime rights between the relevant countries, and the United States should not "play with fire" or interfering in such a situation.[41]

China's growing naval and air advantages over its neighbors have

---

38 Ronald O'Rourke, Congressional Research Service, "Maritime Territorial and Exclusive Economic Zone (EEZ) Disputes Involving China: Issues for Congress," April 22, 2015, pp.17-18, < http://fpc.state.gov/documents/organization/224476.pdf>.

39 Paul Kelly, "Julia Gillard and Barack Obama Recast the Union," *The Australian*, November 17, 2011.

40 Nong Hong and Wenran Jiang, "Chinese Perceptions of U.S. Engagement in the South China Sea," *China Brief*, Vol.11, Issue 12, July 1, 2011, p.7.

41 "U.S. Playing with Fire over South China Sea," *Xinhua News Agency*, May 29, 2015, <http://news.xinhuanet.com/english/2015-05/29/c_134282034.htm>.

increased China's confidence to take assertive actions for protecting this country's sovereignty rights and maritime interests. Guided by the strategy of "rebalancing," the United States has repeatedly confirmed its political will to maintain security commitments to its regional allies and move more defense resources into Asia. However, China's rapid military modernization, along with the potential decline of U.S. power caused by budget sequestration, is reducing the deterrent effect of the U.S. "rebalancing" strategy. In particular, Chinese de facto administration or control over its near-seas area could greatly complicate the operations of the U.S. armed forces in the case of regional contingencies. How to dissuade Beijing from pursuing escalatory actions or coercive diplomacy has become one of Washington's major concerns on handling its relations with China.

VI. Conclusion

When uncertainty about strategic intentions is combined with rising power, especially military capabilities, states usually begin to prepare for the worst scenario. This development can create strategic distrust and power competitions between the existing superpower and the rising great power. Realists believe that the rise of state power is often accompanied by the broadening of national interests and aggressive foreign policies. In this scenario, power competitions and tensions between status-quo and revisionist states will become inevitable.[42]

The U.S.-China extensive interactions and statements have expressed a strong desire to forge a stable relationship between them. The Chinese leaders have sought to advance the concept of a "new type of great power relations" to prevent the United States from responding to a rising China

---

42   Center for American Progress, "A New Model of Major Power Relations: Pivotal Power Pairs as Bulwarks of the International System," in Rudy deLeon and Yang Jiemian (eds), *U.S.-China Relations Toward a New Model of Major Power Relationship* (Washington, DC: Center for American Progress, 2014), p.29.

through a traditional way of "balancing" or "containment." Nevertheless, Washington and Beijing have encountered many uncertainties and challenges on reconciling their differing expectations and concerns towards a "new type" of bilateral relations. China's assertiveness in maritime territorial disputes and a hardened stance against its neighbors have made it difficult for Beijing to win strategic trust from Asian neighbors and the United States. Meanwhile, the United States believes that the rise of comprehensive national power has broadened China's strategic intentions and aggressive foreign policies. Accordingly, an imagination about power competitions between status-quo and revisionist states is already escalating. The current U.S.-China relationship is very similar to an "old type" of competitive relations between great powers.

Xi Jinping's visit to the U.S. in September 2015 underscored that the Obama administration is reluctant to echo the Chinese ideas on "a new type of great power relations." Although it was Xi Jinping's first official state visit to the United States, no comprehensive U.S.-China joint statement was issued after the Obama-Xi summit. On proposing "a new type of great power relations," China wants "equal" status with the United States as great power, so as to build China-dominated security arrangements in Asia and China-led financial institutions in the globe. It should be noted that Beijing's concept of "new type of great power relations" is not to avoid the result of "power transition" between the United States and China. By contrast, Beijing's purpose is to manage the process of such a "power transition," with the expectation to replace the U.S. status of super great power peacefully and without serious disturbance.[43]

The major problem here is that Beijing's vision for new global and regional orders is not shared by the U.S. and many countries in the Asia-

---

43　Yun Sun, "China's Preferred World Order: What Does China Want?" Center for Strategic and International Studies, September 21, 2015, <https://www.csis.org/analysis/pacnet-62-chinas-preferred-world-order-what-does-china-want>.

Pacific region. The sources of mutual distrust result from the structural and deep-rooted elements in both the U.S. and China that are not likely subject to major change. In this sense, strategic distrust and political misperceptions may continue to be the most destabilizing factors in the U.S.-China relations for years to come.

A Japanese Perspective on the U.S.-China Relations and Regional Security Order

Ryo Sahashi[*]

I. Introduction

The regional order in East Asia is in flux. The relative decline of U.S. power in Asia has led to new challenges. The principles, rules, norms and methods for managing the international agenda are being questioned. The willingness of the United States to maintain an active role in East Asia, alongside the behavior of China and key groupings such as ASEAN will define the future of the region. How these key actors respond to the changing security environment will be crucial in determining the future of the security order in East Asia.

Japan today seems to be the strongest supporter in the region for maintaining a U.S.-led order in both the security and economic realms. Surely, in the last decade Japanese government has admitted the relative decline of the U.S. power even in the published documents, including the ones for defense program guideline. However, at the same time it realizes the regional security environment is deteriorating for the defense of its interests, not only by Pyongyang's development and acquisition of nuclear missile capability but also by PLA's assertive behaviors in the surrounding areas of Japanese territory and Chinese growing political influence in the region.

Hence, Japan seeks the way to underpin the presence of the United States through stretching its own defense capability, upgrading military diplomacy in Asia, and transforming its legal platform of security policy.

*   Associate Professor and Director, Department of Law, Faculty of Law, Kanagawa University, Japan.

After the short tenure of former prime minister Yukio Hatoyama, who served from September 2009 to June 2010, Japan lost its desire to be an architect of the regional order. Unlike ASEAN countries, it also fails to show the sign of strategic hedging behavior between the U.S. and China.[1] Instead, Japan has refurbished its defense and alliance policy and securitized its Asian diplomacy to keep a U.S.-led regional order.

In essence, Japan has made its strategic recalculation. It tries to reaffirm the leading role of the United States in East Asian order in all spectrum. Looking back the postwar diplomatic history, Japan sometimes seeks its independent foreign policy, but such momentum is not observed in recent years. Japan realizes solely its own power could not shape the regional balance of power as preferred. This explains why Japan fears, more than any other country, the U.S. grand strategy debate, including offshore balancing or retrenchment, and why it bashes against President Obama's efforts to stabilize U.S.-China bilateral relations. Such moves imply, for the eyes of Japanese policy makers, American counterparts might reach at the different vision on the regional order and Japanese security and political interests would be sacrificed. For Japan, the "status quo" of the regional order, based on American preeminence and commitment, is what it seeks for.

This paper explains Japanese perspective on the regional power politics and order building process. Firstly, it discusses Japan's perception on the United States, and the source of insecurity. Secondly, Japan's pivotal shifts in defense policy are analyzed, asking why and how they are changed. Thirdly, efforts on the alliance and networking are discussed. Throughout this paper, readers will find out the U.S.-China relation is most plausible in explaining the fundamental shifts of Japanese foreign and defense policies.

---

1   Evelyn Goh, "Understanding 'hedging' in Asia-Pacific security," *PacNet*, August 31st, 2006. Darren J. Lim and Zack Cooper, "Reassessing Hedging: The Logic of Alignment in East Asia," *Security Studies*, Vol. 24, Iss. 4 (2015). Lim and Cooper categorize Japan's policy as "resolute ally."

II. Meaning of the Alliance

Seventy years ago, Japan and the United States fought the total war, but through the Occupation (1945-1952) and the Cold War, Prime Minister Shigeru Yoshida and leading Japanese politicians realized the necessity of forming partnership with the U.S. and keep U.S. troops stationing after Japan regaining sovereignty, in order to lessen the fiscal burden of national defense on austerity. Roughly speaking, until around the end of the Cold War, three images of perception of the U.S. had existed among Japanese: *provider, gateway and competitor*.

First, the U.S. provided not only the security commitment for Japan through alliance and forward defense, but also economic assistance and transfer of technology. Such a combined function of alliance is unique and essential for Japan, while the previous experience of alliance with the UK and the Axis failed to provide them. Fortunately, anti-Americanism was not growing strong in Japanese society and the memory of the Pacific War never prevented the formation of the alliance. Even though anti-base and anti-Vietnam demonstration occupied the main street of Tokyo in the 1950s and 60s, and leftist public intellectuals often constituted the majority groups, protests were mainly against Japanese policy makers and the memory of militarism. After the termination of the Vietnam War, the affinity to the U.S. and the support to the alliance has been constantly high among the public.

Secondly, American diplomacy helped Japanese re-entry to international society. It was the U.S. who paved the gateway for Japan to come back to the West order, realizing the importance of Japanese presence as the partner against the communism.

Thirdly, the success of Japanese economic recovery prepared the new stage of the relationship between Japan and the U.S. By the end of 1980s, both regarded each other as economic competitor, or rivals.

The security challenges in the 1990s on Korean Peninsula and Taiwan

Strait, however, forced both governments to re-appreciate the significance of their security institution based on formal alliance. Especially, the development of North Korean nuclear and missile capability made sufficient impacts on Japanese people to keep supporting the alliance. Theater missile defense system had been jointly developed and introduced from then. It is true that Japanese diplomacy made efforts to launch ASEAN Regional Forum and ASEAN Plus Three frameworks in the 1990s, while it successfully invited the U.S. to ARF and upgraded the alliance scheme in 1996-7.

In the wake of the terrorism on 11th of September, 2001, Japanese reaction was rather quick to dispatch naval ships to Indian Ocean as the part of Operation of Enduring Freedom. Prime Minister Junichiro Koizumi also sent the Self-Defense Forces to postwar Iraq for humanitarian missions, and such global cooperation for the U.S. was judged necessary to keep American commitment to East Asia when North Korean crisis had again deteriorated from the fall of 2002.[2] For the key policy makers in Tokyo, global cooperation was required to underpin the U.S. commitment to East Asia.[3]

Japanese perception on the global balance of power has changed. It admits the relative decline of the U.S. power and "the West" in global stage, emerging powers catching up gradually. For example, in 2009 the wise men and women group report to the Prime Minister for the national defense program guideline clearly admits such shift of power. "… [T]he power balance is undergoing a change caused by the emergence of rising powers, including China and India, and other factors. … the scope of U.S. ability

---

2　In late years the operations to refuel multinational forces in the Indian Ocean was suspended by the strong criticism by the non-ruling party and low-rate support from the public.

3　Tsuyoshi Sunohara, Domei Henbo: Nichibei Domei Ittaika no Hikari to Kage [Transformation of the Japan-U.S. Alliance: Balance Sheet of Alliance Integration] (Tokyo: Nikkei, 2007).

to solve problems unilaterally has become narrower than before. As for East Asia in particular, China has been building up its military power as its economy continues rapid development. It is important both for Japan and for the region as a whole that China's rising power will contribute to, rather than disturb, regional stability."[4]

However, by the reason to induce China to contribute to regional stability, Japan expects the U.S. power as the counter-gravity. Since 2008, PLAN ships have passed the straits around Japan to conduct the exercise and operations, which made psychological impacts on defense planners in Tokyo. In addition, incidents in 2010 and 2012 over Senkaku/ Daioyu islands forced Japanese governments to increase patrolling in the areas robustly and to prepare the worst-case. Without any chance of accommodation to China, Japan had no other way other than increasing its own defense efforts and enhancing the alliance. National Security Strategy, which in the first time Japanese government published in 2013, states, "In order to ensure the security of Japan and to maintain and enhance peace, stability, and prosperity in the Asia-Pacific region and the international community, Japan must further elevate the effectiveness of the Japan-U.S. security arrangements and realize a more multifaceted Japan-U.S. Alliance."[5] Even the trade negotiation for Trans Pacific Partnership was emphasized by the reason to shape the liberal regional economic order with the U.S. power in.

Recent private commission report led by former top level policy makers in Tokyo and Washington also recommends joint approach towards China as the top priority of bilateral alliance. "In Asia, the United States and Japan will have to shape the strategic environment by encouraging responsible Chinese behavior and imposing costs for destabilizing activities. To that end, the United States and Japan will have to build up their own power, and use

---

4   Prime Minister of JAPAN and His Cabinet, *The Council on Security and Defense Capabilities Report*, August 2009.

5   Prime Minister of JAPAN and His Cabinet, *National Security Strategy*, December 17, 2013.

it wisely and firmly, to preserve a world order that favors both allies' shared values."[6] The China question is regarded what shapes a coming order and security environment.

Hence, for Japanese interests the U.S. should be *a strong, resolute internationalist*. Recent years with the Obama administration, in Japan the criticism against the U.S. foreign policy is severe. Also, when Obama and Xi had long-hours summit meeting in Sunnylands, it caused insecurity among policy makers in Tokyo, since "a new model of major powers" or any types of bilateral mechanism implies the power consortium, without Japanese presence, to work against its own interests. It does not mean necessarily that Tokyo finds interests in jeopardizing relations between Beijing and Washington. Rather, it tries to preserve the U.S.-led order for the long term and keeps the alliance commitment for the defense of its remote islands. Surely, in the domestic debate over peace-security legislation, some Japanese emphasized the fear of entrapment by enhancing the alliance. However, the expectation on the U.S. as the regional hegemon is credibly raising. In other words, Japan keeps fear for the U.S. accommodating approach to China not only by the memory of "Nixon shock".[7]

---

6 U.S.-Japan Commission on the Future of the Alliance, "The U.S. Japan Alliance to 2030: Power and Principle," Sasakawa Peace Foundation and Center for Strategic and International Studies, April 2016, p.2. <http://spfusa.org/programs/u-s-japan-commission-on-the-future-of-the-alliance-2/>, This report also suggests Chinese future behavior to shape the order by herself. "There will also be further attempts by Beijing to weaken U.S. alliances and construct an Asia-Pacific economic and security order that marginalizes the United States, as suggested by Xi Jinping in Shanghai in the spring of 2014." Ibid., p.6.

7 Ministry of Foreign Affairs' study group report, headed by Professor Yuichi Hosoya, suggested such Japanese vision will be unchanged in the long run. Yuichi Hosoya (ed.), Ministry of Foreign Affairs, *Asia Pacific Order in Twenty Years and the Role of Japan*, March 2015. [In Japanese] <http://www.mofa.go.jp/mofaj/fp/pp/page3_001196.html >, The author of this paper was a co-author and published the unclassified part of his writing as Ryo Sahashi, "How to Analyze Visions of East Asian Security Order," in Masashi Kimiya (ed.), *Nihon no Anzen hosho VI: Higashi Azia to Chosen Hanto* [Series of Japan's National Security: East Asia and Korean Peninsula], 2015 [In Japanese].

III. Stretching Own Assets

Postwar Japanese foreign and defense policy had been under self-imposing restraints. While Japan succeeded in reconstructing its economy after the Pacific War, becoming the second largest economy by 1970, its choice was to keep low profile in military balance of power during the Cold War through the dependence on the United States, its sole ally.

In 1990s, Japanese government made a pivotal shift toward international society by providing UN peace-keeping operations, expanding disaster relief team, and increasing developmental aids. North Korean nuclear and missile development also forced it to install the missile defense system.

Today we might see another pivotal shift of Japanese foreign and defense policy. Japan, especially under Prime Minister Shinzo Abe, has accelerated the change of its security posture, through increasing defense budget (see Figure 1), establishing Japanese national security council secretariat and publishing its first National Security Strategy, relaxing arms embargo policy, and forging security partnership with Australia and some ASEAN nations. It is important to note that such fundamental shift has been caused as the reaction to its perception on China.

Re-organizing National Security Council and creating its back-up bureau at Cabinet Secretariat were done on January 2014.[8] This "Japan-type NSC" was firstly planed under the first Abe administration seven years ago, but after the sudden retirement of the prime minister the plan was abolished by the succeeding administration. While the old institution at the cabinet secretariat called National Security Council was mainly to aim enhanced civilian control over Self-Defensive Forces, with far smaller personnel, the new NSC is envisioned to function strategic planning and contingency

---

8   The revision of National Security Council establishment acts is completed as of December 4, 2012. New legislation is available at http://law.e-gov.go.jp/htmldata/S61/S61HO071. html in Japanese.

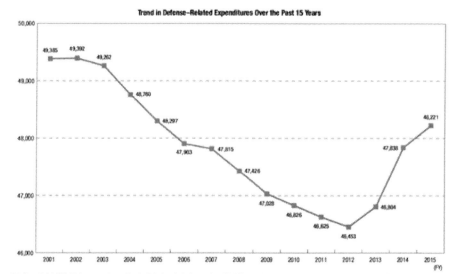

Figure 1: Japanese Defense Budget

response and its staff members are recruited vastly from ministries and agencies, less than half from uniformed.

National Security Strategy was published as the first time in Japanese political history.[9] It shares the basic analysis on the security environment and mission of Japanese defense policy with the renewed National Defense Planning Guideline and five year's Medium Term Defense Program, both of which are approved and publicized at the same day.[10] In short, they emphasize on deteriorated security environment in neighboring area and

---

9   Prime Minister of Japan and His Cabinet, *National Security Strategy*, December 17, 2013, <http://japan.kantei.go.jp/96_abe/documents/2013/__icsFiles/afieldfile/2013/12/18/NSS.pdf>.

10 Prime Minister of Japan and His Cabinet, *National Defense Program Guidelines for FY2014 and beyond*, December 17, 2013, <http://japan.kantei.go.jp/96_abe/documents/2013/__icsFiles/afieldfile/2014/02/03/NDPG.pdf >.

global commons, increasing potential of grey-zone contingencies over Japanese sovereignty and related-rights, hence introduce the new concepts "proactive contribution to peace" and "dynamic joint defense force."[11] Under the new policy, SDFs are acquiring the new capabilities, including amphibious ones to re-take the islands, while the defense budget has experienced, continuously in FY2013 and 2014, the slight increase as the first time in more than fifteen years.

The structure of Self Defense Forces has been shifted with the emphasis to the southward. For example, in January 2016 Ninth Air Wing has been newly formed at Naha, Okinawa, with the new addition of a squadron of F-15J. The main mission of 40 F-15J is to secure Japanese air defense of the South. On March 2016, Ground Self-Defense Forces has opened new radar facility at Yonaguni, the small island close to Taiwan. GSDF will also enhance its facilities at Miyako, Ishigaki, and Amami islands.[12] In addition, Japan Coast Guard strengthened its 11th division with ten newly constructed large patrol vessels, including two with helicopter. It will engage in patrolling Senkaku/ Daioyu areas solely.

The arms exports policy is relaxed. Since 1967, Japanese government prohibited the arms exports, as "Three Principles on Arms Exports and Their Related Policy Guidelines," to states under communism, ban by UN resolutions or conflicts. In 1976, Prime Minister Miki enlarged the scope of regulations to prohibit all weapon-related exports. On 1st of April, 2014, the cabinet published "the Three Principles on Transfer of Defense Equipment and Technology"[13], which replaces the old principles and guidelines.

---

11   On the interesting comparison between Japanese NDPG 2013 and U.S. Quadrennial Defense Review 2014, see Sugio Takahashi, "New QDR, New NDPG, and New Defense Guidelines," *AJISS Commentary* (Association of Japanese Institutes of Strategic Studies), no. 198 (May 15, 2014).

12   *Asahi Shimbun*, March 28th, 2016.

13   Minister of Foreign Affairs of Japan, *The Three Principles on Transfer of Defense Equipment and Technology*, April 1, 2014, <http://www.mofa.go.jp/press/release/press22e_000010.html>.

Criticism points out that under the new principles the government review system is the key but not designed sufficiently to prevent dubious transfer. Asahi Shimbun writes, "[u]nder the new guidelines, Japan can export weapons and other defense equipment to countries that are at great risk of involvement in international conflicts."[14] On the other hand, a security expert who supports this change argues, "[t]he contents of the new principles are conservative and restrictive compared to the U.S.' conventional arms transfer policy, issued in January 2014, and the EU Common Position on Arms Transfer. The Abe administration clearly rejects economic and policy utilization of the new rules, so rapid growth of defense exports is not to be expected."[15]

As of April 2016, the bidding of next generation submarines to Australia is the test case for Japanese arms technology transfer.[16] Japan has also sought to provide old generation surveillance aircrafts to Southeast nations for their capacity building. In addition, this change makes it easier for Japan to join the international development of weaponry system.

Japanese government also revises the charter for developmental cooperation. While it promises avoidance of any use of development cooperation for military purposes or for aggravation of international conflicts, it should be noted that in limited cases armed forces or members of them could be recipient for non-military purposes, "such as public welfare or disaster-relief purposes, such cases will be considered on a case-by-case basis in light of their substantive relevance."[17]

---

14   ASAHI SHIMBUN ,"Japan's arms export rules come with pitfalls, secrecy, limited economic benefits," *Asahi Shimbun (also on Asia& Japan Watch)*, April 2, 2014.

15   Heigo Sato, "From the 'Three Principles of Arms Exports' to the 'Three Principles of Defense Equipment Transfer'", *AJISS Commentary*, no. 197 (May 14, 2014).

16   The potential deal of U.S.-2, long range patrolling aircraft, to India has been under discussion.

17   Ministry of Foreign Affairs, *New Developmental Cooperation Charter*, February 10, 2015.

On the legal platform of security policy, the administration established the wise men group to advise the prime minister on the Constitutional issues, relating to collective self-defense right and collective security. The panel has submitted the final recommendation on May 2014,[18] and the Cabinet has approved its new understanding on July 1st, 2014. Following to this, ruling party coalition submit the legal revisions and the Lower and Upper House has approved, beyond strong resistance from non-ruling parties, the package of revisions by September 2015. It was enacted on the end of March 2016.

Under this new understanding, JSDF could operate for securing the foreign militaries assets and providing ammunitions to foreign militaries. Collective Self-defense right could be exercised under three conditions. The cabinet decision reads, "when an armed attack against a foreign country that is in a close relationship with Japan occurs and as a result threatens Japan's survival and poses a clear danger to fundamentally overturn people's right to life, liberty and pursuit of happiness," "when there is no other appropriate means available to repel the attack and ensure Japan's survival and protect its people," use of force to the minimum extent necessary should be interpreted to be permitted under the Constitution."[19]

Above are the snapshots of the recent development, or transformation, of Japanese foreign and security policy. It includes the institutional and key documents reforms, adopting cross-ministerial approaches, backed up by politicians' strong commitment. While the U.S. has requested the reform of Japanese security policy for a long time, it is rather important to know why Japan has moved now and what is the grand design of foreign and security policy?

---

18 The Advisory Panel on Reconstruction of the Legal Basis for Security, *Report of the Advisory Panel on Reconstruction of the Legal Basis for Security*, Cabinet Secretariat, May 15, 2014. Available at < http://www.kantei.go.jp/jp/singi/anzenhosyou2/dai7/ houkoku_en.pdf>.

19 Prime Minister of JAPAN and His Cabinet, *Cabinet Decision on Development of Seamless Security Legislation to Ensure Japan's Survival and Protect its People*, July 1, 2014, <http://www.mofa.go.jp/fp/nsp/page23e_000273.html>.

China is a crucial factor to explain this. The article by Nikkei, the leading business newspaper in Japan, depicts PM Abe strategy as three-fold: Japan-U.S. alliance, TPP, and value diplomacy, all of which intend to "deter" China. He also makes the most of his occasions to meet foreign leaders to remind the rise of nationalism in China. His determined stance, however, makes it difficult to back down on historical and territorial issues with neighbors, but he accepts the risk of prolonged frozen relationships with two neighbors, this article says.[20] This article was written two years ago, and Sino-Japan relations has been improved with summit meetings, and Abe remarks on the seventieth anniversary since the end of the Pacific War is regarded as softer tone than expected, but the essence of Abe's calculation might be unchanged. Japanese government tries to utilize the influence of the U.S. for the sake of making pressure on China and underpinning a U.S.-centered regional architecture.

IV. Alliance and Networking

i. Japan-U.S. alliance

During the process of Abe administration stretching security policy, the foreign and defense ministerial meeting (2+2) on October 2013 did not conceal the American hope on Japanese new security policy. Its press remarks states, "the U.S. 'welcomed' the recent efforts of Japan on establishing a National Security Council with its first documentation of a National Security Strategy, on making proactive contributions to global and Asian security, on increasing its defense budget and reviewing the National Defense Program Guidelines and, most importantly, on 'the matter of exercising the right of collective self-defense.'" U.S.-Japan alliance has been

---

20 Ken Sato, "Weak Point of Abe Diplomacy (Abe Gaiko No Shikaku)," Nikkei, May 2, 2014. See also Asahi Shimbun political affairs section, *Abe Seiken no Ura No Kao: Koubou Shudanteki Zieiken* [Another Face of Abe Cabinet: Documentary of Political Struggle over Collective Self Defense Right] (Tokyo: Kodan sha, 2015).

positioned "within the broader context of a 'more balanced and effective' partnership in its Asian strategy."[21]

Both governments started to revise their guideline of defense cooperation from 2012, under Democratic Party of Japan's tenure, and reached at its conclusion by April 2015, just before Prime Minister Abe's visit to the United States. The revision of guideline was the first time in eighteen years. The new guideline in its first section put an emphasis on the point that the basic structure of this alliance is not changed. "The two governments will continuously enhance the Japan-U.S. Alliance. Each government will maintain its individual defense posture based on its national security policy. Japan will possess defense capability on the basis of the 'National Security Strategy' and the 'National Defense Program Guidelines'. The United States will *continue to extend deterrence to Japan through the full range of capabilities, including U.S. nuclear forces*. The United States also will *continue to forward deploy combat-ready forces* in the Asia-Pacific region and maintain the ability to reinforce those forces *rapidly*."[22]

Having reconfirmed the basis structure, this guideline aims to improve "the effectiveness of bilateral security and defense cooperation." It lists five areas: seamless, robust, flexible, and effective bilateral responses; synergy across the two governments' national security policies; a whole-of-government Alliance approach; cooperation with regional and other partners, as well as international organizations; the global nature of the Japan-U.S. Alliance.

Seamless responses are projected mostly against grey zone situations. For that purpose, as a whole-of-government approach, alliance coordination

---

21 See also Ryo Sahashi, "Japan-U.S. Security Consultative Committee at Tokyo: From 'Quiet Transformation' to 'Noteworthy Institutionalization' of Alliance," *AJISS Commentary*, no.189, November 21, 2013.

22 Ministry of Defense, *The Guidelines for Japan-U.S. Defense Cooperation*, April 27, 2015. Emphasis added by the author.

mechanism (ACM) is being established. According to Section III-A, "this mechanism will strengthen policy and operational coordination related to activities conducted by the Self-Defense Forces and the United States Armed Forces in all phases from peacetime to contingencies. This mechanism also will contribute to timely information sharing as well as the development and maintenance of common situational awareness." It results in enhanced communication between two governments' security authorities, including the elements of infrastructure and liaison staff. Lessons from their joint operations through Great East Japan Earthquake will be the foundation.

Peacetime cooperation is strengthened by this guideline. Reflecting the new legal platform, it emphasizes the protection of military assets and logistical support from rear-areas (section IV-A).

Section IV-C discusses armed attack on Japan in five areas: airspace, ballistic missile, maritime, ground and cross-domain. At least two points are noteworthy. First, regarding to ground attacks, "The Self-Defense Forces will have primary responsibility for conducting operations to prevent and repel ground attacks, including those against islands... The United States Armed Forces will conduct operations to *support* and supplement the Self-Defense Forces' operations."[23]

Secondly, for the cross domain challenges, "The United States Armed Forces may conduct operations involving the use of strike power, to support and supplement the Self-Defense Forces. When the United States Armed Forces conduct such operations, the Self-Defense Forces may provide support, as necessary. These operations will be based on close bilateral coordination, *as appropriate*."[24]

In addition, the new guideline introduces the cooperation for a large

---

23   Ibid. Emphasis added by the author. While Japan have islands disputes or challenges on Japan's sovereignty of islands from four neighbors, it is only one country who is regarded to make island occupation missions.

24   Ibid. Emphasis added by the author.

scale disaster. The remaining agenda for military cooperation is limited, but it will be discussed continuously between two governments: how to counter anti-access and area-denial (A2AD) capability which China has acquired by precision-strike missiles, and how to impose costs on Chinese military by introducing new technology.

ii. Networking Friends

From the beginning, the prime minister and foreign and defense ministers have spent time for their travel abroad. It is the record breaking that Japanese prime minister visited all ten ASEAN capitals within eleven months, simultaneously visiting the U.S., Europe, Middle East, Africa, Russia, and India within less than eighteen months. Notably, Japan-ASEAN relations had two summit meetings in 2013 and they (multilaterally and bilaterally) agreed on the long list of political, economical, and to some degree strategic cooperation. As of the spring of 2016, the pace of the travel has been constantly high.

National Security Strategy is clearly endorsing that the frequency of diplomacy is to strengthen the foundation for Japan to shape the security environment. It starts to emphasis the partnership with South Korea, Australia, ASEAN and India first.[25]

The partnership between Japan and South Korea has not been developed well when their bilateral relations still has the strong factor of domestic politics. Daniel Sneider, associate director of the Shorenstein Asia-Pacific Research Center at Stanford University, recently argues, "the gaps in strategic understanding and in the readiness to confront the disagreements over history, which are deeply rooted in the politics of identity, remain daunting. The two sides' security perceptions are hardly identical, dictated as

---

25   Ryo Sahashi, "Security Partnerships in Japanese Asia Strategy: Creating Order, Building Capacity, and Sharing Burden," *IFRI Asie*. Visions 61 (Paris: Institut français des relations internationales), February 2013, pp. 1-23. Daniel M. Kliman and Daniel Twining, "Japan's Democracy Diplomacy," *Asia Paper Series*, July 2014, <http://spfusa. org/wp-content/uploads/2015/02/6_Japans_Democracy_Diplomacy.pdf>.

they are by geography and, for South Koreans, by the unresolved Cold War division of the Korean Peninsula."[26]

To the contrary, Australia and Japan have successfully matured their political and security partnership at bilateral and trilateral (with the U.S.) level. In fact, the military cooperation has been upgraded substantially towards operational application. James Schoff, a senior fellow for the Carnegie Endowment for International Peace, points out, "the three countries have placed greater emphasis on operational skills and trilateral interoperability, resulting in less frequent HA/DR-focused trilateral exercises in recent years."[27]

Partnership with Europe is explained in the context of preferred international order. The logic that National Security Strategy suggests is, Europe is a natural partner for Japan to claim rule-based order in the time of power shifts.[28]

iii. Japan's ASEAN Policy[29]

Japan has not always relied on U.S. primacy in Asia. In the past Japan has emphasized the role of regional groups, including the ASEAN+3 and ASEAN+6 mechanisms. Japan also actively pursued its own bilateral diplomacy with Southeast Asian nations as part of the Fukuda doctrine, first established in 1977, which focused on building peaceful and cooperative relations with ASEAN members.

---

26 Daniel Sneider, Advancing U.S.-Japan-ROK Trilateral Cooperation: A U.S. Perspective, Seattle, *National Bureau of Asian Research*, March 31, 2016, <http://www.nbr.org/ research/activity.aspx?id=662>.

27 James L. Schoff, "The Evolution of U.S.-Japan-Australia Security Cooperation," Yuki Tatsumi (ed.), *U.S.-Japan-Australia Security Cooperation: Prospects and Challenges*, April 2015, p.46.

28 Prime Minister of Japan and His Cabinet, *National Security Strategy*, December 17, 2013.

29 This section overlaps substantially with Ryo Sahashi, "Japan's vision for the East Asian security order," *East Asia Forum*, February 23, 2016.

But during the last decade, Japanese foreign policymakers have increasingly viewed Japan's relations with Southeast Asia through the prism of the U.S. alliance. Regardless of the ruling party, Japanese foreign policy has clearly aimed to strengthen U.S. leadership in the region.

To bolster the U.S. alliance framework, Japan enhanced its security cooperation with most of the ASEAN countries, upgrading the substance of bilateral relations with ASEAN countries to include more robust defense exchange. Japan's stance on the Trans-Pacific Partnership negotiations — which it has prioritized above other economic partnerships in the region — also signifies its strong commitment to ensuring continued U.S. engagement in the region. Tokyo policymakers have calculated that it is in their strategic interests to enhance the U.S. position in the region. This view is perhaps more entrenched in Japan than in any other country, including Australia and the United States itself.

In April 2015, Japan and the United States published a new joint statement and updated guidelines on U.S.–Japan defense cooperation, which emphasized bilateral and trilateral collaboration in security capacity-building efforts for Southeast Asian nations. Also, the Abe administration succeeded in a substantial deepening of Japan–India security cooperation, particularly in relation to defense and civil nuclear cooperation. This is indicative of how Japan has 'securitised' its Asian diplomacy.

Japan's behavior is aimed at complementing the so-called American 'pivot' or 'rebalance' to Asia. But this shift in Japanese foreign policy actually predates the U.S. pivot strategy — the first signals of this new foreign policy orientation started under the first Abe administration in 2006–2007.

While some elements of Japan's traditional Asian diplomacy persist in its bilateral engagement, the increasingly prominent role given to security in Japan's Asian diplomacy is the defining development of the last decade. The weight given to security concerns in Japan's foreign policy has led Japanese diplomats to push for a common Japan–ASEAN stance on maritime disputes with China.

The expected role of ASEAN in Japan's foreign policy vision is largely unchanged. Japan wants to encourage a strong ASEAN and promote the ASEAN community building process. In this sense, the legacy of the Fukuda doctrine continues. Even outside government circles, many Japanese specialists value the role of ASEAN in the regional architecture. Comparatively, Chinese policymakers and academics are, at times, more vocal in expressing their doubts over the importance and normative power of ASEAN.

As long as the majority of ASEAN members resist external pressure from any third party, promoting ASEAN will benefit Japan. This is because ASEAN can allow Japan to promote regionalism, while concurrently pursuing economic and security mechanisms that include the United States.

V. Conclusion

"The *primary* geopolitical test for the Alliance is China's rise,"[30] insists the abovementioned study group report. Seemingly, it is the very case at least with Japan.

Japanese behaviors suggest that, in its own strategic re-calculation, maintaining American influence is the key to preserving the regional order. Tokyo recognizes that Japanese power alone is insufficient to shape the regional order. It is therefore crucial for Japan to build coalitions with regional partners that have similar political objectives.

And tensions still remain between the U.S. and Japanese approaches to security in East Asia. Japan is more assertive than its partners in its desire to guard against increasing Chinese influence and to address maritime challenges by implementing rules-based mechanisms. This stance is rooted

---

30   U.S.-Japan Commission on the Future of the Alliance, p.14. Emphasis added by the author.

in Japan's perception of China, which has shifted in response to China's growing political influence and the crises over the Senkaku/Diaoyu islands.

It is uncertain that such Japanese new formation of diplomacy and security build-up would create sufficient gravity to shape the region as it prefers. In addition to the so-called "China gaps" debate over regional powers' perception and way of management with China, Japanese power alone is not able to define the fate of the region. American attitude is still the key, and since Japan realizes this well it fears very much the political debate over the forward defense and alliance in the U.S. presidential election and academia.

Japan-China relation is another important element of game changer for this situation. As Evelyn Goh, professor at Australian National University, explains beautifully, the rivalry between Beijing and Tokyo helped the U.S. centered hierarchical order after the end of the Cold War.[31] If both governments succeed in healing their relationship over territory, historical memory, and international status and order, with the concept of mutually beneficial strategic relationship, they could lead the region as a whole for better direction. However, it looks that their rivalry, in addition to the power rivalry between the U.S. and China, promotes the competition over the desirable regional order in coming decades.

In fact, Japanese diplomacy towards East Asia has experienced a fundamental transformation. As part of this transformation, the strategic vision that underpins the U.S.–Japan alliance has been stretched to underpin Japan's diplomacy for the entire East Asian region. This extension of the logic of the U.S.–Japan alliance undermines the ability of Japan to pursue a truly inclusive regional order. It is high time that Japanese foreign policy embraced the advantages of inclusive multilateralism.

---

31 Evelyn Goh, *The Struggle for Order: Hegemony, Hierarchy and Transition in Post-Cold War East Asia* (Oxford: Oxford University Press, 2013).

The Challenges of Updating ASEAN for the Contemporary Asia-Pacific

Ja Ian Chong[*]

Growing tensions over competing South China Sea claims coupled with China's increasing economic influence are sharpening longstanding cleavages within the Association of Southeast Asian Nations (ASEAN). Unless its members relook and reconfigure the way ASEAN operates, the organization risks irrelevance. A diminished ASEAN means not only a reduced role for its members, but also an East Asian region where major power frictions become increasingly direct. Whatever the faults of 'ASEAN-centrality' in regional cooperation, it can be a useful fiction that allows regional actors to coalesce around some lowest-common denominator to avoid escalating tensions and even seek cooperation. An ASEAN whose members are less able to find common ground on basic issues may mean that diffusing tensions and delaying divisive decisions can become more challenging.

Unfortunately, for ASEAN members and perhaps the Asia-Pacific more broadly, there is too much reticence over updating ASEAN to more adequately address the needs of contemporary regional politics. ASEAN members continue to emphasize consensus, autonomy, non-interference, and ASEAN's 'centrality' in regional cooperation along with a desire 'not to choose sides' between the United States and China. This translates into inaction over some issues and sporadic attention to others, even as member states address national concerns at some expense to collective action.

---

*   Associate Professor, Department of Political Science, National University of Singapore, Singapore.

A consequence is an ASEAN that appears somewhat out of sync with a changing regional environment, but as yet does not have a concrete response to the situation.

I. ASEAN Adrift

ASEAN was unquestionably the premier regional organization in Southeast, if not East, Asia coming out of the Cold War. Successful intra-ASEAN coordination and cooperation with the United States and China facilitated an end to Vietnamese occupation of Cambodia in 1989.[1] ASEAN was starting to take the lead on regional issues in the early 1990s, advancing economic dialogue through the Asia-Pacific Economic Cooperation (APEC) forum as well as discussions on political and security issues through the ASEAN Regional Forum (ARF).[2] ASEAN members were discussing not only community building, but also ideas for confidence building, preventive diplomacy, and conflict resolution.[3] The grouping was pushing ahead on the engagement of larger neighbors through the ASEAN+3 exchanges with China, Japan, and South Korea as was as with China alone through the ASEAN+1 framework.[4] The late 1990s saw ASEAN expand to incorporate Cambodia, Laos, Myanmar, and Vietnam, adding to the memberships of Brunei, Indonesia, Malaysia, the Philippines, Thailand, and Singapore.

Momentum began to peter out in the late 1990s, culminating in

---

1   Muthiah Alagappa, "Regionalism and the Quest for Security: ASEAN and the Cambodian Conflict," *Australian Journal of International Affairs*, vol. 47, no. 2 (1993), pp. 189-209.

2   Mark Beeson, *Institutions of the Asia-Pacific: ASEAN, APEC, and Beyond* (Abingdon, Oxon: Routledge, 2009), Chs. 2-4.

3   Desmond Ball and Amitav Acharya [eds.], *The Next Stage: Preventive Diplomacy and Security Cooperation in the Asia-Pacific Region*, Canberra Papers on Strategic and Defence No.131 (Canberra, ACT: Strategic and Defence Studies Centre, Australian National University, 1999).

4   Richard Stubbs, "ASEAN Plus Three: Emerging East Asian Regionalism?," *Asian Survey*, vol. 42, no. 3 (May/June 2002), pp. 440-455.

increasingly obvious divergence within ASEAN. With the 1997-8 Asian Financial Crisis, ASEAN started differing on the degree to which the organization's traditional emphasis on consensus should restrict efforts to move ahead on initiatives some members were not ready to fully undertake. Proposals to bring member states closer together, such as the ASEAN Economic Community (AEC), ASEAN Security Community (ASC), and ASEAN Social-Cultural Community (ASCC), were slow to gain traction.[5] fforts to move toward a Code of Conduct for the South China Sea still seem stuck.[6] ASEAN's two-decade attempt to tackle the smog that periodically blankets parts of the region has limited success.[7] The relative success of the ASEAN-China Free Trade Area (ACFTA), ASEAN Plus frameworks, and the Chiang Mai Initiative Multi-lateralized (CMIM) currency swap mechanism, and cooperation over the Mekong River during the 2000s seemed driven by non-ASEAN initiative.[8] Debate continues over whether the ASEAN Free Trade Area (AFTA) drove the growth in post-2000 intra-regional trade.[9]

By the 2010s, ASEAN members further differed over how to approach

---

5   Association of Southeast Asian Nations (ASEAN), *Cebu Declaration on the Acceleration of the Establishment of an ASEAN Community by 2015*, January 13, 2007, <http://www.asean.org/cebu-declaration-on-th-acceleration-of-the-establishment-of-an-asean-community-by-2015/>, accessed March 20, 2016.

6   Mark Valencia, "A South China Sea Code of Conduct is Still the Holy Grail of Regional Diplomacy—and Just as Likely to be Discovered," *South China Morning Post*, November 15, 2015, <http://www.scmp.com/comment/insight-opinion/article/1878572/south-china-sea-code-conduct-still-holy-grail-regional>, accessed March 15, 2016.

7   Apichai Suchindah, "Transboundary Haze Problem in Southeast Asia: Reframing ASEAN's Response," *ERIA Discussion Paper Series*, ERIA-DP-2015-82, Economic Research Institute for ASEAN and East Asia, December 2015.

8   Evelyn Goh, "Developing the Mekong: Regionalism and Regional Security in China-Southeast Asian Relations," *The Adelphi Papers*, No. 387 (May 18, 2007), Chalongphob Sussangkarn, "The Chiang Mai Initiative Multilateralization: Origin, Development and Outlook," ABDI Working Paper Series, No. 230 (July 2010).

9   Masahiro Kawai and Ganeshan Wignaraja [eds.], *Asia's Free Trade Agreements: How is Business Responding?* (Cheltenham: Edward Elgar, 2011).

key challenges facing the region. Disparate views over whether to even mention South China Sea issues led to a failure to a to deliver an ASEAN post-ministerial meeting joint statement for the first time in 2012.[10] ASEAN members with the exception of Vietnam remained silent toward a 2014 Filipino effort to have the Permanent Court of Arbitration (PCA) determine the nature of a number of South China Sea maritime features Manila disputes with Beijing.[11] Malaysia's use of a chair's statement in lieu of a joint statement after the 2015 ASEAN Defense Minister Meeting (ADMM) seemed like a papering over of differences to reach a joint position, placing the organization's ability to manage splits in the hands of the annually rotating ASEAN chair.[12] This makes progress susceptible to the widely varying institutional capabilities of the government holding the chair. ASEAN and its Human Rights Commissioners too were silent during the 2012 and 2015 Rohingya refugee crises, even as people were perishing at sea.[13]

The organization's voice too was notably absent in the wake of reports that Chinese Coast Guard vessels forcibly retrieved a Chinese-flagged fishing vessel from the custody of Indonesian fisheries enforcement authorities

---

10 "ASEAN nations fail to reach agreement on South China Sea," *BBC News* ,July 13, 2012, <http://www.bbc.com/news/world-asia-18825148>, accessed March 12, 2016.

11 Prashanth Parameswaran, "Vietnam Launches Legal Challenge Against China's South China Sea Claims," *The Diplomat* ,December 12, 2014, <http://thediplomat. com/2014/12/vietnam-launches-legal-challenge-against-chinas-south-china-sea-claims/>, accessed March 20, 2016.

12 Razak Ahmad, "Hisham Issues Chairman's Statement as Defence Chiefs Vow to Bridge Differences," *The Star* ,November 5, 2015, < http://www.thestar.com.my/ news/nation/2015/11/05/ministers-fail-to-reach-consensus-hisham-issues-chairmans-statement-as-defence-chiefs-vow-to-bridge>, accessed March 25, 2016, See Seng Tan, "Claims of ASEAN Disunity at Summit Unfounded," *Straits Times* ,November 26, 2015, <http://www.straitstimes.com/opinion/claims-of-asean-disunity-at-summit-unfounded>, accessed March 25, 2016.

13 Betsy Nolan, "ASEAN 'Cannot Stay Out of Rohingya Crisis,'" *Jakarta Post* , June 18, 2015, <http://www.thejakartapost.com/news/2015/06/18/asean-cannot-stay-out-rohingya-crisis.html>, accessed March 27, 2016.

apparently in Indonesian waters in March 2016.[14] Reports that there were about a hundred Chinese fishing vessels heading toward Malaysian claimed waters about a week later likewise drew no response from ASEAN. Individual ASEAN members apart from the governments directly involved too did not voice any opinion in public.[15] Similarly, American and Australia efforts to engage in Freedom of Navigation Operations (FONOPs) in disputed South China Sea waters did not draw much public reaction from either ASEAN or ASEAN member states.[16] This suggests that divisions within ASEAN over how to deal with disputes in the South China Sea as well as friction between China, the United States, and U.S. allies in the region continues to persist.

II. Enduring Cleavages, Hidden Divisions

ASEAN ultimately remains a collection of different states whose basis for cooperation rests largely on convenience, even though there is some sense of self-identity among elites. Integration within the organization remains limited. ASEAN members' preferred mode for dealing with issues, especially difficult ones, remains ad hoc expediency, with a premium placed on presenting outward consensus even as members tried to find basic compromises behind closed doors. This often means shying away from a clear position individually or as a group. Member states often claim that this is the 'ASEAN Way,' which enables them to avoid discord. Such

---

14 Joe Cochrane, "China's Coast Guard Rams Fishing Boat to Free it From Indonesian Authorities," *New York Times*, March 21, 2016, <http://www.nytimes.com/2016/03/22/world/asia/indonesia-south-china-sea-fishing-boat.html>, accessed March 28, 2016.

15 "A Hundred Chinese Boats Encroach in Malaysian Waters: Minister," *Reuters*, March 25, 2016, <http://www.reuters.com/article/us-southchinasea-malaysia-idUSKCN0WR03H>, accessed March 26, 2016.

16 "U.S., ASEAN Agree on Freedom of Navigation Principle," *Bangkok Post*, February 17, 2016, <http://www.bangkokpost.com/news/asia/867532/us-asean-agree-on-freedom-of-navigation-principle>, accessed March 26, 2016.

characteristics supposedly allow ASEAN and its members consistently 'not choose sides' among major powers while maintaining the grouping's 'centrality' in East Asia.

Behind member states' apparently discordant approaches to cooperation lie overriding concerns about their own individual country positions. Mainland ASEAN members, for instance, may be willing to forego a more united position on South China Sea issues littoral states care about in favor of assurances over land disputes, riparian issues, and economic goals.[17] Low-income ASEAN economies may find bilateral arrangements over such issues as commodity export and infrastructure development preferable to shared positions with other ASEAN members.[18] Middle and higher income members may be willing to do the same for capital investment or access to export markets for manufactures and services. Such member actions discount joint ASEAN efforts to advance cooperation.

Fears of an overbearing ASEAN secretariat that restricts the autonomy of individual members, possibly unfounded, prompt member states to underinvest in that body. They also encourage member states to limit the Secretariat's formal responsibilities for coordination, much less for monitoring and enforcing ASEAN agreements.[19] ASEAN members have almost a thousand annual meetings that a Secretariat can theoretically oversee but has no authority to do so. Moreover, ASEAN members cap

---

17 "China allies leave ASEAN split over statement on South China Sea," *Japan Times*, August 5, 2015, <http://www.japantimes.co.jp/news/2015/08/06/asia-pacific/politics-diplomacy-asia-pacific/china-allies-leave-asean-split-statement-south-china-sea/#. VwKTG2Mkcm8>, accessed March 27, 2016.

18 Agnes Isnawangsih, Vladimir Klyuev, Longmei Zhang, "The Big Split: Why Did Output Trajectories in the ASEAN-4 Diverge after the Global Financial Crisis?" *IMF Working Paper*, WP/13/222, October 2013, <https://www.imf.org/external/pubs/ft/wp/2013/wp13222.pdf>, accessed March 27, 2016.

19 ASEAN, *Agreement on the Establishment of the ASEAN Secretariat Bali*, 24 February, 1976, <http://www.asean.org/?static_post=asean-secretariat-basic-documents-agreement-on-the-establishment-of-the-asean-secretariat-bali-24-february-1976-2>, accessed March 28, 2016.

annual contributions to the Secretariat at a little less than $2 million each.[20] These realities constrain the Secretariat's ability to function, hampering its overall effectiveness and ability to support member states. A Secretariat better able to perform these functions can help manage persistent problems and offer much needed assistance to member states with more resource and capacity limitations, especially when they serve as ASEAN chair.

Apprehensions about a potentially overbearing ASEAN stem from the organization's roots. ASEAN originated from concerns of conservative, nationalist, and anti-communist political elites, most of whom participated in recent struggles against colonial rule. This was certainly the case with Indonesia, Malaysia, the Philippines, and Singapore. The exception was Thailand, which had maintained its formal political autonomy in the face of British, French, and Japanese pressure. All these governments were amid continuing processes suppressing domestic resistance to their rule while looking anxiously to the growing success of Communist-led forces in Indochina at the point of ASEAN's founding in 1967.[21] ASEAN's founding members too looked toward each other as potential sources of threat. In fact, Indonesia had only ended the Konfrontasi against Malaysia in 1965, even as communist and ethnic insurgents continued to be a nuisance in Thailand, the Philippines, and along the Thai-Malaysian border.[22]

The circumstances facing ASEAN's ruling elites at the organization's inception made its founding members highly suspicious toward outside political interference, challenges to territorial control, and limits on external political autonomy. They viewed such conditions are potentially developing into affronts to the continued rule of their regimes domestically. ASEAN's founding members resolved to protect these core interests in any and all

---

20 Quratul-Ain Bandial, "ASEAN Secretariat Getting Funds to Raise Staff Salaries," *Brunei Times*, November 29, 2014, <http://www.bt.com.bn/news-national/2014/11/29/asean-secretariat-getting-funds-raise-staff-salaries>, accessed March 29, 2016.

21 Beeson, *Institutions of the Asia-Pacific*, Ch. 2.

22 Ibid.

efforts to promote regional cooperation despite their shared interests in resisting the spread of communism. Such considerations contributed to earlier attempts to develop anti-communist regional cooperation, such as the South-East Asian Treaty Organization modeled after NATO, the Association of Southeast Asia (ASA), and Maphilindo.[23] They institutionalized these apprehensions in ASEAN's founding documents, which enshrined territorial integrity, mutual non-interference, and consensus decision-making as core principles of the organization.

ASEAN elites institutionalized their apprehensions in the grouping's founding documents, which enshrined territorial integrity, mutual non-interference, and consensus decision-making as core principles of the organization. The 1976 Treaty of Amity and Cooperation in Southeast Asia (TAC) which lays out the principles of both intra-ASEAN relations and interactions with non-Southeast Asian partners laws out this sentiment most clearly. Article II of the TAC states:

In their relations with one another, the High Contracting Parties shall be guided by the following fundamental principles:

a. Mutual respect for the independence, sovereignty, equality, territorial integrity and national identity of all nations.
b. The right of every State to lead its national existence free from external interference, subversion or coercion.
c. Non-interference in the internal affairs of one another.
d. Settlement of differences or disputes by peaceful means.
e. Renunciation of the threat or use of force.
f. Effective cooperation among themselves.[24]

Given that the TAC continues to provide the basis for ASEAN and

---

23   Ibid.

24   ASEAN, *Treaty of Amity and Cooperation in Southeast Asia, Indonesia*, February 24, 1976, <http://www.asean.org/treaty-amity-cooperation-southeast-asia-indonesia-24-february-1976/>, accessed March 20, 2016.

ASEAN-related activities, there is no ambiguity about how the grouping and its members envisions regional politics and cooperation.

ASEAN's core principles enabled its founding members to set aside differences and establish some basis for coordination. In particular, a shared commitment toward mutual respect for and mutual restraint from intervening within each other's borders eased fears among ASEAN members. The focus on consensus in decision-making ensured that no member state felt bound or forced to follow some organizational position and could preserve maximum autonomy. Consensus also forced member states to negotiate over differences if they wished to work together, encouraging ASEAN states to either set aside or discuss contentious issues. This created an incentive to avoid escalation of tensions, or even to actively seek de-escalation and hold disputes dormant until such time there can be a mutually acceptable resolution. This shared understanding permitted ASEAN members to come together to oppose the Vietnamese invasion and occupation of Cambodia between 1979 and 1989, and work with the United States and China to diplomatically isolate the Vietnamese-backed Cambodian government.[25] Vietnamese actions at the time were clear threats to the core ASEAN principles of territorial integrity and non-intervention.

The experience of coordination over issues and the shelving of contentious disputes enabled political and diplomatic elites in the original ASEAN members and Brunei, which joined on independence in 1984, to lower mutual mistrust and possibly develop some sense of commonality. Such perspectives helped give rise to confidence behind ASEAN expansion after the end of the Cold War and efforts to put the organization in the 'driver's seat' for regional cooperation. Leaders in the original five members plus Brunei, or the ASEAN Six, believed that the 'ASEAN Way' of shelving disputes and seeking collaboration was a way to 'socialize' both Southeast Asian states as well as major powers active in the region into more

---

25   Alagappa, "Regionalism and the Quest for Security."

stable, predictable, and amicable modes of interaction, even cooperation. Emphasizing 'ASEAN centrality' while doing so further aimed to draw major power attention and give major powers like the United States, China, Japan, and India stakes in ASEAN. For the major powers, this approach seemed like a potential vehicle to buffer their mutual competition by ceding some leadership over regional matters to ASEAN.

ASEAN's successes and development are unable to fully offset the very real structural fault lines within the grouping, however. As an organization, ASEAN remains more adept at promoting dialogue, reducing tensions, and putting off contentious issues. Such functions are important in helping to promote stability and avoid the escalation of disputes, but are fundamentally different from promoting cooperation or building a strong sense of community beyond political and diplomatic elites. Absent clearer mechanisms for coordination or binding members to commitments, ASEAN is more susceptible to coordination and collective action problems. Sensitivity over interference in domestic affairs also prevents more binding arrangements that allow the monitoring and enforcement of agreements that relate to domestic issues. ASEAN members are able to help shelve disputes such as Thai-Cambodian differences over the status of Preah Vihear, Filipino-Malaysian contention over Sabah, border jurisdiction between Thailand and Myanmar, and the Malaysia-Indonesia dispute over Ambalat.[26] Any resolution tends to come from third-party arbitration, as seen in the case of Malaysia-Singapore over Pedra Branca, Middle Rocks, and South Ledge

---

26   John Aglionby, "War of Blame after Thai-Burmese Border Clashes," *Guardian*, February 13, 2001,<http://www.theguardian.com/world/2001/feb/13/thailand>, accessed March 26, 2016; Stephen C. Druce and Efri Yoni Baikoeni, "Circumventing Conflict: The Indonesia–Malaysia Ambalat Block Dispute," in Mikio Oishi [ed.], *Contemporary Conflicts in Southeast Asia: Towards a New ASEAN Way of Conflict Management* (Singapore: Springer, 2016), pp. 137-56; K. Kesavapany, "ASEAN and the Cambodia-Thailand Conflict," *East Asia Forum*, March 1, 2011,<http://www.eastasiaforum. org/2011/03/01/asean-and-the-cambodia-thailand-conflict/>, accessed March 26, 2016; Salim Osman, "The Dispute Over Sabah," *Straits Times*, March 6, 2013, <http://www. straitstimes.com/singapore/the-dispute-over-sabah>, accessed March 26, 2016.

as well as Malaysia-Indonesia over Sipadan and Ligatan.[27]

Left to their own devices, ASEAN members seem to have trouble more fully complying with agreements they entered into, as seen in the relative ineffectiveness of the ASEAN Haze Action Plan and agreements on Trans-Boundary Haze, which involves domestic compliance.[28] 'ASEAN centric' frameworks such as the ARF, APEC, and even the East Asian Summit are largely fora for discussions. ARF, in particular, is unable to achieve its goal of creating mechanisms for preventive diplomacy much less conflict resolution. This is the case even though it seems to have some success in confidence building, as seen in the shelving of intra-ASEAN disputes and promotion of cooperation despite the persistence of differences.

Even the multilateral military exercises that take place under the aegis of the ADMM and ADMM Plus, which includes Australia, China, India, Japan, New Zealand, Russia, South Korea, and the United States, focus on low hanging fruit. In this case, exchanging best practices in areas such as military medicine and humanitarian assistance and disaster relief (HADR).[29] Efforts that demonstrate consistent and prolonged commitment to cooperation by

---

27 International Court of Justice (ICJ), Sovereignty over Pedra Branca/Pulau Batu Puteh, Middle Rocks and South Ledge (Malaysia/Singapore), Cases, March,2001, <http:// www.icj-cij.org/docket/index.php?p1=3&p2=3&k=2b&case=130&code=masi&p3=5>, accessed March 26, 2016; ICJ, *Sovereignty over Pulau Ligitan and Pulau Sipadan (Indonesia/Malaysia), Cases*, November,2, 1998, <http://www.icj-cij.org/docket/index.ph p?p1=3&code=inma&case=102&k=df>, accessed March 26, 2016.

28 ASEAN, *ASEAN Agreement on Transboundary Haze Pollution*, June 10, 2002,<http:// environment.asean.org/wp-content/uploads/2015/06/ASEANAgreementonTransbou ndaryHazePollution.pdf>, accessed March 28, 2016; ASEAN, *Regional Haze Action Plan*, December 23, 1997, <http://cil.nus.edu.sg/rp/pdf/1997%20Regional%20Haze%20 Action%20Plan-pdf.pdf>, accessed March 28, 2016; Mong Palatino, "Haze Exposes ASEAN Failure," *The Diplomat*, June 27, 2013, <http://thediplomat.com/2013/06/haze-exposes-asean-failure/>, accessed March 28, 2016.

29 Chiang Chie Foo, "Insights on the ADMM and the ADMM Plus: The Road to Realisation, and What Lies Ahead," <http://news.ntu.edu.sg/Search/Pages/default.aspx?cx=0099096 68336905004361:jkblgzxtphk&cof=FORID%3A10&ie=UTF-8&q=site%3Anews.ntu. edu.sg%2FSAFNTU%20Chiang%20Chie%20Foo>, accessed March 28, 2016.

ASEAN members include only a small subset of members and operate outside ASEAN, as seen in the Indonesia-Malaysia-Singapore Malacca Strait patrols and eye-in-the-sky surveillance operations.[30] These anti-piracy patrols only began in the face of pressure from potential American patrols in those waters, despite the fact that all three countries have a clearly shared interest in reducing piracy in those waters.

Moreover, efforts to preserve the diplomatic autonomy of ASEAN members through the insistence on consensus makes every single member state a veto player on virtually all matters relating to ASEAN. In short, any member government can derail any discussion or agreement at their discretion. Failure to deliver a joint statement that included any reference to the South China Sea at the ASEAN Ministerial Meeting in Phnom Penh in 2012 resulted largely from Cambodian opposition, for instance.[31] Failure to reach consensus similarly doomed earlier Thai attempts to enhance the coordinating role of ASEAN in the wake of the Asian Financial Crisis. To be sure, these collective action, coordination, and veto challenges have been with ASEAN since its inception. However, the expansion of ASEAN to include countries with very different developmental needs and political proclivities, not to mention a focus on mainland and riparian issues, in the 1990s magnified the intensity of and risks associated with these existing cleavages.

China's prominence and major power friction further compounds the challenges facing intra-ASEAN cooperation, widening intra-ASEAN fractures and encumbering organizational initiative. Opportunities that China offers in terms of markets, tourist dollars, investments, and low-interest loans give ASEAN members more reason to cooperate bilaterally with China rather than share benefits and navigate intricacies of ASEAN

---

30 Anthony S. Massey, "Maritime Security Cooperation in the Strait of Malacca," Thesis, Naval Post Graduate School, June 2008.

31 "ASEAN nations fail to reach agreement on South China Sea."

politics.[32] This adds to the existing opportunities that America offers in terms of investment, markets, and security cooperation that may at times prove more attractive to ASEAN members than intra-ASEAN cooperation. These unintended, second-order effects place more pressure on the fault lines already present within ASEAN, and which members are reluctant to directly address, exacerbating longstanding collective action problems. Individual ASEAN members may find more incentive and reason to defect from fuller commitment to cooperation within the grouping given the presence of such temptations.

Growing differences between China on one hand and the United States and Japan on the other as well are making intra-ASEAN coordination trickier. Member states more attracted by one side or another on an issue have more reason to depart from a joint ASEAN position, even as they claim to be 'not choosing sides.'[33] Additionally, different ASEAN capitals may 'not choose sides' in ways that are not mutually consistent, even contradictory. ASEAN as well as member states who wish to keep ties with major powers on an even keel as well have to worry more about not alienating one side or another while dealing with a more complicated and uncertain context. A net result of such dynamics is greater incoherence for the grouping, even if the national policies and strategies of ASEAN members remain internally consistent. Less effective coordination within ASEAN spells less leadership and direction for regional organizations that stress 'ASEAN centrality,' potentially paving the way for greater disarray or more unembellished friction between major powers like China, Japan, and the United States.

---

32 Nargiza Salidjanova and Iacob Koch-Weser, "China's Economic Ties with ASEAN: A Country-by-Country Analysis," *U.S.-China Economic and Security Review Commission Staff Research Report*, March 17, 2015; Sarah Y. Tong and Lim Wen Xin, "China-ASEAN Economic Relations: An Update," *EAI Background Brief* No. 1081 (November 18, 2015).

33 S. Mahmud Ali, *Asia-Pacific Security Dynamics in the Obama Era: A New World Emerging* (London: Routledge, 2012), Ch. 4; Institute of Southeast Asian Studies, *Developing ASEAN-China Relations: Realities and Prospects* (Singapore: Institute of Southeast Asian Studies, 2004), pp. 12-15.

III. The Risks and Comfort of Inaction

A key challenge now facing ASEAN is the situation where longstanding positions and approaches to regional politics are beginning to experience diminishing returns, seen from the mounting difficulties the grouping seems to be facing. This creates an imperative for fresh approaches to ASEAN cooperation. ASEAN members and their partners can benefit from serious efforts to rethink ways to go beyond existing practices and make ASEAN more suited for today's more contentious and uncertain East Asia. Governments with an active interest in the regional may wish to seriously consider possible next steps, including ones that depart from the comfort of established approaches. This could involve considering ways to invest in ASEAN's organizational capacities and also some examination of alternatives should serious reforms of the grouping prove intractable. Choices worth considering range from invigorating ASEAN's ability to take a leading regional position to devolving the organization from East Asia's security and economic architecture.

That said, business-as-usual still promises some substantive benefits for ASEAN and its members to be sure. The emphasis on slow consensus-building and dialogue is useful in easing escalation and defusing tensions within ASEAN, even creating some sense of commonality. That long-standing territorial disputes among various ASEAN members remained dormant or saw resolution through third party arbitration are testaments to the effectiveness of ASEAN in easing friction among its members. Malaysia and the Philippines have effectively frozen their dispute over the Malaysian state of Sabah on North Borneo, just as Malaysia and Indonesia seem to have done the same for their dispute over Ambalat.[34] Singapore and Malaysia used the International Court of Justice to arbitrate over ownership of Pedra Branca, Middle Rocks, and South Ledge, while Indonesia and Malaysia

---

34   Druce and Baikoeni, "Circumventing Conflict," pp. 137-56; Osman, "The Dispute Over Sabah."

did the same for Sipadan and Ligatan.[35] Occasional flare-ups, such as those along the Thai-Myanmar and Thai-Cambodian borders, are infrequent and localized.[36] Intra-ASEAN economic exchanges continue to grow as do trade and investment with non-ASEAN partners and with them economies.[37] Just that the net gains member states accrue from being in ASEAN are likely to decrease over time if the effectiveness of the grouping decays and individual members begin losing a key platform to highlight their concerns in a broader regional setting.

Given the real and serious but incremental intensification of the challenges facing ASEAN, the grouping is at an important crossroad whether member states fully recognize this or not. They can choose to look into the fundamental institutional characteristics of the organization and consider ways to best address and even resolve core issues dogging better coordination and more effective cooperation. Such reform is unlikely to take place quickly, but pushing them off is likely to allow existing pressure on ASEAN to build further and problems to fester more. Trying to fix these issues now may already be a little too late, especially given the long lead time needed to decide on and implement any changes. However, taking on the challenges facing ASEAN head on going forward may be preferable to scrambling when a crisis arises.

Another option is for ASEAN members to continue to do more of

---

35 ICJ, Sovereignty over Pedra Branca/Pulau Batu Puteh, Middle Rocks and South Ledge (Malaysia/Singapore); ICJ, Sovereignty over Pulau Ligitan and Pulau Sipadan (Indonesia/ Malaysia).

36 Aglionby, "War of Blame after Thai-Burmese Border Clashes"; Kesavapany, "ASEAN and the Cambodia-Thailand Conflict."

37 ASEAN, *ASEAN Economic Community 2015: Progress and Key Achievements* (Jakarta: ASEAN Secretariat, 2015); Ahmad Ahsan et al, Association of Southeast Asian Nations (ASEAN) Integration Monitoring Report: A Joint Report by the ASEAN Secretariat and the World Bank (Jakarta: The ASEAN Secretariat; Washington, DC: The World Bank, 2013); "ASEAN's Bright Future: Growth Opportunities for Corporates in the ASEAN Region," J.P. Morgan Website, <https://www.jpmorgan.com/country/US/EN/cib/ investment-banking/trade-asean-future>, accessed March 28, 2016.

the same — seeking to maximize and enjoy what immediate benefits they can without worrying too much about the grouping's future. This may put ASEAN, its members, and even partners in a situation akin to being the proverbial frogs in slowly boiling water. Yet, I fear the ease, comfort, and familiarity of not choosing and simply going with the flow, along with the expected risks and costs that come with any serious reform efforts, is likely to make inaction the preferred choice for ASEAN and its individual members. It is far simpler to not worry about longer time horizons and kick the can down the road for future leaders to handle. Whether they can realistically do so or not at a critical juncture with the all the baggage of past omission and inattention is another matter altogether.

IV. Parameters, Possibilities, and Obstacles

Next steps for ASEAN in the face of the complications presented by China's rise and growing major power friction can start with a serious commitment toward improving coordination and sharing information within the grouping. Better intra-ASEAN coordination and transparency means working out areas of overlap, unnecessary redundancy, identifying potential for collaboration, and encouraging cooperation both across different ASEAN initiatives and among member states. Such efforts can involve facilitating the development of joint ASEAN positions, including but not limited to the preparation for key meetings.

Better coordination can allow consistent support for ASEAN governments during their term as the grouping's rotating chair, which may be particularly crucial if the chair government has less institutional capacity to spare to handle more complex regional issues. Higher levels of transparency among member states as well as between member states and the ASEAN Secretariat can further allow better understanding of different perspectives and smooth the way to better decision-making and coordinated policy implementation. Tangible areas that can benefit from better coordination and transparency include developing greater clarity within ASEAN on basic features of a Conduct of Parties in the South China Sea and more credible ways to implement cross-border attempts to manage haze.

The ASEAN Secretariat is probably best placed to facilitate greater transparency and enhanced coordination functions given its neutrality among member states and central position within the organization. Movement in this direction will likely entail enhancements to the Secretariat's institutional capacity. Developments in this direction involve the rather pedestrian steps. They can include expanding the Secretariat's staffing numbers, increasing its budget by raising member annual contributions, and re-organizing the structure of the Secretariat to more closely reflect key issue clusters. ASEAN members can also increase the numbers of civil servants from member governments who serve rotations at the Secretariat as well as to have larger permanent national representation at the Secretariat. These changes merely propose to improve how the Secretariat and organization approaches existing tasks and responsibilities without increasing authority or expand functions. Such a build-up of the ASEAN Secretariat's effectiveness in discharging existing responsibilities do not entail the increase in authority or rise of European Union-like structures that pool aspects of sovereignty. Changes like these should not threaten or erode sovereignty.

Another useful step to consider is to enhance monitoring and transparency among ASEAN members, especially on issues where there are substantive agreements. Work on the haze, human trafficking, crime, the spread of disease, refugees, Humanitarian Assistance and Disaster Relief (HADR), as well as compliance with arrangements for behavior in the South China Sea tends to face difficulties with monitoring and transparency. Too often, member states tend to be less informed about developments in fellow neighboring ASEAN members even if these issues may have repercussions that extend beyond the borders of any one state. As a result, neighboring states may find themselves having less reaction time when critical events occur. Steps to further coordinate the collection and dissemination of information relating to such transnational issues can be of great benefit to ASEAN, ASEAN members, as well as partners going forward. Again, the ASEAN Secretariat seems best placed to take on this role. Note that improved monitoring and sharing of information need not imply the necessity of a formal enforcement mechanism, something that most if not all ASEAN members are likely to resist.

The ideas to begin updating ASEAN I propose above are evolutionary and clearly nothing radical. They aim to help the organization as well as the member states and partners it serves operate better in a contemporary regional political environment. This is a setting now characterized by more centripetal pressure of the grouping and its members as well as less surety that the competition among major powers in the region will necessarily remain within the same old comfort windows. Specifically, they thoughts above seek to help ASEAN members work with each other more effectively through the organization, bearing in mind the sensitivities embedded in Southeast Asian regional relations. Movement in this direction can enable ASEAN and its members to extend greater clarity and certainty in its interactions with key partners. Approaching such outcomes can benefit region stability and cooperation at moments of flux.

Any initial move toward updating ASEAN, no matter how modest, is likely to run into strong opposition regardless. A key source of this resistance comes from the over-cautiousness of many, if not most, political and diplomatic elites across Southeast Asia discussed earlier. This group tends to dominate policy-making circles among member states, and tend to prioritize state foreign policy autonomy and non-interference.[38] They often view almost any modification of the ASEAN Secretariat that does not weaken that body as an affront to their belief in non-interference and autonomy. Parochial

---

38   Alex Bue, "ASEAN Should Get People Back as Its Focus," *Jakarta Post*, (April 10, 2015, <http://www.thejakartapost.com/news/2015/04/10/asean-should-get-people-back-its-focus.html>, accessed March 28, 2016.

bureaucratic interests like the use of ASEAN meetings to obtain supplements to income through travel allowances may create opposition to the placement of more coordination activities within the Secretariat from the civil servants of various member governments.[39] Major powers accustomed to being able to pay on ASEAN differences may also be less amenable to a more effective ASEAN. That the institutional design of ASEAN allows all members to veto any process or decision means that reforming the organization in the face of the above conditions will be particularly trying.

V. Conclusion: An Uncertain Future Ahead for ASEAN?

At stake in updates in the institutional design and organizational structure of ASEAN are the broader, longer-term interests of individual ASEAN members as well as the intensity of competition in East Asia. As detailed earlier, greater temptation to stay away from common positions and the heightened intensity of major power competition exacerbates long-standing, deep-seated fissures within ASEAN. This degrades ASEAN's effectiveness to advance cooperation and the interests of its member states. Insofar as ASEAN members' ability to play a consequential and lasting role in the region and beyond depends on their position within a well-functioning organization, ASEAN reform is a serious matter and should take some precedence over concerns short-term, immediate benefits. An ASEAN that can help coordinate regional issues under the useful myth of 'ASEAN centrality' can help major power distance themselves from elements of competition and contestation that may raise friction and even fuel confrontation. This may be especially true for areas of sharper contention among the major powers. Unfortunately, even such modest steps may be a

---

39 See, for instance, ASEAN, "Annex 1: ASEAN+3 Regional Training Course on Thailand's Land Management for Rural Development and Poverty Eradication Scheme," *ASEAN Cooperation Document*, pp. 24, 24, 36; United States Agency for International Development (USAID), *Audit of the ASEAN Watershed Project*, Audit Report No. 2-498-88-06, May 5, 1988, pp. 14-5, Appendix 1.

bridge too far for almost all the actors concerned at this point.

Of course, revising ASEAN to make it more suited to the contemporary regional politics is not the only option. An alternative is to fundamentally reconfigure the features of regional economic and security architecture. This possibility may involve moving past older institutional structures like ASEAN and reimagining different ways to manage the mode of interaction across Northeast and Southeast Asia. A ground-up redesign may resolve many of the structural problems that now dog ASEAN and 'ASEAN driven' organizations. How Southeast Asian governments should navigate and negotiate such solutions under the shadow of heightened major power differences, or whether major powers are willing and able to bear the burden of such far-reaching changes remain unclear.

Since the end of the Cold War ASEAN members have sought to manage regional relations, major powers, and tensions by 'not choosing sides' between the United States and China. Sometimes this seems to result in an overly cautious approach to regional politics that exacerbates longstanding challenges within ASEAN that may leave the organization and its members worse off. The benefits of reinvigorating ASEAN are clear, but member states and other stakeholders seem too ready to succumb to other temptations at present. This focus on immediate concerns may mean that actors active in the Asia-Pacific may have to face the much more difficult task of re-working regional architecture in the years and decades ahead.

Friend or Foe: The Coopetition between the U.S. and China in Asia

Nathan K. H. Liu[*]

I. Cooperation or Competition

Ever since Samuel Huntington published his "Lonely Superpower" in 1999 describing the unipolar system after the collapse of the USSR and the end of Cold War, the US, as the only superpower, has exerted its influences of "soft power" and "hard power"to almost every corner of the world.[1] The U.S. has therefore been able to take the leading position in all aspects of international affairs, ranging from political, economic, technological and cultural fields and maintaining that leverage is of course the first priority of their national strategy formulation. Any emerging power that might threat that leverage, as a result, becomes the focal point that the U.S. has to pay attention to.

The 21st Century witnessed the great change of the nature of the international system. The so-called lonely superpower is no longer lonely and the emergence of states such as China, India, and Russia are beginning to challenge the dominance of the U.S., especially in Asia. Among the emerging powers, China looks more and more like a potential candidate to challenge American hegemony in Asia.[2] It appears that the rise of China due

---

[*]   Associate Professor and Director, International Affairs and Diplomacy Master's / Bachelor's Program, Ming Chuan University, Taiwan.

[1]   Samuel P. Huntington, "The Lonely Superpower," *Foreign Affairs*, Vol.78, No.2 (March / April, 1999). Joseph S. Nye believes that the US owns both the soft and hard power and Pax Americana will continue due to that leverage. See Joseph S. Nye, *The Paradox of American Power: Why the World's Only Superpower Can't Go It Alone* (New York: Oxford University Press, 2002), pp. 17-18.

[2]   Robert S. Ross, "The Geography of the Peace: East Asia in the Twenty-first Century," *International Security*, Vol.23, No.4 (spring, 1999), pp. 83-86.

to the rapid economic development in the past 35 years and the consequent growth of comprehensive national power has posed as a threat to the presence of the U.S. in Asia. The U.S.'s "Pivot to Asia" or "Rebalance Asia" seems to be the strategy in response to that potential threat. In the meantime, it seems that comprehensive national power of the U.S. is decreasing after getting involved in a series of regional conflicts, including the two Gulf Wars and campaign in Afghanistan. Recent development in the Syrian Conflict seems to demonstrate that the U.S.'s ability to resolve security issues is diminishing.

From the realist perspective, competition among states is zero-sum game, in which one side's gain means the other side's loss. Therefore, the rise of China implies the relative weakening of U.S. influence. If the U.S. intends to maintain the influence, the U.S. will need to seek measures to restrain China's challenges to its dominance. The most effective ways are as a result to adopt competition and confrontational strategies as it successfully did to USSR in the past: containment strategy.

From the liberalist point of view, international interdependence and reciprocal effects should go through international transaction. So cooperation should serve as the major means to reach that goal in the globalized world. Consequently, in order to maintain the U.S. hegemonic status in Asian region, engagement strategy that focuses on interaction and cooperation with China should be the correct measures.

As it appears that U.S. government's China policy is neither realist nor liberal. As a matter of fact, it seems to have been vacillating between containment and engagement trajectory. For example, George H.W. Bush Administration emphasized containment strategy while Clinton Administration seemed to pay more attention to engagement strategy. In his first term, George W. Bush appeared to be more competitive but went back to engagement trajectory later. Whereas, Obama appeared more flexible in his first term but is now taking a more hardline position in the end of his second term--as seen from the confrontations between the two countries in the SCS in early 2016. Consequently, it does not seem to far-fetched as to say that the U.S.'s China policy has been inconsistent in the past 30 years.[3]

Having said that, the relation between the U.S. and China has been comparatively more peaceful and cooperative than confrontational and competitive ever since the end of the Cold War, that is, if the recent development between the two countries is put aside. For one thing, the relation between the two countries is not as tense and hostile as that between the U.S. and the USSR in the Cold War Era. Second, neither side has the intension to conduct confrontational strategy regardless of the recent development between the two countries in the SCS. In other words, the two sides seem to have maintained a relation of "struggle without breaking."[4]

To sum up, never in modern history have two great powers been so deeply intertwined yet so suspicious and potentially antagonistic. The relationship between the U.S. and China involves an uneasy and ever shifting blend of cooperation and competition. This kind of relationship is best described by a coined word "coopetition" which means cooperative competition, emphasizing the part of competition. This also means that the two sides will face the daunting tasks of simultaneously managing competition and maximizing cooperation. As a result, it is reasonable to assume that the strategic landscape in Asia is bound to change.

This article will first describe the general relationship between the U.S. and China so as to lay the groundwork for following discussions. The cooperation in economic, political, environmental as well as security aspects between the two countries will then be discussed in detail. The following

---

3   Peter Cai, "From Engagement to Containment, A Shifting Strategy on China," *China Spectator*, May 15, 2015, <http://www.businessspectator.com.au/article/2015/5/15/china/engagement-containment-shifting-strategy-china>, accessed on March 2, 2016.

4   Chong-Pin Lin, "China's Maritime Embroilments: Behind Rising East Asian Maritime Tensions with China Struggle without Breaking," *Asian Survey*, Vol. 55, No. 3 (May/June, 2015), pp. 478-501.

section will focus on the competition between the two countries because even the two engage in a so-called new type of great-power relations; the reality is that the two countries are still competitors. Ideas and thoughts on the new strategic landscape in Asia will be brought up to the last section of the article.

II. Cooperation between the Two Countries

Although the competition between China and the U.S., mainly in the economic and security realms, intensify greatly especially in the past few years, the cooperation between the two countries has never stopped and still appears promising.

i. Trans-Pacific Partnership

Trans-Pacific Partnership (TPP) is a good starting point for the discussion of the cooperation between the two countries. As early as 2014, China already expressed its interest in participating in the TPP so as to integrate with the global trade system. Many in China believe that by doing so China could provide a necessary boost to its domestic economic reforms.[5] Regardless of the willingness to join the TPP, China was not included in the TPP as the 12 countries signed the agreement in October, 2015.[6] Some argue that China does not really care about its being excluded in the TPP in that China continues to actively engage its neighbors and trading partners. Bilateral agreements between China and other countries and other trade blocs such as the Regional Comprehensive Economic Partnership (RCEP) come so handy. So it really does not mean that much to China for being not

---

5   Shannon Tiezzi, "Will China Join the Trans-Pacific Partnership?" *The Diplomat*, October 10, 2014, <http://thediplomat.com/2014/10/will-china-join-the-trans-pacific-partnership>, accessed on March 4, 2016.

6   Sara Hsu, "China and the Trans-Pacific Partnership," *The Diploma*t, October 14, 2015, < http://thediplomat.com/2015/10/china-and-the-trans-pacific-partnership/>, accessed on March 4, 2016.

a TPP member.[7]

However, the lack of TPP membership will prevent China from enjoying new tariff reductions and preferential market access. As a result, it will divert trade and manufacturing from China to TPP members. Furthermore, according to estimation, losses coming to China from the TPP will be over $46 billion by 2025 and if China joins the TPP, income gains for China could be over $800 billion by 2025.[8] The TPP will also serve as the platform for the two largest economies in the world to establish a solid and long term economic cooperation.

This is not to say that TPP is the cure to the U.S.-China economic relationship that has been beset with challenges, both real and perceived. However, issues like market-access and regulatory barriers in China, an uneven playing field between favored Chinese state-owned enterprises and U.S. firms, inadequate enforcement of intellectual property laws in China, and consumer anxiety about Chinese product safety will be better taken care of with the availability of the TPP platform.

ii. Climate Change

Another realm for the two countries to work together is on climate change mitigation, adaptation, and consequence management. Scientific evidence is clear that human activities are partly responsible for extreme weather events that the world is already experiencing at an increasing rate.[9] The U.S. and China, the two biggest economies and largest emitters

---

7   Peter K Yu, "How China's Exclusion from the TPP could Hurt Its Economic Growth," *Fortune*, October 19, 2015, <http://fortune.com/2015/10/19/china-exclusion-tpp-economic-growth/>, accessed on March 4, 2016.

8   Joshua P. Meltzer, "Why China should Join the Trans-Pacific Partnership," *Order from Chaos*, The Brookings Institution, September 21, 2015, <http://www.brookings.edu/blogs/order-from-chaos>, accessed on March 4, 2016.

9   National Oceanic And Atmospheric Administration, *New report finds human-caused climate change increased the severity of many extreme events in 2014*, November 5th, 2015, <http://www.noaanews.noaa.gov/stories2015/110515-new-report-human-caused-climate-change-increased-the-severity-of-many-extreme-events-in-2014.html>, accessed

of greenhouse gases in the world hold the key to the success of long-term global efforts to combat climate change.[10]

Without the cooperation of the two countries, it is highly possible that global climate change will lead to climate-induced humanitarian disasters and infrastructure destruction. The world would have to face expensive relief operations at the global level with costly and long-term adaptation process. The social and political instability in many areas of the world then increases, especially in emerging economies and developing countries. The U.S.-China cooperation in all these areas will as a result serves as the ground, on which the world could cooperate and effectively respond to the potentially existential threat posed by global climate change. The two countries obviously realized the severity of the situation and bilateral cooperation on climate change has made remarkable progress, highlighted by the historic climate change agreement signed by the two countries in November 2014.[11] The agreement also plays a critical role in the success of the Paris climate change conference in 2015.[12]

iii. Strategic and Economic Dialogue

Regardless of the saber-rattling between the U.S. and China in the SCS recently, the two countries have never stopped attempting to cooperate on critical global, regional, economic as well as security realms. The Strategic and Economic Dialogue (S&ED) is a typical example.

---

on March 4, 2016.

10   Mengpin Ge, Johannes Friedrich and Thomas Damassa, "6 Graphs Explain the World's Top 10 Emitters," *World Resources Institute*, November 25, 2014, <http://www.wri.org/blog/2014/11/6-graphs-explain-world%E2%80%99s-top-10-emitters>, accessed on March 5, 2016.

11   The White House Office of the Press Secretary, *US-China Joint Announcement on Climate Change*, November 11, 2014,<https://www.whitehouse.gov/the-press-office/2014/11/11/us-china-joint-announcement-climate-change>, accessed on March 5, 2016.

12   Julie Makinen and Chris Megerian, "China, US Relationship Key in Climate Agreement," *Los Angeles Times*, December 13, 2015, <http://www.latimes.com/world/asia/la-fg-china-u-s-climate-20151213-story.html>, accessed on March 5, 2016.

As a broad and high level exchange between the U.S. and Chinese governments, the latest S&ED took place in Washington DC in late June 2015 as scheduled. This was the 7th session and discussions focused on a wide range of bilateral, regional, and global issues of strategic and economic importance in the immediate and long term, including security issues such as military relation, confidence building measures, strategic dialog, and non-proliferation.[13] The S&ED mechanism is aimed to facilitate robust engagement and progress between dialogues through coordination with existing bilateral dialogues and working-level interactions.

iv. Regional issues

The two countries even worked together in an attempt to bring peace back to Afghanistan as the Quadrilateral Coordination Group was made up in early 2016.[14] Both U.S. and China have an interest in a peaceful and self-sustaining Afghanistan and China's inclusion in the talk is crucial to the success of the talk since its influence on Pakistan will enable it to serve as a mediator in Afghan peace and reconciliation process, which is something the U.S. lacks.[15]

As a matter of fact, Afghanistan presents challenges and opportunities for both the U.S. and China. The two countries, by working together, could fix the significant problems, energize high-level diplomacy, and provide a future model for U.S.-China cooperation.

In addition to regional security issues, the two countries should consider

---

13 Media Note, "US-China Strategic & Economic Dialogue Outcomes of the Strategic Track," Office of the Spokesperson, US Department of State, June 24, 2015. <http://www.state.gov/r/pa/prs/ps/2015/06/244205.htm>, accessed on March 6, 2016.

14 Shannon Tiezzi, "China Joins Afghanistan, Pakistan, and US for Talks on Afghan Peace Process," *The Diplomat*, January 12, 2016, <http://thediplomat.com/2016/01/china-joins-afghanistan-pakistan-and-us-for-talks-on-afghan-peace-process/>, accessed on March 6, 2016.

15 David Caragliano and Noah Coburn, "Could Afghanistan Be a Model for US-China Cooperation?" *The Diplomat*, April 21, 2015, <http://thediplomat.com/2015/04/could-afghanistan-be-a-model-for-us-china-cooperation/>, accessed on March 6, 2016.

working with each other on broader regional issues such as joint natural disaster relief, joint rescue and patrol, and anti-terrorism exercises, as well as mitigating tensions on the Korean Peninsula.

v. Cybersecurity

Regardless of the thorny accusation from the U.S. that China has launched state-backed hacking against U.S. companies, stealing business secrets, the two countries still managed to work together on enhancing cybersecurity.[16] The two technological powers signed an agreement in the end of 2015 and set up a "hotline" to facilitate the communication and also have agreed their agencies will work together to tackle terrorism, child exploitation and online crime like fraud and the theft of trade secrets.[17]

There were different voices, however. It was said that the attacks had continued in the three weeks since the two countries signed the cyber security agreement. Some expressed skepticism that the agreement would lead to concrete changes in a Chinese policy, which has been accused of being permissive with those who have plundered secrets from companies in the United States. The skepticism is likely to put new pressure on the two countries' agreement to limit attacks on private companies.[18]

vi. U.S.-China Space Dialogue

Ever since China successfully launched Shenzhou 5, the country's first manned spacecraft, in 2003, China became the third country to carry

---

16 Mark Ward, "Does China's Government Hack US Companies to Steal Secrets?" *BBC News*, September 23, 2015, <www.bbc.com/news/technology-34324252>, accessed on March 7, 2016.

17 Richard Bejtlich, "To Hack, or Not to Hack? ," *The Brookings Institution*, September 28, 2015, <http://www.brookings.edu/blogs/up-front/posts/2015/09/28-us-china-hacking-agreement-bejtlich>, accessed on March 7, 2016.

18 Paul Mozur, "Cybersecurity Firm Says Chinese Hackers Keep Attacking US Companies," *The New York Times*, Oct. 19, 2015, <http://www.nytimes.com/2015/10/20/technology/cybersecurity-firm-says-chinese-hackers-keep-attacking-us-companies.html?_r=0>, accessed on March 30, 2016.

astronauts to an orbital space station.[19] As the outer space became more crowded, a mechanism for communication and exchange of ideas between the two countries becomes necessary, thus, to guarantee the peaceful exploration and use of outer space. As a result, the first U.S.-China Space Dialogue meeting was held on Sep. 28, 2015 in Beijing. The two sides exchanged information on respective space policies. They conducted discussions on further collaboration related to space debris and the long-term sustainability of outer space activities. Both sides also exchanged views on issues related to satellite collision avoidance, civil Earth observation activities, space sciences, space weather, and civil Global Navigation Satellite Systems.[20]

To sum up, as it is described above, the U.S. and China has been already in cooperation with each other in many realms, including trade, climate change, regional stability, cybersecurity, and even space development. Given the increasingly interconnected and extraordinarily turbulent challenges in the future at global level, it is imperative for the two countries to deepen the cooperation to address urgent global challenges. As China proposed to build up a "new type of great power relationship" with the U.S., which also has the intension of engaging China, it seems reasonable for the two to work together to address looming, and long-term global challenges that are beyond the capacity of any nation to solve alone.

III. Competition between the Two Countries

However, there has also been steadily rising competition in the relationship regardless of the fact that the U.S. and China seem to have

---

19   Dragon Space, "China Successfully Completes First Manned Space Flight," *Space Daily*, Oct 16, 2003, <http://www.spacedaily.com/news/china-03zo.html>, accessed on March 7, 2016.

20   US Department of State, *The First Meeting of the US-China Space Dialogue*, September 28, 2015, <https://www.state.gov/r/pa/prs/ps/2015/09/247394.htm>.

cooperated wherever they can. Some even argue that the competition is dominating the relationship between the two countries, which is not limited to strategic competition, but covers commercial, ideological, political, diplomatic, technological, even in the academic world.[21]

i. The increasing mutual distrust

The mutual distrust in the both sides increases at astonishing speed, which is especially true in the general public of the both sides. As it is pointed out by a 2015 Pew Research Center survey that 54% of Americans expressed an unfavorable opinion of China and this negative sentiment has exceeded 50% in each of the last three years. A decade ago, in 2006, just 29% of Americans had an unfavorable opinion of China. A more alarming sign is that 56% would use military force to defend an Asian ally such as Japan, South Korea or the Philippines if it was attacked by China.[22] By the same token, only 44% of Chinese have positive views of Americans and 54% say the U.S. is trying to prevent China from becoming a nation as powerful as the U.S. In fact, most believe the U.S. is trying to contain a rising China.[23]

The two governments have been in a climate of mutual suspicion and doubt throughout the entire 2015 and seem to be now in danger of entering a phase of mutual strategic suspicion, a state of affairs that looks unlikely to be eased in the near future. Issues that will deepen the mutual mistrust include alleged Chinese cyberattacks on U.S. targets, regardless of the fact that two sides have already agreed to work together on the issues, the alleged U.S.'s

---

21 David Shambaugh, "In a Fundamental Shift, China and the US are Now Engaged in All-out Competition," *South China Morning Post*, June 11, 2015, <http://www.scmp.com/comment/insight-opinion/article/1819980/fundamental-shift-china-and-us-are-now-engaged-all-out?page=all>, accessed on Feb. 23, 2016.

22 Bruce Stokes, "American Fear of China Weighs on US Election," *Asian Review*, January 29, 2016, <http://asia.nikkei.com/Viewpoints/Viewpoints/American-fear-of-China-weighs-on-US-election>, accessed on March 8, 2016.

23 Richard Wike, "Six Facts about How Americans and Chinese See Each Other," *Pew Research Center*, September 22, 2015, <http://www.pewresearch.org/fact-tank/2015/09/22/6-facts-about-how-americans-and-chinese-see-each-other/>, accessed on March 8, 2016.

containment strategy, and China's island-building in the SCS.[24]

The source of strategic distrust between the U.S. and China is threefold. For one thing, the difference between the political traditions, value systems, and cultures is huge. As the U.S. sees China as an undemocratic country with human right violation records, China regards the U.S. as a hostile country aimed to undermine its authority and legitimacy. Second, the two countries do not understand each other's decision-making process, which leads to suspicion of each other's intention. As the U.S. suspects that the economic activities of China's state-own business are part of its grand strategy, China often sees American NGO's activities as CIA operations. Third, there is a decreasing power gap between the two countries. Most Americans believe that China is going to take over the US role as a hegemon, at least in Asia in the near future.[25]

ii. Intensified Security Competition

The security competition between the two countries has been intensified due to the mutual distrust discussed above and recent developments in certain hot spots, including East China Sea (ECS) and SCS. In the ECS, as Japan decided to purchase three of the five disputed Diaoyutai islands from their private Japanese owner in 2012, the territorial dispute escalated from a minor irritant between China and Japan to a major security concern in the region.[26]

As a matter of fact, ever since 2012, the U.S. has taken steps to clarify

---

24   Wei Pu, "Strategic Mistrust Deepens Between China and the US," *Radio Free Asia*, Sep. 23, 2015, <http://www.rfa.org/english/commentaries/mistrust-09232015110426.html>, accessed on March 9, 2016.

25   Kenneth Lieberthal and Wang Jisi, *Addressing US-China Strategic Distrust*, (Washington DC: The John L. Thornton China Center at Brookings, 2012), pp. 35-36.

26   Scott Cheney-Peters, "How Japan's Nationalization Move in the East China Sea Shaped the US Rebalance," *The National Interest*, October 26, 2014, <http://nationalinterest.org/feature/how-japans-nationalization-move-the-east-china-sea-shaped-11549>, accessed on March 10, 2016.

the U.S. role in deterring any coercive action by China. Furthermore, the US and Japanese forces have conducted regular exercises to strengthen defense of Japan. The U.S. policymakers also clearly stated that the U.S. will defend Japan against any aggression, and the U.S. Senate in the same year passed a resolution accompanying the 2013 National Defense Authorization Act to demonstrate congressional support for the Obama administration's commitment to Japan's defense. In other words, as a security treaty ally of Japan, it is not unlikely that the US would be dragged into an unintended Sino-Japan conflict.[27]

In the SCS, the disputes in the region are focused on two pillars, of which the first pillar is the transformation of the U.S. role in the region from a relatively neutral one to a participatory one. The second pillar is the more aggressive attitude of Vietnam and the Philippines toward sovereignty claims over the SCS. In terms of U.S. attitude, the country, not a claimant state, actually functioned as a coordinator and mediator of the region over security issues and focused on peaceful means to solve the sovereignty disputes, including safe passage of the sea lane in the region before 2000. The U.S. even refused to put the conflicts between the Philippines and claimant states over sovereignty in the region under the coverage of the Mutual Defense Treaty between U.S. and the Philippines.[28]

Ever since 2000, the U.S. has started to actively express its concern over the development in the SCS and even got involved in the regional issue, which has been connected deeply with the rise of China.[29] For example, USS Impeccable was said to be harassed by five Chinese boats while

---

27   Sheila Smith, "A Sino-Japanese Clash in the East China Sea," *Contingency Planning Memorandum No. 18*, Council on Foreign Relations, April 2013, <http://www.cfr.org/japan/sino-japanese-clash-east-china-sea/p30504>, accessed on March 10, 2016.

28   Ian James Storey, "Creeping Assertiveness: China, the Philippines and the South China Sea Dispute," *Contemporary Southeast Asia*, Vol. 21, No. 1 (April, 1999), pp. 95-118.

29   Kristin Deasy, "US Wades into South China Sea Dispute," *Global Post*, July 12, 2012, <http://www.globalpost.com/dispatch/news/regions/americas/united-states/120712/us-wades-south-china-sea-dispute#1>, accessed on April 5, 2013.

conducting survey operation in the region 120 km south of Hainan Island. The incident escalated to a small scale standoff between the two countries. The U.S. claimed that Impeccable was unarmed while China accused the ship of intruding into China's EEZ zone and collected PLAN intelligence.[30] The situation escalated into quasi-military level as U.S. destroyer Lassen navigated within 12 nautical miles of the emerging land masses in the Spratly Islands In October 2015.[31] In November 2015, two U.S. B-52 strategic bombers flew near artificial Chinese-built islands in the area of the Spratly Islands.[32] After the routine patrol of the U.S. aircraft carrier Stennis in the SCS, the U.S. asserts that the U.S. Air Force will continue to fly daily missions over the region despite a buildup of Chinese surface-to-air missiles and fighter jets in the contested region.[33]

These actions of "freedom of navigation" conducted by the US, against the background of China's island-building operations, might lead to unexpected armed clashes between the two countries and thus intensify the security competition in the region.

iii. Formation of anti-Chinese Alliance

As China and the U.S. poised for the SCS confrontation, China's sovereignty disputes with other claimants on the region, especially with Vietnam and the Philippines, is intensifying. The tension consequently leads to the formation of an anti-Chinese alliance, which is understandably

---

30   Mark Valencia, "The Impeccable Incident: Truth and Consequences," *China Security* Vol. 5 No. 2 (Spring,2009), pp. 22-28.

31   Andrea Shalal and David Brunnstrom, "US Navy Destroyer Nears Islands Built by China in South China Sea," *Reuters*, Oct 26, 2015, <http://www.reuters.com/article/us-southchinasea-usa-idUSKCN0SK2AC20151026>, accessed on March 12, 2016.

32   "US B-52 Bombers Flew Near Disputed Islands in South China Sea, Says Pentagon," *The Guardian*, November 12, 2015, <http://www.theguardian.com/world/2015/nov/13/us-b-52-bombers-flew-near-disputed-islands-in-south-china-sea-says-pentagon>, accessed on March 12, 2016.

33   "US General: Air Force to Keep Flying Over South China Sea," *The New York Times*, March 8, 2016, <http://www.nytimes.com/aponline/2016/03/08/world/asia/ap-as-south-china-sea-us-air-force.html?emc=eta1&referer>, accessed on March 12, 2016.

contributed by the sovereignty disputes between China and the two Southeast Asian countries.

China's dispute with Vietnam over Paracel islands in 1974 resulted in an armed conflict between the two countries. It was a significant turning point for China in that the war completed China's control over the Paracel Islands.[34] In 1988, the so-called Johnson South Reef skirmish broke out. China has captured 6 islands within the Johnson South Reef while Vietnam has maintained control over Collins Reef and Lansdowne Reef after the conflict.[35] In January , 2005, Chinese patrol ships fired upon two Vietnamese fishing boats from Thanh Hoa province, killing 9 people and detaining one ship with 8 people on Hainan Island.[36] In May, 2011, the clash involved a Vietnamese survey ship and three Chinese maritime patrol vessels occurred. The event stirred up unprecedented anti-China protests in Vietnam.[37] In June, 2011. A Vietnamese seismic conducting ship clashed with another three Chinese fishery patrol vessels within Vietnam's Exclusive Economic Zone. Vietnam claimed that its exploration cables were deliberately cut.[38] The most recent conflict happened in May 2014 when Chinese state oil company put an oil rig in the waters of disputed Paracel Islands, where Vietnam believes are part of Vietnam' own economic zone.[39]

---

34   Roby Arya Brata, "Open War in the South China Sea," *Jakarta Post*, July 28, 2012, <http://www.thejakartapost.com/news/2012/07/28/open-war-south-china-sea.html>, accessed on April 3, 2013.

35   Neil Connor, "Johnson South Reef Skirmish," *The Daily Star*, November 29, 2012, <http://www.dailystar.com.lb/Entity/People/3351339208/Johnson-South-Reef-Skirmish.ashx#axzz2PNm4Z0Cl>, accessed on April, 2013.

36   Lan Storey, "Conflict in the South China Sea: China's Relations with Vietnam and the Philippines," *The Asia-Pacific Journal: Japan Focus*, April 30, 2008, <http://www.japanfocus.org/-ian-storey/2734>, accessed on April 3, 2013.

37   "South China Sea: Vietnamese Hold Anti-Chinese Protest," *BBC News*, June 5, 2011, <http://www.bbc.co.uk/news/world-asia-pacific-13661779>, accessed on April 3, 2013.

38   Ibid.

39   Paul J. Leaf, "Learning From China's Oil Rig Standoff with Vietnam," *The Diplomat*, August 30, 2014, <http://thediplomat.com/2014/08/learning-from-chinas-oil-rig-standoff-with-vietnam/>, accessed on March 13, 2016.

China's dispute with the Philippines is no less complex. In 1995, the Philippines increased patrol of the surrounding area of Mischief Reefs after realizing that China was building up military structure on the Reefs, which led to numerous arrests of Chinese fishermen and naval clashes with Chinese patrol vessels.[40] In February 2011, a Chinese frigate fired three shots at the Philippine fishing boats in the vicinity of Jackson atoll.[41] In April 2011, a Philippine warship was involved in a standoff with two Chinese surveillance vessels in the Scarborough Shoal. The incident led a series of political protests and negotiations and a fishing ban in 2012.[42]

Japan is of course part of the alliance as the tension between Japan and China over the sovereignty on Diaoyutai islands tightens. In fact, the Philippines and Japan have stepped up their security cooperation as the Philippine President Aquino embarked on a four-day state visit to Tokyo, hoping to rally greater international support against China, which was of great strategic importance to both countries as the Philippines needs Japan's military capability while Japan needs the Philippines' diplomatic support.[43]

To make the situation worse, it was said that Vietnam and the Philippines are discussing security cooperation and South Korea and Vietnam have also discussed common security interests.[44] Some even go

---

40 "Showdown at Mischief Reef," *The Baltimore Sun*, August 5, 1995, <http://articles. baltimoresun.com/1995-08-05/news/1995217032_1_south-china-sea-spratly-islands-mischief-reef>, accessed on April 3, 2013.

41 Tessa Jamandre, "China Fired at Filipino Fishermen in Jackson Atoll," *ABS@CBN News. com*, June 3, 2011, <http://www.abs-cbnnews.com/-depth/06/02/11/china-fired-filipino-fishermen-jackson-atoll>, accessed on April 3, 2013.

42 Gary Li, "Scarborough Shoal Standoff: Bluster or War?" *Caixin Online*, January 23, 2013, <http://gulfnews.com/news/world/philippines/declare-scarborough-shoal-as-rocks-not-island-philippines-1.1136624>, accessed April3, 2013.

43 Richard Javad Heydarian, "Made in Beijing: An Anti-China Alliance Emerges," *The National Interest*, June 13, 2015, <http://nationalinterest.org/feature/made-beijing-anti-china-alliance-emerges-13104?page=2>, accessed on March 13, 2016.

44 Craig Hill, "China's Aggression could See Formation of a Powerful Anti-China Alliance," *China Daily Mail*, June 14, 2014, <http://chinadailymail.com/2014/06/14/

further to say that military exercises between India and the U.S., Japan's possible action of patrolling the SCS, and Australia's announcement that it is going to modernize its Navy are all part of the "ganging up on China."[45]

An anti-Chinese coalition seems emerging.

iv. Accidental outbreak of military conflicts

As China sped up its island-building constructions and became more active in its sovereignty claim over the SCS, the U.S. also started to test China's resolute to protect its sovereign rights in the region. As mentioned above, U.S. destroyer Lassen navigated within 12 nautical miles of the claimed islands. Not long after, two U.S. B-52 strategic bombers flew over the disputed area and the U.S. aircraft carrier Stennis also entered the area. The U.S. even asserts that they will continue to fly daily missions over the region. However, by sending warships and bombers to patrol the adjacent waters off the disputed islands and test China's bottom line, the U.S. also has to face the risk of accidental outbreak of military conflicts in the region, which might be worsened to an uncontrollable level.[46]

There are some possibilities that military conflicts between China and the U.S. could break out in the SCS. For one thing, If U.S. ships or bombers keep entering the territorial waters China claims on a routine basis and China conducts a militarized response, leading to serious damage or great casualties in the U.S. troops. The tension may be escalated into an all-out war. Second, if China declares SCS Air Defense Identification Zone (ADIZ),

chinas-aggression-could-see-formation-of-a-powerful-anti-china-alliance/>, accessed on March 14, 2016.

45   Lira Dalangin-Fernandez, "Aggression in South China Sea will See New anti-China Coalition – Golez," *Interaksyon*, February 20, 2016, <http://interaksyon.com/article/124322/aggression-in-south-china-sea-will-see-new-anti-china-coalition---golez>, accessed on March 14, 2016.

46   Global Conflict Tracker, "Territorial Disputes in the South China Sea," *Council on Foreign Relations*, March 14, 2016, <http://www.cfr.org/global/global-conflict-tracker/p32137#!/conflict/territorial-disputes-in-the-south-china-sea>, accessed on March 15, 2016.

the U.S. may respond similarly as they did when China Declared ECS ADIZ in 2013.[47] The tension in the SCS sky may tighten up as China enforces the ADIZ and the U.S. challenge it. Possible fighter intercepts and encounters may lead to aircraft collisions, if not dogfighting, and escalate the situation.[48]

Other possibilities for the outbreak of military conflicts may be caused by U.S.'s unintentional involvement in the territorial disputes between China and other U.S. allies or neighboring countries, which may drag the two nuclear-armed powers into a conflict that could escalate perilously.

Given the background of "Pivot to Asia" and the rise of China, it seems that the U.S. has been strengthening the security connection with its allies, including Japan and the Philippines, with the intention of "containing" China. In addition, the U.S. also has improved relations with Vietnam, a former enemy.

What should not be ignored is that China has territorial disputes with Japan in the ECS and territorial disputes with the Philippines, an ally, and Vietnam in the SCS. What is worse is that the U.S. also has mutual security defense agreement with Japan and the Philippines. If the situations between China and Japan/the Philippines turn sour, or if Japan and the Philippines decide to initiate provocative actions given the U.S. support, it would be very likely that the U.S. would be dragged into a major conflict with China.[49]

Even the conflicts between China and Vietnam, a non-U.S. ally,

---

47 Robert Farley, "3 Ways China and the US Could Go to War in the South China Sea," *The National Interest*, June 6, 2015, <http://nationalinterest.org/feature/3-ways-china-the-us-could-go-war-the-south-china-sea-13055>, accessed on March 15, 2016.

48 Elisabeth Rosenthal and David E. Sanger, "US Plane in China after It Collides With Chinese Jet," *New York Times*, April 2, 2001, <http://www.nytimes.com/2001/04/02/world/us-plane-in-china-after-it-collides-with-chinese-jet.html?pagewanted=all>, accessed on March 15, 2016.

49 Ivan Eland, "Let's Not Get Into It with China," *The Huffington Post*, September 21, 2015, <http://www.huffingtonpost.com/ivan-eland/lets-not-get-into-it-with_b_8170776.html>, accessed on March 15, 2016.

might drag the U.S. into the military clash with China, especially when the U.S. and Vietnam are gradually promoting a "comprehensive cooperative partnership."[50] As a matter of fact, the progress on U.S.-Vietnam security cooperation not only affects the two countries' strategic military plans, but also exerts considerable influence on the overall geostrategic environment in the SCS region. As a result, if Vietnam is emboldened by that partnership and military conflicts between China and Vietnam occurs. The U.S. send in troops to the SCS, unlikely to join the fight, with the intention to protect the sea lane of communication, which is so vital to shipping in that over $5 trillion in trade passes through the sea annually, including more than half of the world's trade in liquid natural gas and over 33 percent of trade in crude oil.[51] The miscalculation and accidental outbreak of conflicts between the U.S. and China is not entirely unimaginable.

v. Competition for the dominance of the region

As China surpassed Japan to become the world's second-largest economy in 2011, it seems reasonable to assume that China would grow into a regional power too. This assumption is based on the belief that the rise of military power usually parallels with the growth of economic power.[52] Thus, an emerging China coping with the incumbent hegemon, the U.S., becomes something inevitable, especially in Asia.

Even with the growth of military strength, it is still clear that China does not currently possess a formidable military enough to pick a fight with the U.S., even in the Asia-Pacific region. However, there are non-military means to compete for the dominance of the region. For one thing, at the heart of

---

50   Fact Sheet, "US-Vietnam Comprehensive Partnership," Office of the Spokesperson, US Department of State, December 16, 2013, <http://www.state.gov/r/pa/prs/ps/2013/218734. htm>, accessed on March 17, 2016.

51   Joshua Kurlantzick, "A China-Vietnam Military Clash," Contingency Planning Memorandum No. 26, *Council on Foreign Relations*, September 2015, <http://www.cfr. org/china/china-vietnam-military-clash/p37029>, accessed on March 17, 2016.

52   Paul Kennedy, *The Rise and Fall of the Great Powers* (London: Unwin Hyman, 1987), p. xxii.

China's "One Belt, One Road" lies the creation of an economic land belt that includes countries on the original Silk Road through Central Asia, West Asia, the Middle East and Europe, as well as a maritime road that links China's port facilities with the African coast, pushing up through the Suez Canal into the Mediterranean.

The project appears to aim at redirecting the country's domestic overcapacity and capital for regional infrastructure development to improve trade and relations with ASEAN, Central Asian and European countries. However, by offering substantial investment in infrastructure as well as burgeoning trade and economic benefits, it is actually a strategy designed to draw countries across Eurasia, the Middle East and Africa into its plans and thereby blunt the U.S.'s "pivot to Asia."[53]

As mentioned above, the TPP could serve as the platform for China and the U.S. to establish a solid and long term economic cooperation. TPP includes 12 nations bordering the Pacific and account for roughly 40% of global gross domestic product, 30% of global exports and 25% of global imports. However, China is not included in the TPP and has its own version of global trade RCEP, which would include nations with about 30% of global GDP but exclude the U.S. The proposed pact would include the 10 ASEAN countries, Australia, India, Japan, New Zealand and South Korea. Even if it was claimed that the RCEP is not aimed to provide a real alternative to the TPP, it will no doubt function as the center of East Asia's trade regime.

It seems that the two countries have tried to use TPP and RCEP to benefit themselves and keep each other out of their respective regional economic arrangements. As a matter of fact, it is not difficult to imagine that China would hope that the economic size of the RCEP is huge enough

---

53   Peter Symonds, "One Belt, One Road: China's Response to the US 'Pivot," *World Socialist Website*, December 4, 2015, <https://www.wsws.org/en/articles/2015/12/04/obor-d04.html>, accessed on March 18, 2016.

to cut across the economic and strategic bloc established through the TPP.[54] Overlapped membership in TPP and RCEP is another example of the intense competition between the US and China--Australia, Brunei, Japan, Malaysia, New Zealand, Singapore, Vietnam are all included in the both agreements.

Another non-military means to cope with the U.S. dominance is the proposition of the establishment of the Asian Infrastructure Investment Bank (AIIB). Given China's economic strength, China is disproportionately represented in the International Monetary Fund (IMF) and World Bank. It has been proposed in IMF to give China more say. However, the reforms have been delayed for years and even if they go through, America will still retain far more power. As a result, AIIB is aimed to provide a regional alternative to IMF and World Bank based on the Bretton Woods system.

As 58 member nations, including France, Germany, South Korea, and the United Kingdom, joined the bank regardless of the U.S. warnings, China appears to have the confidence to set up an alternative economic world order. To take a step back, if it is too early for China to set a new world order, China could at least use the new bank to expand its influence in Asia with the hope of surpassing the established powers, the U.S. and Japan.[55]

IV. Conclusion: Changing Strategic Landscape in Asia

From the analysis above, it is clear that the Asian strategic landscape is facing a great change, which stemmed primarily from the sustained rapid economic growth of China over the past 35 years. China is now the world's second largest economy followed by Japan. Rapid economic growth has also

---

54   Jingyang Chen, "TPP and RCEP: Boon or Bane for ASEAN? ," *In Asia*, September 9, 2015, <http://asiafoundation.org/in-asia/2015/09/09/tpp-and-rcep-boon-or-bane-for-asean/>, accessed on March 20, 2016.

55   The Economist explains, "Why China Is Creating a New 'World Bank' for Asia," *The Economist*, Nov. 11, 2014, <http://www.economist.com/blogs/economist-explains/2014/11/economist-explains-6>, accessed on March 20, 2016.

enabled China to devote greater resources to military modernization and build-up, contributing to change in the strategic landscape in Asia.

As the incumbent hegemon, the U.S. will of course continue to be the dominant power in the region for at least decades to come, given China's growing but still limited military strength. The two countries could cooperate with each other in many aspects including economic, environmental, cyber-security, or even military fields. However, it seems the competition between the two countries is getting stronger as the U.S. strengthens its military deployment in the Asian-Pacific region and deepens its military cooperation with its traditional allies. Especially with Japan, the U.S. has virtually encouraged Japan to amend its security-related laws so as to give Japan the power to fully exercise the right to collective self-defense and enable Japanese troops to fight abroad. Furthermore, the US is getting actively involved in the sovereignty claims in the ECS and SCS with the intention to maintain its hegemony in the Asia Pacific region.

As a result, the dynamics between the U.S. and China is bound to change--the earlier equilibrium between the two is apparently being broken. Judging from the factors discussed above, the new strategic situation in the region could be presented in several aspects.

First, the relation of "struggle without breaking" could be unfortunately broken given the uncertainties caused by the competition between the U.S. and China in many aspects. Accidents may occur due to strategic misunderstanding or misjudgment of both or even the third party, intensifying the tension in the region.

Second, as the competition intensifies, it seems Asian countries are also forced to take sides between the U.S. and China. It was reported that China received the permission of Malaysia to dock warships at Kota Kinabalu whereas Vietnam and the Philippines may be happy to see a U.S. challenge to China's claims in the disputed SCS waters.[56] In addition, regardless of the fact that South Korea has been an U.S. ally for decades and the U.S.'s opposition to its traditional allies and partners signing on to the AIIB, it joined the bank anyway for the founding member status.[57] As mentioned earlier, overlapped membership of Australia, Brunei, Japan, Malaysia, New Zealand, Singapore, Vietnam in both TPP and RCEP is another indicator that countries in the Asian region may need to take sides sooner or later.

Third, the tension in the Asian region is harmful to the economic growth in the region, especially to the investment and business environments. Nor does the regional tension meet the primary interests of many Asian countries that desire for regional stability for development.

Last, it seems the U.S. is confident in its ability to maintain the regional stability. However, maintaining the regional stability does not seem as easy as it did when the American power in Asia was at its height, especially after the rise of China and the consequent change of geostrategic landscape in the region. The regional stability or equilibrium maybe disturbed due to miscalculation or accidents.

To sum up, the U.S. is still the only superpower of the world regardless of the fact that China is now the second largest economy and is rapidly increasing its military buildup. Nonetheless, it is not entirely far-fetched to say that China is catching up.

The million dollar question then is: Will China overthrow the existing order set by the U.S. and replace its role in the region or will China coexist peacefully with the U.S.?

---

56 Elizabeth Shim, "China: US Forcing Countries to 'Take Sides' on South China Sea Dispute", *UPI*, Nov. 20, 2015, <http://www.upi.com/Top_News/World-News/2015/11/20/China-US-forcing-countries-to-take-sides-on-South-China-Sea-dispute/4161448036062/>, accessed on March 23, 2016.

57 Ankit Panda, "South Korea Joins the AIIB," *The Diplomat*, March 28, 2015, <http://thediplomat.com/2015/03/south-korea-joins-the-aiib/>, accessed on March 23, 2016.

We do not know as of now. Maybe we do not have to wait too long to know the answer.

My Lawn is Greener than Yours: The American and Chinese Views on the International Order[*]

Yeh-Chung Lu [**]

I. Introduction

Perceptions and misperceptions of decision-makers continue to affect foreign policy in the case of Chinese foreign policy, in that Chinese top leaders tend to assess the external environment in which China operates and interacts with others, and then make decisions they see fit or prudent accordingly.

The end of the Cold War and the financial crisis of 2008 had a significant impact on China's worldview. The end of Cold War led Chinese leaders to foresee the commencement of a multipolar world. This perception, to certain extent, finally contributed to China's relatively confrontational policy toward the United States in the mid-1990s. Since the global financial crisis in 2008, many Chinese analysts have begun to predict, once and again, the decline of the U.S. Accordingly, China has become more confident to propose initiatives that may transform its role from rule-taker to rule-maker.

This development leads us to ponder two distinct but related questions: What is China's view on the current international that is considered to be led by the United States? To what extent would China expect to shape this

---

[*] Earlier versions of this paper were presented at the International Conference on U.S.-China Relations and the Changing Security Dynamics in East Asia, organized by the Graduate Institute of International Affairs and Strategic Studies (GIIASS), Tamkang University, Taipei, Taiwan, April 30, 2016, and at the annual meeting of American Political Science Association (APSA), Philadelphia, USA, August 31 to September 1, 2016.

[**] Associate Professor, Department of Diplomacy; Director, International Master's Program in International Studies, National Chengchi University, Taiwan.

order? To answer these questions, this paper proceeds as follows: After the introductory section, section two describes how China perceives the political power structure in international politics in recent years. With the examination on Chinese perceptions in relation to the U.S., this paper concludes that at least for now, China has become more pragmatic in promoting its view of international order vis-à-vis the U.S.-led world order.

II. China's Views on International Power Distribution after the Global Financial Crisis of 2008[1]

When the U.S. began to face economic downturns in 2008, China began to see the decline of the U.S. has become reality. With this judgement in mind, China's U.S. policy seemed to be less accommodative.

Some evidence supports China's optimism. For instance, after thirty years of economic reform and opening up, the increase of China's gross domestic production (GDP) has been impressive, surpassing Japan as the second largest economy in the world in 2010. With confidence and thanks to the Obama administration's "strategic reassurance", more and more Chinese scholars and analysts do not see the decline of the U.S. as a prerequisite for the rise of China.

The international environment has changed rapidly seems to be a shared understanding among Chinese scholars and analysts. In the meantime, the external environment is full of uncertainty under the impact of the financial crisis. In the bluebook on International Situation and China's Foreign Affairs (2010/2011), edited by the think tank of China's Ministry of Foreign Affairs, also known as China Institute of International Studies (CIIS), analysts concluded that the trend of multipolarization in world affairs is further

---

1   Part of this paper is from Yeh-chung Lu, "Déjà Vu? China's Assessments on the World in the Early 1990s and Late 2000s," *Tamkang Journal of International Affairs*, Vol.18, No.2 (October 2014), pp. 25-58.

advanced and becomes more evident, due to the rise of newly emerged powers and tardy recovery in world economy.[2] This official view champions power reconfiguration and multipolarization in world politics.

Nevertheless, other analysts provide more diverse views on the international structure with several major arguments. Among them, a group of scholars contends that the U.S. decline is for real this time, and other rising powers would continue to rise.[3] The U.S. decline this time is attributed to the war on Iraq and economic downturns.

Nevertheless, another group of analysts tends to judge that the U.S. is "wounded" but not "dead" yet. Through the angle of Marxism, this group of scholars contends Capitalism represented by the U.S. is doomed to fail in the long run but not now, given the fact that the U.S. continues to meddle in regional affairs in the Asia-Pacific with the policy dubbed as "rebalancing".[4] Still others see U.S. declinism ungrounded and this declinism is wide-spread mainly due to rising nationalism in developing countries which seems to cloud top leaders' judgment on world politics.[5]

---

2   "Preamble," in Chu Xing, ed., *Guoji Xingshi he Zhongguo Waijiao Lanpishu* (2010/2011) [Bluebook on International Situation and China's Foreign Affairs (2010/2011)] (Beijing: Shishi Chubanshe, 2011), pp. 1-13.

3   Wang Tien, "Meiguo shuailuo yu qunxong xueqi" [The Decline of the U.S. and the Rise of Other Powers], *Renmin Ribao*, May 30, 2008, p. 3; Peng Guangqian, "Meiguo qiangquan zoxiang xiangdue shuailuo de guaidian" [The U.S. Decline has Passed the Point of No Return], *Xiandai Guoji Guanxi*, No. 5 (2007), pp. 8-10; Peng Guangqian, "Quanqiu jinrong weiji dui guoji geju de yingxiang" [The Impact of Global Financial Crisis on the International Structure], *Xiandai Guoji Guanxi*, No. 4 (2009), pp. 26-28.

4   Li Shenming, "Meiguo 'Yatai Zaipingheng Zhanglue' de Mudi yu Shouduan" [The Ends and Means of U.S. Rebalancing to Asia], in Li Shneming and Zhang Yuyan, eds., *Quanqiu Zhengzhi yu Anquan Baogao (2014)* [Annual Report on International Politics and Security (2014)] (Beijing: Shehuei Keshue Chubanshe, 2014), pp. 21-32. A latest account on China's views on U.S. rebalancing policy, please refer to Richard Weixing Hu, "The Chinese Response to the U.S. Rebalancing Strategy: Sino-U.S. Relations and Washington's Pivot to Asia," in David W.F. Huang ed., *Asia Pacific Countries and the U.S. Rebalancing* (N.Y.: Palgrave MacMillan, 2016), pp. 69-84.

5   Li Chuanyuan and Fan Jianzhong, "'Meiguo Shuailuolun' Xilun" [An Analysis on the U.S. Declinism], *Xiandai Guoji Guanxi*, No. 8 (2009), pp. 30-36.

While the abovementioned views present the debate over whether the decline of the U.S. is a precondition for the rise of China, most Chinese scholars view a strong U.S. with a hostile policy constitute a sufficient challenge to China's rise.[6] However, while interpreting the U.S. rebalancing as ill-intended, the majority of the analysts and scholars do not hint that a head-on conflict with the U.S. is desirable.[7]

In reaction to U.S. rebalancing strategy, Chinese strategists pay more attention on how much burden China needs to share in world affairs or as some dubbed as the "Olson Trap", and less on promoting the idea of multipolarization.[8] In the meantime, they caution against the U.S. intention of advocating the idea of "G-2."[9]

The aforementioned discussion suggests that the U.S. declinism is more real than that was in the early 1990s. Lately Chinese scholars continue to see the trend of multipolarization as inevitable, but are fully aware that the U.S.-China relations are characterized by competition rather than cooperation.[10] Nevertheless, most of the discussion concludes with the suggestion that

6   Robert S. Ross, "The Problem with the Pivot," *Foreign Affairs*, Vol. 91, No. 6 (November/ December 2012), pp. 70-82; Li Changjiu, "Guoji geju duanqinei buhui fasheng genbanxing bianhua" [The International Structure would not Change fundamentally in the Short-term], *Xiandai Guoji Guanxi*, No. 4 (2009), pp. 11-13.

7   Li Boya, etc., "Zhanglue Shousuo haishi Yituei Weijin?" [Strategic Restraint or One Step back, Two Steps forward?], *Renmin Ribao*, April 1, 2014, p. 23.

8   Wen Xian, Liao Zhengjun, and Li Boya, "Meiguo Kucheng Shijie 'Laoda'" [The U.S. is Working hard to Maintain its Superpower Status], *Renmin Ribao*, May 30, 2014, p. 3; "Qin Yaqing: Major-country Diplomacy Must Steer Clear of Three Traps that Could Hinder China's Rise," *Chinese Social Sciences Today*, June 11, 2015, http://www.csstoday.com/ Item/2179.aspx.

9   Li Changjiu, "Guoji geju duanqinei buhui fasheng genbanxing bianhua" [The International Structure would not Change fundamentally in the Short-term], *Xiandai Guoji Guanxi*, No. 4 (2009), pp. 11-13.

10   Zhang Jie, "Zhongguo zuobien anquan xingshi: bienhua, gojian yu tiaozhan" [China's Regional Security Environment: Changes, Construction, and Challenges], in Zhang Jie ed., *Zhongguo Zuobien Anquan Xingshi Pinggu: 2015* [China's Regional Security Environment Review: 2015] (Beijing: Social Sciences Academic Press, 2015), pp. 12-31.

China needs to be pragmatic and it is unwise to challenge the U.S. head on.

III. Implications of this New International Order

In addition to the above discussion, Yuan Peng from CICIR contends that China sees the international system as moving into its fourth transformation: from the Westphalian system of 1648, the Versailles-Washington system of 1918, the Yalta system of 1945, to the one after the global financial crisis. This stage of great transformation is characterized by four trends: the power shift from the West to rising powers, it is the first time in history that dominant powers in the West are all facing economic difficulties and political problems, non-state actors are playing a key role in world politics, and the world as a whole is facing global problems.[11]

In accordance to this interpretation, Yuan Peng continues to argue that China cab grasp the moment of great transformation in the international system to shape the rules of major mechanisms. It is worth noting that China has a long tradition seeing the international system as illegitimate and only representing the triumph of the strong over the weak since Mao Zedong.[12] Therefore, when China perceives its own success in modernization, it calls for the revision of the rules in the international system corresponding with its material power and status.

Fu Ying, the Chairperson of Foreign Affairs Committee of National People's Congress, opines that China sees itself as sitting under the same roof with the U.S., and China's goal is to improve the international order and global governance while the U.S. seems to be deeply concerned with its own

---

11 Yuan Peng and Nina Hachigian, "Global Roles and Responsibilities," in Nina Hachigian, ed., *Debating China: The US-China Relationship in Ten Conversations* (NY: Oxford University Press, 2014), p. 89.

12 Jeffrey Bader, *How Xi Jinping Sees the World... and Why* (Washington, DC: The Brookings Institution, 2016).

dominance.[13]

Table 1: China's Views on the International Order

	China	The U.S.
Preferred Terminology	**International order**	**World order**
Basic Content	International institutions under the United Nations structure, in which China plays a contributing role as others; acting with legitimacy.	Global hegemonic power system, underpinned with monetary system, military alliances, and values altogether contributing to U.S. dominance.
Goals	How to improve international order and global governance; China has neither the intention nor ability to overturn the current system.	How to maintain world dominance; Full of doubt on China's intention.
Nature	Inclusive	Exclusive
Role of UN	Facilitating China's economic growth and making China's voice to be heard.	U.S. as designer and supporter to UN, but bypasses it when necessary.

Please be noted that in this table the U.S. part refers to how China interprets U.S. perspective on the international order.

Source: Adapted from Fu Ying, "Under the Same Roof: China's View of Global Order," *New Perspectives Quarterly*, Vol. 33, No. 1 (January 2016), pp. 45-50.

By suggesting the term "international order" in relation to U.S.-preferred "world order," China implies that it has not only benefited from the extant international system, but been dedicated to preserve the order organized by the U.S. (and China) along with others after the WWII. In other words, China is in pursuit of status quo, not a revisionist power.

It is noteworthy that with the perception that China's rise is inevitable and more legitimate in relation to U.S. hegemony, China has redefined its

---

13   Fu Ying, "Under the Same Roof: China's View of Global Order," *New Perspectives Quarterly*, Vol. 33, No. 1 (January 2016), pp. 45-50.

national interests in recent years accordingly.[14] The conception of national interest in China is not static or fixed, and since the 1990s, China has put more emphasis on economic and technological capabilities than pure military power as their western counterparts have emphasized.[15] Besides, economic growth indeed helped transform China's image from "enemy" to "engine of growth" and the power as a buyer granted China with more influence.[16] This power of buying makes China to unavoidably broaden its definition of national interests. As the other side of the same coin, being as one of the most important factories in the world also equipped China with the power of selling. Combined together, growing quest for resources also constitutes part of China's national interests.[17]

On top of those discussions, Wang Jisi succinctly points out the sovereignty, security, and economic development can be seen as China's core interests.[18] Sovereignty issues relating but not limited to Taiwan, Tibet, and Xinjiang are of significance in Chinese foreign policy making, from the very beginning of the establishment of PRC. However, Wang continues, the three prongs of sovereignty, security, and development may not necessarily lead to clarity of what China's national interests really are, because sometimes these three prongs are in tension and there seems no clear hierarchy among these three. With the nature of core interests as non-negotiable, the result is China is in lack of a consistent and organizing principle for foreign policy. In other words, there are rooms for maneuver to define and redefine Chinese national interests.

---

14 The author would like to thank the discussant at the APSA annual meeting for highlighting this point.

15 Yong Deng, "The Chinese Conception of National Interests in International Relations," *The China Quarterly*, No. 154 (1998), pp. 308-329.

16 David M. Lampton, *The Three Faces of Chinese Power: Might, Money, and Minds* (Berkeley, CA: University of California Press, 2008), pp. 88-96.

17 Elizabeth C. Economy and Michael Levi, *By All Means Necessary: How China's Resource Quest is Changing the World* (Oxford: Oxford University Press, 2014).

18 Wang Jisi, "China's Search for a Grand Strategy," *Foreign Affairs*, Vol. 90, No. 2 (March/April 2011), pp. 68-79.

Wang's opinion can be further evidenced by China's latest attempt to build "One Belt, One Road" (OBOR). According to some, OBOR serves the top leadership's interests in presenting effective political performance to China's general public, so Xi Jinping has promoted this initiative among other issues, including the South China Sea issue.[19] The OBOR initiative represents the dimensions of economic development and security, but the South China Sea is highly related to sovereignty and security but less so to economic development. When more dimensions are involved in a given issue, more policy advocates or stakeholders there can be in the process of decision-making, which makes the issue less likely to be effectively solved.

IV. Exit, Voice, Loyalty, or What?

Lack of clarity in the definition of core interests and of a clear grand strategy, this paper finds the saying that China aims and is capable of taking over the hegemonic status in world politics is in question. Several decades ago, Albert Hirschman argued that there are two types of response to unsatisfactory situations in one's firm, organization or country. The first is "exit," or "leaving without trying to fix things." The second is "voice," or "speaking up and trying to remedy the defects." Loyalty can modify the response, causing one to stand and fight (voice) rather than cut and run (exit).[20] This argument has later become a well-accepted analogy when one wants to explain a state's behavior vis-à-vis the international environment.

China's reference to the benefits in joining the international institutions seems to demonstrate a degree of "loyalty" to the extant international system. And yet, with the growing material capabilities, China under Xi Jinping has begun to proactively propose the ways to better shape the international

---

19   Wenjuan Nie, "Xi Jinping's Foreign Policy Dilemma: One Belt, One Road or the South China Sea?" *Contemporary Southeast Asia*, Vol. 38, No. 3 (2016), pp. 422-444.

20   Albert O. Hirschman, *Exit, Voice, and Loyalty: Responses to Decline in Firms, Organizations, and States* (Cambridge, Mass.: Harvard University Press, 1970).

system – an act that can be understood by "voice". However, some experts interpret China's behavior as an "exit" strategy, with which China aims to present an alternative to the U.S.-led international order.[21]

China is also eager to reflect its influence in existing international organizations, as indicated in the revision of proportional voting system of IMF and World Bank. China's reservation on certain articles of the United Nations Convention on Law of the Seas (UNCLOS) is another indication. These institutions all fall under what China describes as the "international system."

However, it would be too soon to argue that China is trying to overthrow and replace the U.S.-led world order for the time being – an act of "exit". The extent to which China perceives these initiatives as deliverables remains unclear, especially when domestic issues are a real danger to the Chinese leadership under Hu and Xi. And, China has been assuming, more or less, the role as stakeholder in the international arena. For instance, over the past years, China has dispatched more than 21,000 personnel on UN peacekeeping missions, and been more in line with other major countries on regional flashpoints such as Darfur, Afghanistan, Iran, and lately North Korea.

From the U.S. perspective, Assistant Secretary of State Daniel Russel's latest remarks indicated China's compliance to the U.S.-led world order and international norms is mixed.[22] On the issues pertaining to climate change, nuclear nonproliferation, combating disease and terrorism, and wildlife protection, China has demonstrated high degree of compliance and cooperation. Even on the issues more sensitive in the past, such as the Trans-

---

21 Michael Pillsbury, The Hundred-Year Marathon: China's Secret Strategy to Replace America as the Global Superpower (N.Y.: St. Martin's Griffin, 2016); Barry Buzan, "The Logic and Contradictions of 'Peaceful Rise/Development' as China's Grand Strategy," The Chinese Journal of International Politics, Vol. 7, No. 4 (June 2014), pp. 381-420.

22 Daniel Russel, "Remarks at 'China's Growing Pains' Conference," US Department of State, April 22, 2016.

Table 2: China's Initiatives on Parallel Institutions

CHINA-CENTERED AND PAN-ASIAN INSTITUTIONS	KEY FEATURES	PARALLEL TO
Financial and Monetary Policy		
BRICS New Development Bank (NDB)	Development bank with a focus on infrastructure, founded in July 2014 with headquarters in Shanghai; Indian presidency for the first five years.	World Bank, regional development Banks
Asian Infrastructure Investment Bank (AIIB)	ADB members were invited to join in; fifty-seven founding countries (as of May 2015).	ADB
BRICS Contingency Reserve Arrangement (CRA)	Reserve pool (100 billion USD) for crisis liquidity (signed in July 2014).	IMF
Mechanisms for internationalizing the RMB	Twenty-eight agreements on direct exchange of RMB with other currencies; treaties on clearing banks in nine countries; seven country-specific Renminbi Qualified Foreign Institutional Investor (RQFII) quotas; twenty-eight swap agreements with central banks.	Established currency market Mechanisms
Shanghai as global financial center with RMB-denominated futures markets	State Council decision (2012) to turn Shanghai into a global financial center; approval of Shanghai Free-Trade Zone (August 2013). RMB-denominated futures markets for crude oil, natural gas, petrochemicals (August 2014); gold trading platform (fall 2014); six other international commodities futures markets are in the planning stage.	Established centers for financial, commodities, and futures markets

China International Payment System (CIPS)	CIPS for international RMB transactions (April 2012); Sino- Russian negotiations on alternatives to SWIFT (fall 2014).	Established payment systems (CHIPS, etc.)
Transregional Infrastructure Projects		
One Road, One Belt	Large-scale infrastructural and geostrategic projects (announced by President Xi Jinping in November 2013) that aim at opening up new land and maritime trading corridors across Eurasia.	New Silk Road (United States, 2011), Eurasian Economic Union (Russia)
Security		
Conference on Interaction and Confidence-Building Measures in Asia (CICA)	A security forum originally initiated by Kazakhstan (1999); China serves as chair 2014-16.	ARF
Shanghai Cooperation Organization (SCO)	An international organization (established in 2001) by China, Russia, Kazakhstan, Kyrgyzstan, Tajikistan, and Uzbekistan with a security focus. In 2014, India, Iran, and Pakistan applied for membership.	CSTO, ARF
Diplomatic Forums		
Boao Forum for Asia (BFA)	An annual forum founded in 2001 for decision-makers from politics, business, and academia with a regional focus on Asia.	WEF/Davos
Pan-Asian Trade, Finance, Monetary Policy		
Regional Comprehensive Economic Partnership (RCEP)	A free trade agreement planned to be concluded by the end of 2015 and to encompass three billion people and 40 percent of world trade.	TPP, TTIP

| Chiang Mai Initiative Multilateralization (CMIM); ASEAN Plus Three; Asian Macroeconomic Research Office (AMRO) | Reserve pool (increase to 240 billion USD in effect since July 2014) for crisis liquidity ("Multilateralization" started in March 2010; AMRO established in April 2011, status as international organization since October 2014). | IMF |

Source: Olin Wethington and Robert A. Manning, *Shaping the Asia-Pacific Future: Strengthening the Institutional Architecture for an Open, Rules-Based Economic Order* (Washington, DC: Atlantic Council, 2015), Table 1, p. 17.

Pacific Partnership (TPP) and military-to-military dialogues, China has been willing to interact with the U.S. counterparts. The Asian Infrastructure Investment Bank (AIIB) now also has the ink of existing institutions – by moving toward adopting the standard and accountability from the Asia Development Bank (ADB).

With more vehicles that can bear China's ideals of political and economic development, some are concerned about the possibility that it would be more likely for China to diffuse its model and dominate the world. Nevertheless, from Russel's comments, China's signature AIIB somewhat seems to be working in tandem with the U.S.-led ADB and World Bank.[23] Some scholars in the West also begin to argue that due to domestic constraints, it is unlikely for rising powers including China to provide the public good to the international community, which in turn makes it more difficult for rising powers to garner support to replace a U.S.-led international system.[24] To make sure rising powers would continue to uphold the rule-based current international system, some suggest that a consultation

---

23   A critical assessment of the influence of the Beijing Consensus is Mark Beeson and Fujian Li, "What Consensus? Geopolitics and Policy Paradigms in China and the United States," *International Affairs*, Vol. 91, No. 1 (2015), pp. 93-109.

24   William I. Hitchcock, Melvyn P. Leffler, and Jeffrey W. Legro, eds., *Shaper Nations: Strategies for a Changing World* (Cambridge, M.A.: Harvard University Press, 2016).

rather than confrontation with rising powers are in need, especially when sovereign states are expected to meet their own obligations in the future.[25]

The caveat here is, China is eager to secure its status in East Asia, and is "an Asia-Pacific regional power with some global reach." As a result, China hardens its position on maritime issues in recent years as noted by both Russel and Bader. Besides, even if China upholds the UN system, its involvement remains selective to be in line with its core interests.

V. By Way of Conclusion

China's growing economic and political influence makes observers to doubt if it is having a secret plan to take over the U.S. as the dominant power in world politics. The evidence in this research suggests that at this moment China's ambition is still limited to reshape but not replace the international structure. This is a way for China to demonstrate the willingness to avoid the "Thucydides Trap" – an inevitable conflict between China as a rising power and the U.S. as a status quo power.

However, when the issues are significant to core interests and a peaceful and stable surrounding environment, China are less willing to show the sense of self-constraint. In the meantime, Daniel Russel opines that the U.S.-led world order is rule-based, and that the U.S. shall continue to avoid the accommodationist trap where accepting China's "core interests" is the price for trade benefits and global cooperation. This is a statement that requires China's leaders to ponder.

---

25   Richard Haass, "World Order 2.0: The Case for Sovereign Obligation," *Foreign Affairs*, Vol. 96, No. 1 (January/February 2017), pp. 2-9.

The End of the "Hidden Light"? Rationalist and Reflectivist Perspectives on China's Foreign Policy

Hsin-Wei Tang[*]

I. Introduction

Between January 19 and 23, 2016, President Xi Jinping paid state visits to Saudi Arabia, Egypt, and Iran. According to the Chinese Foreign Minister, Wang Yi, the motivations underlying President Xi Jinping's visits were peace, development, and reconciliation. Consequently, they attracted considerable attention and heightened expectations within the region and the international community.[1]

However, some have argued that by courting U.S. allies such as Saudi Arabia,[2] cooperating with African countries such as Egypt,[3] and engaging with countries such as Iran,[4] the PRC is, in fact, challenging the US. This

---

1 Yi Wang, "Foreign Minister Wang Yi's Comments on President Xi Jinping's Visits to Saudi Arabia, Egypt, Iran and Headquarters of League of Arab States: Renew Friendship, Discuss Cooperation and Seek Common Development," *Ministry of Foreign Affairs of the People's Republic of China*, January 24, 2016, <http://www.fmprc.gov.cn/mfa_eng/topics_665678/xjpdstajyljxgsfw/t1335155.shtml/>.

2 Robert G. Sutter, "China's Regional Strategy and Why it May Not be Good for America," in David Shambaugh ed., *Power Shift: China and Asia's New Dynamics* (Berkeley: University of California Press, 2005), pp. 289-305; Gill Bates, *Rising Star: China's New Security Diplomacy* (Washington, DC: Brookings Institution, 2007).

3 Akwe Amosu, "China in Africa: It's (Still) the Governance, Stupid," *Foreign Policy in Focus*, March 9, 2007, <http://fpif.org/china_in_africa_its_still_the_governance_stupid/>; Moises Naim, "Rogue Aid," *Foreign Policy*, No. 159 (March/April,2007), pp. 95-96.

4 Robert Kagan, "Ambition and Anxiety: America's Competition with China," in Gary J. Schmitt ed., *The Rise of China: Essays on the Future Competition* (New York: Encounter Books, 2009), pp. 1-24; Stephanie Kleine-Ahlbrandt and Andrew Small, "China's New

view that the PRC is deliberately challenging the international status quo established by the U.S. is widely held.[5] This raises the question of whether such claims have reasonable foundations. Alternatively, is Beijing continuing to maintain its previous status quo policy? This paper engages with these questions from the perspectives of both rationalism and reflectivism, as defined by Robert Keohane.[6]

II. Rationalist Perspectives

In the landmark rationalist exposition titled Theory of International Politics, Kenneth Waltz identified two methods that could be used by a country to maintain balance with another power: external balancing (forging alliances) or internal balancing (military buildups).[7] Similarly, if a rising power is inclined to revise the international status quo upheld by the dominant power, it may resort to one of two ways of accumulating sufficient capabilities through attracting allies and increasing military capabilities to challenge the latter. Power transition theorists, self-labeled as being the rationalist,[8] have focused on the above two strategies[9] to assess whether or

Dictatorship Diplomacy: Is Beijing Parting with Pariahs?" *Foreign Affairs*, Vol. 87, No. 3 (January/February, 2008), pp. 38-56.

5   See: for example, John J. Mearsheimer, *The Tragedy of Great Power Politics* (New York: W. W. Norton, 2014), pp. 360-411; Andrew F. Krepinevich, Jr. "How to Deter China: The Case for Archipelagic Defense," *Foreign Affairs*, Vol.94, No.2, (March/April, 2015), pp.78–86.

6   Robert O. Keohane, "International Institutions: Two Approaches," *International Studies Quarterly*, Vol. 32, No. 4 (December, 1988), pp. 379-396. Also: Milja Kurki and Colin Wight, "International Relations and Social Science," in Tim Dunne, Milja Kurki, and Steve Smith eds., *International Relations Theories: Discipline and Diversity*, (Oxford: Oxford University Press, 2013), pp. 23-24

7   Kenneth Waltz, *Theory of International Politics* (Mass: Addison-Wesley, 1979).

8   Ronald L. Tammen et al., *Power Transitions: Strategies for the 21st Century* (New York: Chatham House, 2000), p. 6.

9   Douglas Lemke, *Regions of War and Peace* (Cambridge: Cambridge University Press, 2002), pp. 99-109.

not a power is satisfied with the international status quo.

i. Alliance Portfolios and the PRC's Alliance Policy

A potential aggressor against the international order is likely to have an alliance portfolio that differs from that of the dominant power. Kim has operationalized the concept of satisfaction or dissatisfaction with the international order based on the following procedure.[10] He always begins with the assumption that the dominant nation is satisfied. Next, he calculates the coefficients for the similarity between the dominant nation's alliance portfolio and that of another power. A positive coefficient indicates satisfaction of the non-dominant power, and a negative coefficient indicates its dissatisfaction. Kim has applied this assessment procedure in his follow-up studies on war and peace at the global level[11] and at the regional level of East Asia.[12] Accordingly, he has concluded that dissatisfaction with the status quo has a significant positive effect on the onset of wars.

Similarly, alliance portfolios are evidently the predominant and the most widely used measure of dissatisfaction with the international status quo in a large number of statistical analyses that have tested power transition theory.[13]

---

10 Woosang Kim, "Alliance Transitions and the Great Power War," *American Journal of Political Science*, Vol. 35, No. 4 (November, 1991), pp. 833-850.

11 Woosang Kim, "Power Transitions and Great Power War from Westphalia to Waterloo," *World Politics*, Vol. 45, No. 1 (October, 1992), pp. 153-172; "Power Parity, Alliance, and War from 1648-1975," in Jacek Kugler and Douglas Lemke ed., *Parity and War* (Ann Arbor: University of Michigan Press, 1996), pp. 93-106.

12 Woosang Kim, "Power Parity, Alliance, Dissatisfaction, and Wars in East Asia, 1860-1993," *Journal of Conflict Resolution*, Vol. 46, No. 5 (October, 2002), pp. 654-671.

13 Douglas Lemke and William Reed, "War and Rivalry among Great Powers," *American Journal of Political Science*, Vol. 45, No. 2 (April, 2001), pp. 457-469; Brian Efird, Jacek Kugler and Gaspare M. Genna, "From War to Integration: Generalizing Power Transition Theory," *International Interactions*, Vol. 29, No. 4 (October-December, 2003), pp. 293-313; Gaspare M. Genna and Taeko Hiroi, "Power Preponderance and Domestic Politics: Explaining Regional Economic Integration in Latin America and the Caribbean, 1960-1997," *International Interactions*, Vol. 30, No. 2 (April-June, 2004), pp. 143-164; Margit Bussmann and John R. Oneal, "Do Hegemons Distribute Private Goods?—A Test of Power-Transition Theory," *Journal of Conflict Resolution*, Vol. 51, No.1 (February,

In the event that the PRC is attempting to challenge the U.S.-led international order, Beijing is likely to form an alliance system to increase its external resources in a manner similar to the alliance formed by Nazi Germany with Italy and Japan prior to World War II. As the dominant power within the international order, the U.S. has been allied with nations in the Western Hemisphere through the Organization of American States (OAS), with Canada and most of the European nations through the North Atlantic Treaty Organization (NATO), and with Japan, South Korea, and the Philippines in the West Pacific region. By contrast, the PRC has only one unreliable formal ally—North Korea. Russia and China are close, but not allies.[14] Therefore, the PRC and the U.S. have significantly different alliance portfolios. According to Kim and many other power transition theorists, this indicates that the PRC is dissatisfied with the current U.S.-led international order.

Kastner and Saunders[15] have argued that Kim's measure of alliance portfolios is not a suitable one for the PRC, because Beijing has only one formal ally. In fact, the PRC has not attempted to form any aggressive alliances to challenge the overwhelmingly powerful U.S. alliance system.[16] We may also interpret this as evidence that the PRC supports rather than opposes the international status quo. Moreover, if the PRC were to reach a military pact with an ally of the U.S., Washington would not view this as a positive indicator for including the PRC in the status quo camp. Last but not least, the PRC's alliance system has remained the same in recent decades, while the U.S. has only added a few small Eastern European powers as allies. Thus, the alliance portfolios of the U.S. and the PRC are as dissimilar

---

2007), pp. 88-111.

14   Ying Fu, "How China Sees Russia: Beijing and Moscow are Close, but not Allies," Vol. 95, No. 1 (January-February, 2016) *Foreign Affairs*, pp. 96-105.

15   Scott L. Kastner and Phillip C. Saunders, "Is China a Status Quo or a Revisionist State? Leadership Travel as an Empirical Indicator of Foreign Policy Priorities," *International Studies Quarterly*, Vol. 56, No. 1 (March, 2012), pp. 163-77.

16   Mearsheimer observed this as well. Mearsheimer, *op. cit*, p. 362.

now as they were in the past. This fact cannot explain the difference between the foreign policies of Xi Jinping and Jiang Zemin or Hu Jintao. If the PRC starts to pursue military alliances, like some scholars think,[17] it will be an alarming to the U.S. So far, Beijing does not plan to do so.

ii. The PRC's Military Buildup

Bridging power transition theory and the literature on the arms race and its buildup, Werner and Kugler[18] and Lemke and Werner[19] have proposed a measure for assessing dissatisfaction with the international status quo. They have argued that a country can be deemed dissatisfied if, over a decade, it increases its military expenditure at a rate that exceeds its past expenditure rate, and amasses a greater military buildup than that of the dominant state. Werner and Kugler[20] have utilized this measure in their research at the global level, while Lemke has employed it in a multiple-hierarchical model applied at the global and regional levels.[21]

According to data obtained from the Stockholm International Peace Research Institute, the military expenditure of the U.S. increased from about 552 billion U.S .dollars in 1989 to about 578 billion U.S. dollars in 2014,

---

17 Feng Zhang, "China's New Thinking on Alliances," *Survival*, Vol. 54, No. 5 (2012), pp. 129-148.

18 Suzanne Werner and Jacek Kugler, "Power Transitions and Military Buildups: Resolving the Relationship between Arms Buildups and War," in Jacek Kugler and Douglas Lemke ed., *Parity and War: Evaluations and Extensions of the War Ledger* (Ann Arbor: University of Michigan Press, 1996), pp. 187-207.

19 Douglas Lemke and Suzanne Werner, "Power Parity, Commitment to Change, and War," *International Studies Quarterly*, Vol. 40, No. 2 (June, 1996), pp. 235-260.

20 Suzanne Werner and Jacek Kugler, "Power Transitions and Military Buildups: Resolving the Relationship between Arms Buildups and War," in Jacek Kugler and Douglas Lemke ed., *Parity and War: Evaluations and Extensions of the War Ledger* (Ann Arbor: University of Michigan Press, 1996), pp. 187-208.

21 Douglas Lemke, *Regions of War and Peace* (Cambridge: Cambridge University Press, 2002), p. 105.

while that of the PRC increased from 18 billion to 191 billion U.S. dollars. There was an increase in the rate of the PRC's military expenditure both in relation to the previous year and to that of the U.S. in the same year during the following years: 1992, 1994, 1995, 1996, 1998, 1999, 2001, 2004, 2005, 2006, 2009, 2011, 2012, and 2014.[22]

Between 1989 and 2014, the average annual growth rate of the PRC's military expenditure was about 9.84%, which was much higher than that of the U.S. but was comparable to the PRC's economic growth rate. Moreover, between 2005 and 2014, the PRC's military expenditure growth rate was lower than it was between 1995 and 2004. As the pace of economic growth has declined, the official military budget of the PRC will increase by only 7.6% in 2016, as revealed by Prime Minister Li Keqiang's annual report presented to the legislature.[23] Thus, the measure of military expenditure does not clearly indicate that the PRC is a dissatisfied revisionist power.

In fact, a study illustrates that China's military is corrupted,[24] some even argue that the PRC's military is "far from able to successfully carry out all its most pressing military tasks within China's borders;"[25] "China is at a much lower technological level than the leading state, and the gap separating Chinese and U.S. military capabilities is much larger than it was in the

---

22 Stockholm International Peace Research Institute, "SIPRI Military Expenditure Database," *Stockholm International Peace Research Institute*, 2016, <http://www.sipri.org/research/armaments/milex/milex_database >.

23 Chris Buckley and Jane Perlez, "China Military Budget to Rise Less Than 8%, Slower Than Usual," *New York Times*, March 4, 2016, <http://www.nytimes.com/2016/03/05/world/asia/china-military-spending.html?_r=0> ; Sam Perlo-Freeman, "Economics Trumps Geopolitics as China Announces Lowest Defense Budget Increase in Years," *Stockholm International Peace Research Institute*, March 7, 2016, <http://www.sipri.org/media/expert-comments/china-defence-budget>.

24 Peng Wang, "Military Corruption in China: The Role of Guanxi in the Buying and Selling of Military Positions," *China Quarterly*, Vol. 228 (2016).

25 Andrew Scobell and Andrew J. Nathan, "China's Overstretched Military," *The Washington Quarterly*, Vol. 35, No. 4 (2012), pp. 135-148.

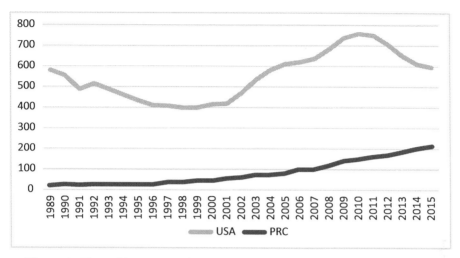

Figure 1: The military expenditure of the US and the PRC (1989–2015)

Source: Stockholm International Peace Research Institute, 2016.
Note: one unit on the Y-axis denotes one billion US dollars (at a constant value in 2014).

past."[26] Even acknowledging the improvement of PRC's missile, sensor, guidance, and other technologies, the U.S. is still able to deny China military hegemony in the Western Pacific.[27] Considering the huge disparity between the military budgets of the U.S. and the PRC, it is unlikely that the latter would spend more than the former within a period of a decade. The PRC's military efforts appear less impressive than those of the U.S., as shown in Figure 1.

Although the presence of an extraordinary military buildup within a nation does imply its dissatisfaction with the international status quo, its absence does not necessarily indicate its satisfaction. As Lemke and Reed

26 Stephen G. Brooks and William C. Wohlforth, "The Rise and Fall of the Great Powers in the Twenty-first Century: China's Rise and the Fate of America's Global Position," *International Security*, Vol. 40, No. 3 (winter 2015/2016), pp. 7-53.

27 Stephen Biddle and Ivan Oelrich, "Future Warfare in the Western Pacific: Chinese Antiaccess/Area Denial, U.S. AirSea Battle, and Command of the Commons in East Asia," *International Security*, Vol. 41, No. 1 (summer 2016), pp. 7-48.

have pointed out, the extraordinary military buildup measure "does not provide [the] means to identify satisfied states."[28] Furthermore, Kugler and Lemke have argued that "this measure is limited to only indicating [if] a state is dissatisfied as parity approaches."[29] It is assumed that the absence of such a buildup indicates satisfaction, and while this may hold true, it is very likely not the case. Thus, whether or not the PRC is satisfied cannot be clearly distinguished using this measure.

iii. Territorial Disputes between the PRC and its Neighbors

Evidently, neither alliance portfolios nor military buildups clearly indicate that the PRC is a dissatisfied challenger of the global order established by the U.S. Nevertheless, Beijing could still pose a threat at the regional level. When Lemke operationalized and applied the concept of satisfaction to local international systems, he found that every war occurred within the pre-existing context of a territorial disagreement.[30] Kacowicz even viewed territorial arrangements as representing a status quo at local levels.[31] Recent studies have reaffirmed that territorial disputes exert an indisputable influence on war and peace.[32]

---

28   Douglas Lemke and William Reed, "Regime Type and Status Quo Evaluations: Power Transitions and the Democratic Peace Proposition," *International Interactions*, Vol. 22, No. 2 (June 1996), pp. 143-164.

29   Jacek Kugler and Douglas Lemke, "The Power Transition Research Program: Assessing Theoretical and Empirical Advances," in Manus I. Midlarsky ed., *Handbook of War Studies II* (Ann Arbor, MI: The University of Michigan Press, 2000), pp. 129-163.

30   Douglas Lemke, *Regions of War and Peace* (Cambridge: Cambridge University Press, 2002), p. 102.

31   Arie Kacowicz, "Explaining Zones of Peace," *Journal of Peace Research*, Vol. 32, No. 3 (August, 1995), pp. 265-276.

32   Dominic D.P. Johnson and Monica Duffy Toft, "Grounds for War: The Evolution of Territorial Conflict," International Security, Vol. 38, No. 3 (winter 2013/2014), pp. 7-38; John A. Vasquez and Marie T. Henehan, *Territory, War, and Peace* (New York: Routledge, 2010).

As noted by Mearsheimer, the PRC is involved in various territorial disputes in the locations of the South China Sea, the East China Sea, and the PRC's southwestern frontier with India.[33] The territorial dispute between China and India has lasted for decades, but these two giant countries have demonstrated strong political will and incentives to develop their bilateral relations despite their unsolved border dispute.[34] The East China Sea dispute concerning oil, gas, and islets had become serious under Hu Jintao's presidency.[35] Although Japan extends its dispute with China from the East China Sea to the South China Sea,[36] the East China Sea itself seems to cool down in 2016.[37]

More recently, the South China Sea dispute has risen to prominence, becoming even more heated than the disputes concerning the East China Sea and the Taiwan Straits. The PRC's tense relations with Vietnam and the Philippines have become more apparent, and the U.S. and Japan have consequently provided these two Southeast Asian countries with military support for possible use against China. For example, Japan held a navy exercise with the Philippines[38] and donated two large patrol vessels to that country.[39] The U.S. President just has announced to lift the embargo

---

33   Mearsheimer, *op. cit*, pp. 368-373.

34   Hongzhou Zhang and Mingjiang   Li, "Sino-Indian Border Dispute," *Analysis*, No. 181, (June 2013), pp. 1-9.

35   Mark J. Valencia, "The East China Sea Dispute: Context, Claims, Issues, and Possible Solutions," *Asian Perspective*, Vol. 31, No. 1, Special Issue on "Reconciliation between China and Japan" (2007), pp. 127-167; Sheila A. Smith, "Japan and The East China Sea Dispute," *Orbis*, Vol. 56, No. 3 (Summer, 2012), pp. 370–390.

36   Ian Storey, "Japan's Maritime Security Interests in Southeast Asia and the South China Sea Dispute," *Political Science*, Vol. 65, No. 2, (December, 2013), pp. 135-156.

37   "Turning Down the Heat: China and Japan Agree to Cool Tensions over the East China Sea," *South China Morning Post*, August 24, 2016.

38   "Japan to Supply Philippines with Military Equipment," *Japan Times*, February 28, 2016, <http://www.japantimes.co.jp/news/2016/02/28/national/japan-to-supply-philippines-with-military-equipment/>.

39   "Japan to Provide Philippines with 2 Large Patrol Vessels," *Chicago Tribune*, September 6, 2016, < http://www.standard.net/World/2016/09/06/Japan-to-provide-Philippines-with-

on the sale of military equipment to Vietnam.[40] Although these disputes have not escalated to the point where the PRC can be identified as a global challenger to the U.S. power, Asian countries are beginning to feel that the PRC has abandoned its previous foreign policy of maintaining a low profile. Nevertheless, the President of the Philippines Rodrigo Duterte's visit to China in October 2016 indicates a probable reconciliation between Manila and Beijing.

On the other hand, over the last decade, the Taiwan issue, which has been the most prominent among the existing insular disputes within the West Pacific region, has temporarily subsided.[41] If cross-straits relations turn hostile again, the PRC's international image will suffer further.

III. Reflectivist Perspectives

The reflectivist perspective differs from the above-discussed rationalist approach. Whereas rationalists adopt a positivist stance, assuming that an objective fact needs to be measured, reflectivists disagree. As noted by Sørensen, following the emergence of constructivism as another mainstream approach within the field of international relations from the 1990s, many European constructivists have focused their attention on exploring the role of discourses in mediating and constructing social reality in continental Europe.[42] David Lampton, an established American expert on China, also

---

2-large-patrol-vessels >.

40   Franz-Stefan Gady, "US Arms Sales to Vietnam: A Military Analysis," *Diplomat*, June 06, 2016, <http://thediplomat.com/2016/06/us-arms-sales-to-vietnam-a-military-analysis/>.

41   Scott L. Kastner, "Is the Taiwan Strait Still a Flash Point? Rethinking the Prospects for Armed Conflict between China and Taiwan," *International Security*, Vol. 40, No. 3 (winter 2015/2016), pp. 54-92.

42   Camilla T. N. Sørensen, "The Significance of Xi Jinping's 'Chinese Dream' for Chinese Foreign Policy: From 'Tao Guang Yang Hui' to 'Fen Fa You Wei'," *Journal of Chinese International Relations*, Vol. 3, No. 1 (2015), p. 57.

disagrees with rationalist Mearsheimer's theoretical approach, seeking to understand the PRC on its own terms to better predict Chinese behavior and suggesting that Chinese foreign policy is rooted in the PRC's self-perception in relation to its neighbors.[43]

The following discourse analysis, mainly based on the works of Lampton and especially of Sørensen, is aimed at identifying and analyzing the official Chinese discourse sourced from texts by Chinese foreign policy leaders and international relations scholars.

Some Chinese scholars have argued that during the leadership transition from Hu Jintao and Xi Jinping, the PRC's diplomatic perspective shifted from a focus on revolution and nationalism to one on development and globalization. Consequently, the PRC abandoned the role of challenger to the existing international order.[44] As compared to the Mao Zedong era, the intensity of contemporary nationalism in the minds of Chinese political leaders has evidenced a gradual reduction.[45] However, the question being addressed here is whether or not Xi Jinping has continued to pursue Deng Xiaoping's foreign policy of maintaining a low profile.

On November 15, 2012, Xi Jinping made a public speech. At the outset, he introduced the six other members of the Standing Committee, presented a brief review of the PRC's history, and noted people's expectations. This comprised standard rhetoric, but in the latter part of the speech, Xi Jinping stressed serious governmental challenges, especially corruption and bribe-

---

43   David M. Lampton, *Following the Leader: Ruling China, From Den Xiaoping to Xi Jinping* (Berkeley: University of California Press, 2013), pp. 7, 8, 110.

44   Baijia Zhang, "Perspectives Shifts during the Development of Chinese Diplomacy: From Revolution and Nationalism to Development and Globalization," in Shao Binhong ed., *The World in 2020 According to China: Chinese Foreign Policy Elites Discuss Emerging Trends in International Politics* (Leiden: Brill, 2014), p. 13.

45   Yinhong Shi, "Perspectives Shifts during the Development of Chinese Diplomacy: From Revolution and Nationalism to Development and Globalization," in Shao Binhong ed., *The World in 2020 According to China: Chinese Foreign Policy Elites Discuss Emerging Trends in International Politics* (Leiden: Brill, 2014), p. 35.

taking by some party members and cadres; being out of touch with the people, and placing undue emphasis on formality and bureaucracy.[46] These observations reflected Xi Jinping's awareness of a serious domestic crisis threatening the legitimacy of the rule of the Communist Party of China (CPC), or at any rate, this was the message that he intended to deliver to his audience.

With Xi Jinping's ongoing anti-corruption campaign, many important party figures, for example, Bo Xilai, have been placed under arrest. It is possible that the reaction of the corrupted elite could endanger the Chinese leadership from another direction before the anti-corruption campaign gains popular support for the reconsolidation of the CPC. This sheds light on the proposal of the "Chinese Dream" as a new pillar of the CPC's regime by Xi Jinping's administration.

Here I summarize key points emerging from Sørensen's study to explore what Xi Jinping and other Chinese foreign policy leaders have said about the PRC's international role and developments in their speeches and statements about the "Chinese Dream."[47] The three key points emerging from the observations of Sørensen and others on contemporary Chinese diplomacy relate to the continuation, innovation, and assertiveness.

1. **Continuation** of the "Chinese Dream" and peaceful development. In his article titled "Implementing the Chinese Dream," State Councilor, Yang Jiechi, elaborated on the links between the "Chinese Dream" and Chinese foreign policy and stressed that "the 'Chinese Dream' requires peaceful and stable international and neighboring environment[s], and China is committed to realizing the dream through peaceful development."[48] Yang further noted that "since the 'Chinese Dream'

---

46   Kerry Brown, *The New Emperors: Power and the Princelings in China* (London: Tauris, 2014), p. 102.

47   Sørensen, *op. cit.*, pp. 59-73.

48   Jiechi Yang, "Implementing the Chinese Dream," *The National Interest*, September 10,

is closely linked to the dreams of other peoples around the world, China is committed to helping other countries, developing countries, and neighboring countries in particular." Such statements indicate that the Chinese leadership is attempting to promote the "Chinese Dream" internationally as a continuation of China's peaceful development strategy.

At the third group study session of the Political Bureau of the 18th CPC Central Committee, Xi Jinping also emphasized both peaceful development and "Chinese Dream"—a peaceful international environment is a precondition for realizing Chinese Dream.[49] Xi made the same connection when he spoke at the Moscow State Institute of International Relations.[50]

Peace and development are still key ideas in recent Xi Jinping's speech at the 8th BRICS Summit in October 2016.[51] However, some innovative elements have also been introduced in Xi's era. The speeches and statements of Chinese leaders often refer to a "new type of international relations" (xin xing guo ji guan xi) that China is working to foster based on win-win cooperation and the peaceful resolution of international and regional disputes. Generally, expressions such as "new type" and "new approach" are prominent in the speeches and statements made by Chinese leaders. As Qin Yaqing has argued, continuity and change

---

2013, <http://nationalinterest.org/commentary/implementing-the-chinese-dream-9026>. Cited in Sørensen, *op. cit.*, p. 59.

49 Jinping Xi, "Strengthen the Foundation for Pursuing Peaceful Development," *The Governance of China* (Beijing: Foreign Languages Press, 2014), pp. 271-272.

50 Jinping Xi, "Follow the Trend of the Times and Promote Global Peace and Development," *The Governance of China* (Beijing: Foreign Languages Press, 2014), pp. 297-305.

51 Jinping Xi, "Xi Jinping Attends the 8th BRICS Summit and Delivers Important Speech, Stressing to Cement Confidence and Seek Common Development and Announcing China to Host the 9th BRICS Summit," *Ministry of Foreign Affairs, the People's Republic of China*, October 17, 2016, <http://www.fmprc.gov.cn/mfa_eng/zxxx_662805/t1406785.shtml>.

coexist, although the former is a central theme relating to strategic goals, designs, and policies as a whole.[52]

2. **Innovation.** Some scholars have traced the trajectory of the PRC's new diplomacy, commencing from the early 1990s.[53] However, the concept of "a new type of major-power relationships" (xin xing da guo guan xi) has evolved to characterize more recent relations between the PRC and the U.S.[54] This is presented as "a strategic choice made based on full review of the experience and lessons of history as well as being an inherent requirement of the 'two centenary goals' and the overall strategy of peaceful development."[55]

In his speech titled "China at a New Starting Point," delivered at the UN General Assembly in September 2013, the Foreign Minister, Wang Yi, explicitly stated that "various versions of [the] China threat have surfaced. However, what happened in the past cannot be applied indiscriminately to today's China. The outdated Cold War mentality has no place in the new era of globalization." He further sought to provide reassurance that "China would never seek hegemony in the world."[56] Wang Yi also stated that the PRC's participation in global affairs would

---

52   Yaqing Qin, "Continuity through Change: Background Knowledge and China's International Strategy," *Chinese Journal of International Politics*, Vol. 7, No. 3 (Autumn, 2014), pp. 285-314.

53   Zhiqun Zhu, *China's New Diplomacy: Rationale, Strategies and Significance* (Surrey: Ashgate Publishing Company, 2013), pp. 1-18.

54   Jinping Xi, "Build a New Model of Major-country Relationship between China and the United States," *The Governance of China* (Beijing: Foreign Languages Press, 2014), pp. 306-308; David M. Lampton, "A New Type of Major-Power Relationship: Seeking a Durable Foundation for US–China Ties," *Asia Policy* 16 (July 2013): pp. 51–68. *China's New Diplomacy: Rationale, Strategies and Significance* (Surrey: Ashgate Publishing Company, 2013), pp. 1-18.

55   Yang, *op. cit.*

56   Yi Wang, "China at a New Starting Point: Statement at the General Debate of the 68th Session of the UN General Assembly," *United Nations*, September 27, 2013, <http://gadebate.un.org/sites/default/files/gastatements/68/CN_en.pdf>. Cited in Sørensen, *op. cit.*, p. 59.

be more active and comprehensive, entailing close cooperation with all other countries, handling complex global challenges jointly with others, and solving all kinds of difficult issues facing the human race.

Along the same lines, Yang Jiechi[57] has emphasized innovation, along with new strategic ideas and diplomatic initiatives in the development of a "diplomatic theory with Chinese characteristics" (zhong guo te se wai jiao li lun) under Xi Jinping's administration. He further stated that the PRC's diplomacy under Xi Jinping "display[s] such features as rich ideas, clear priorities, firm positions, flexible approaches and distinctive styles." Such statements clearly indicate that there is an ongoing movement away from the formulation of central guidelines for Chinese foreign policy strategies according to the concept of "Hidden Light" (tao guang yang hui).[58]

3. **Assertiveness.** Scholars have also pointed out a tougher Chinese approach aimed at safeguarding Chinese sovereignty and core interests.[59] This is especially apparent in the context of Xi Jinping's emphasis on the PRC's rejuvenation through the regaining of its international status, rights, and power.[60] Yang Jiechi has also emphasized that Xi Jinping while being "firmly committed to peaceful development,

---

57   Yang, *op. cit.*

58   Sørensen, *op. cit.*, p. 61.

59   Nien-Chung Chang Liao, "The Sources of China's Assertiveness: the System, Domestic Politics or Leadership Preferences?" *International Affairs*, Vol. 92, No. 4 (July 2016), pp. 817-833; Bama Andika Putra, "China's Assertiveness in the South China Sea: Have ASEAN's Endeavors in Establishing Regional Order Truly Failed," *Journal of Politics and Law*, Vol. 8, No. 4 (2015), pp. 178-184; Michael Yahuda, "China's New Assertiveness in the South China Sea," *Journal of Contemporary China*, Vol. 22, (2013), pp. 446-459.

60   See: for example, Jinping Xi, "To Inherit from the Past and Use it for the Future, and Continuing What Has Passed in Beginning the Future: Continue to Forge Ahead Dauntlessly Towards the Goal of the Great Rejuvenation of the Chinese People - speech at the 'Road Towards Rejuvenation' exhibition," *Ren Min Net*, November 29, 2012, <http://cpc.people.com.cn/shipin/n/2012/1130/c243284-19755158.html>. Cited in Sørensen, *op. cit.*, p. 62.

will never forsake the legitimate interests or compromise on China's core interests."[61] Thus, contrary to the perceptions of many Western observers that recent Chinese actions in the South China Sea and those relating to the Diaoyu/Senkaku Islands dispute in the East China Sea demonstrate aggression, Chinese leaders have presented these actions as being reactive or defensive attempts to protect territories. However, Xi Jinping's speeches and statements also reveal that he wants to "shape" the international system to a greater degree than previous leaders did.[62] At the summit meeting of the Conference on Confidence-Building Measures in Asia (CICA), held in Shanghai in May 2014, Xi Jinping outlined his thoughts on the future of security within Asia: establishing new security mechanisms other than military alliances made by the U.S. He further noted that the PRC would lead new regional security practices and mechanisms, emphasizing the point that Asian security was best dealt with by Asians.[63] According to Wang Yizhou, a Chinese international relations scholar, it is possible for Xi Jinping to seek to promote a more positive or "rational" nationalism, because "current Chinese leaders are less weighed down by historical memories and more driven by future ambitions."[64]

Sørensen has summed up the key points extracted from the speeches and statements referring to the "Chinese Dream" made by Xi Jinping and other Chinese leaders on foreign policy. First, the PRC under Xi Jinping intends

---

61   Yang, *op. cit.*

62   Sørensen, *op. cit.*, p. 62.

63   Jinping Xi, "Xi Jinping's speech at the fourth summit meeting of the Conference on Confidence-Building Measures in Asia: Actively Establishing the Asian Security Perspective; Commonly Creating the New Security Situation," *Xin Hua Net*, May 21, 2014, <http://news.xinhuanet.com/world/2014-05/21/c_1110796357.htm>. Cited in Sørensen, *op. cit.*, p. 63.

64   Yizhou Wang, "China's New Foreign Policy: Transformations and Challenges Reflected in Changing Discourse," *Asan Forum*, March 21, 2014, <http://www.theasanforum. org/chinas-new-foreign-policy-transformations-and-challenges-reflected-in-changing-discourse/>. Cited in Sørensen, *op. cit.*, p. 64.

not only to assume more international responsibilities but also to "shape" the international system to a greater degree than previously, increasingly offering Chinese proposals and solutions to international conflicts and crises. Second, the PRC desires respect and treatment on an equal footing. Third, the PRC will never compromise on its sovereignty and core interests.[65]

In October 2013, Xi Jinping hosted a conference on Chinese regional diplomacy that was attended by all members of the Standing Committee of the CPC. In his speech at the conference, Xi Jinping strongly urged Chinese diplomats to adopt the principles or guidelines of "Fen Fa You Wei" (strive for achievement), "GengjiaJiji" (be more active) and "GengjiaZhudong" (take greater initiative).[66] Professor Zhai Kun, the Director of the Institute of World Political Studies at the China Institute of Contemporary International Relations (CICIR) has argued that there are three evident manifestations of this proactive stance. The first is the establishment of the new National Security Commission. The second entails efforts to combine the use of different types of instruments (economic, political, military, and non-governmental) in a comprehensive and integrated way within Chinese foreign policy. The third manifestation entails efforts to combine strength and gentleness in relation to major hot spot issues and questions concerning the PRC's rights and interests.[67]

While it is still not clear whether there have been any new, officially sanctioned broad guidelines for formulating Chinese foreign policy, a movement away from Deng Xiaoping's guidelines seems to be evident. Why? Professor Yan Xuetong has argued that the Chinese leadership's overall assessment of the PRC's security environment is changing. Instead of "peace and development," the dominant view is that the probability

---

65   Sørensen, *op. cit.*, p. 65.

66   Bonnie Glaser and Deep Pal, "Is China's Charm Offensive Dead?" *China Brief*, Vol. 14, No. 15 (2014), pp. 1-4. Cited in Sørensen, *op. cit.*, p. 66.

67   Zhai Kun, "The Xi Jinping Doctrine of Chinese Diplomacy," *China and US Focus*. March 25, 2014. Cited in Sørensen, *op. cit.*, p. 66.

of conflict with other states is increasing.[68] Therefore, the general trend indicates that the PRC needs to confront rather than avoid the issue of conflict. Another reason to account for this change comes from domestic politics within China.[69] Glaser and Pal[70] have also claimed that Beijing has quietly discarded Deng Xiaoping's guidelines. They support this argument by highlighting how several of their Chinese sources have revealed that Deng's "Tao Guang Yang Hui" directive is no longer referenced at internal meetings and in party documents.

IV. Conclusion

From the rationalist perspective, we find little evidence indicating that the PRC has changed from being a status quo power to a revisionist power at the global level. Beijing is not attempting to form any military alliance against the U.S. bloc. Although the PRC's military expenditure is rapidly increasing, it does not meet the criteria of "extraordinary buildup" within the definition offered by power transition theorists. At the regional level, Beijing's territorial disputes with neighboring countries are becoming more apparent. Thus, it is reasonable to posit that the PRC's rise at the regional level is of more concern than it is at the global level.

From the reflectivist perspective, it is inappropriate to divide the PRC's foreign policy simply into two distinct categories: status quo or revisionist. While the Chinese leadership publicly still insists that it is pursuing peaceful development, it is also demonstrating a more assertive stance when dealing

---

68   Xuetong Yan, "From Keeping a Low Profile to Striving for Achievement," *The Chinese Journal of International Politics*, Vol. 7, No.2 (2014), pp. 153-184, <http://cjip. oxfordjournals.org/content/7/2/153.full.pdf+html>. Cited in Sørensen, *op. cit.*, p. 67.

69   Mikael Weissmann, "Chinese Foreign Policy in a Global Perspective: A Responsible Reformer "Striving For Achievement," *Journal of China and International Relations*, Vol. 3, No. 1, (2015), pp. 151-166.

70   Glaser and Pal, *op. cit.*, pp. 8-11.

with foreign issues. In sum, while it is too early to conclude that Beijing has become a dissatisfied great power, it is clear that Beijing has already deviated from its previous attitude of maintaining a low profile.

This research relies on Sørensen's work to conduct a discursive analysis of Chinese foreign policy makers' speeches. In future studies, we may examine more original speeches and statements from leaders of China, and consult more scholars' works to identify and understand the meaning of these words. Then, compare these speeches and what the PRC's actual diplomatic and military action. Thus, we may combine both the rationalist and reflective approaches to comprehending China's foreign policy.

Tragedy of Great Power Politics? Re-examining US-China Relations in the 21st Century

Andrea, Pei-Shan Kao[*]

I. Introduction

According to Mearsheimer and offensive realists, a war sooner or later will certainly happen between the United States and China. However, if one examines US-China relations since they established formal diplomatic relations from 1979 until present, a war has never happened between them. Although many crises have happened between the two; for instance, the 1989 Tiananmen Incident, the 1999 Bombing of Chinese embassy in Belgrade, the plane collision in South China Sea in 2001, and their WTO negotiations and trade disputes, etc.; every time they peacefully and successfully resolved the problems and disputes, in the end, by means of negotiations and consultations. This therefore has raised the questions: can offensive realism be used to explain the relationship of the United States and China? This paper therefore wants to test offensive realist approach on US-China relations in the 21st century. This research will explain first the theoretical assumptions of offensive realism hence apply them to examine the development of the relationship of the United States, the unique offshore balancer, and China, the rising power, in the 21st century. This will include their bilateral contacts and exchanges in different sections, and most importantly, their competition in some contending issues hence to make conclusions. That is to say, this research will first find out the data and numbers of their trade and economic contacts, social, cultural and educational exchanges, including the comparison of their national powers. Then, it will investigate and examine the contending issues between the two

[*]   Associate Professor, Department of Border Police, Central Police University, Taiwan.

great powers and their methods and ways to resolve problems. By means of examining the development of U.S.-China relations since the 21st century and their crisis bargaining model, one can demonstrate if offensive realism can be used to explain this relationship. If the answer is yes, how much of U.S.-China relations can be explained by Mearsheimer's theory? If not, what kind of U.S.-China relationship will it be in the near future?

II. Theoretical and Research Concepts

The roots of offensive realism can be traced back to classic realism which is the most long-lasting and dominant theory in the field of International Relations. Classic realism suggests the following assumptions: the nation-states are the key unit of analysis in the modern world; states are unitary rational actors who pursue their own national interests, own autonomy and own security; states will struggle for power so that power constitutes politics; conflict cannot be avoided.[1] For realists,[2] the research of international politics focuses on the origins and reasons for the happening of wars and the status of peace; international organisations are of importance though they cannot explain all the sectors of international relations. They consider that anarchy is the origin of security dilemma which will eventually cause the occurrence of war. Hans Morgenthau who suggested "six principles" of political realism has been considered as the representative of classic realism. According to Morgenthau, politics is governed by objective laws which have their root in human nature; the key to understand international politics is the concept of interest defined in terms of power; the forms and nature of state power will vary in time, place and context while the concept of interest remains consistent; universal moral principles don't

---

1   On the assumptions of class realism, can see Hans Morgenthau, *Politics among States* (New York: McGraw-Hill, 1985).

2   See Ole R. Holsti, "Theories of International Relations" (Handout or online: http://people. duke.edu/~pfeaver/holsti.pdf).

guide state behavior; there is no universally agreed set of moral principles; and the political sphere is autonomous from every other sphere of human concern.[3]

However, following with its popularity, more and more scholars criticised(criticized) that realism could not completely explain and depict international politics.[4] The new generation of IR scholars such as Kenneth Waltz therefore revised and developed a new model that emphasised (emphasized) the importance of "structure"; that is, the so-called "Neo-Realism".[5] Waltz defined international system by reference to three features: the principle by which the parts are arranged, namely, anarchy rather than hierarchy; the characteristics of the units are functional un-differentiation, that is, all units do the same thing; the distribution of capabilities across the units, namely, polarity. The first two elements are constant and permanent features of all international systems while the third feature will vary historically. Following with the criticism of neo-realism,[6] some scholars attempted to revise realism hence to develop new approaches. Among them, "offensive realism" is the one created and labelled by John Mearsheimer. To develop his approach, John Mearsheimer combined Morgenthau's assumption of "maximisation (maximization) of power" and Waltz's assumption of structural realism. His theory is built on five assumptions:

> "there is anarchy in the international system, which means that there is no hierarchically superior, coercive power that can guarantee limits

---

3 See Hans Morgenthau, *Politics among States*, chapters 11-14.

4 On the criticism of Classic Realism, can see Ole R. Holsti, "Theories of international Relations", pp. 5-7.

5 On Waltz's theory can see Kenneth Waltz, *Theory of International Politics* (MA: Addison-Wesley, 1979), chapters 5-9.

6 On the criticism of neo-realism, see Robert Keohane (ed.), *Neorealism and Its Critics* (New York: Columbia University Press, 1986); and Robert Keohane, "Theory of World Politics: Structural Realism and Beyond," in Robert Keohane (ed.), *International Institutions and State Power: Essays in International Relations Theory* (Boulder: Westview Press, 1989), pp. 35-74.

on the behavior of states…; all great powers possess offensive military capabilities, which they are capable of using against other states…; states can never be certain that other states will refrain from using those offensive military capabilities…; states seek to maintain their survival (their territorial integrity and domestic autonomy) above all other goals…; states are rational actors, which means that they consider the immediate and long-term consequences of their actions, and think strategically about how to survive."[7]

According to Mearsheimer,[8] international system is anarchic; states can only "self-help" themselves, the aims of states' policies are "security", power is the "means" to reach this objective. For Mearsheimer, it is difficult to change international politics which is cruel and dangerous and that is why states want to and must maximise (maximize) their military power.[9] For offensive realists like Mearsheimer, states are pretty much concerned with the change and distribution of power in the international society and its "relative powers" as well. To assure their national security, states must become the most powerful and dominant country in the international system and eliminate any possibility from the challenges of its adversary. When a state becomes a hegemon, it will hope to maintain the status quo.

On his book published again in 2014, Mearsheimer used the last chapter in particular to explain US-China relations. He claimed that once China rises, its interests will be likely to clash with the dominant great power in the Asia-Pacific region, that is, the United States.[10] In addition, China

---

7   John Mearshimer, *The Tragedy of Power Politics* (New York: W.W. Norton & Company, 2001), pp. 30-31.

8   On the hypotheses of offensive realism can see John Mearshimer, *The Tragedy of Power Politics*.

9   On the explanations and defense for Mearsheimer's theory, can see Peter Toft, "John J. Mearsheimer: an offensive realist between geopolitics and power," *Journal of International Relations and Development*, December 2005, Vol. 8, Number 4, pp. 381-408.

10 Regarding John Mearsheimer's argument on US-China relations, can see his talks on

cannot live peacefully neither with its neighbors such as Japan and India. According to Mearsheimer, following with the rise of China's economic power, it will have much more resources to build its military forces so that it can dominate Asia. This hence will be contained by the United States and China's neighbors; and there will be an intense security competition in the Asia-Pacific region. As the United States now is the dominant power in Asia-Pacific region; it will secure its status in the region. However, China is not a hegemony yet, according to offensive realism, China will definitely search for its aim to be a hegemon, but this will encounter with the opposition of the United States and other powers. If one applies offensive realism to examine US-China relations, a war will seem to eventually happen between the two. However, since the two established formal diplomatic relations in 1979 until present, a war has not happened between them. Although many crises did happen between the two, they resolve the problems and conflicts by means of negotiations and consultations. This paper therefore wants to test offensive realism to review and exam the relationship between the United States and China hence to make conclusions.

III. US-China Bilateral Exchanges and Contacts

In this section, the paper wants to examine the contacts and exchanges between the United States and China, that is to say, their bilateral trade and investment, cultural, social and educational interactions, and official contacts as well.

1. Bilateral Trade and Investment

First, on the bilateral trade, according to the US Census Bureau, US trade in goods with China in 2015 was $598.96 billion as Table 1 showed.

Harper Lecture of University of Chicago. John Mearsheimer, "Harper Lecture with John J. Mearsheimer: Can China Rise Peacefully?", *University of Chicago Social Sciences*, December 18, 2013, <http://m.youtube.com/watch?v=0DMn4PmiDeQ>.

The United States exported $116.18 billion to China, and imported $481.88 billion in goods from China. The bilateral trade rose greatly from $116.4 billion to close to $600 billion in the past fifteen years, namely from 2000 to 2015. It grew over 5 times; needless to say, from only $4.9 billion from 1980 as Table 2 showed. China now is the United States' second-largest trading partner, its third-largest export market, and also its biggest source of imports. China is one of the fastest-growing export markets for Americans. It is expected that the Chinese market will be much more important for Americans in the years ahead although the United States trade deficit with China is the largest in the world. The US trade deficit with China increased from $2.7 billion in 1980 to $365.69 billion in 2015, many trade disputes therefore have happened between the two. However, after China's entry in 2001 into the World Trade Organisation (WTO), a rule-based organisation, all trade disputes have been resolved through the Dispute Settlement Body (DSB).[11] Moreover, the WTO also has a monitor-review mechanism; these all can increase the likelihood of states' cooperation. That is to say, if there is any trade dispute happened between the two, it can be better resolved within this multilateral regime, hence to ensure the smooth flow of trade.

Table 1: U.S. trade in goods with China in 2015

Unit: $ in millions

Month	Exports	Imports	Balance
January 2015	9,552.0	38,158.4	-28,606.4
February 2015	8,699.8	31,240.1	-22,540.3
March 2015	9,887.2	41,121.9	-31,234.7
April 2015	9,316.8	35,795.1	-26,478.3
May 2015	8,758.8	39,211.2	-30,452.4

---

11 Since China joined the WTO in 2001 until December 2015, it has in total 49 trade disputes with other countries and has appealed to the DSB; among them, 26 cases are complained or responded by the United States. See: World Trade Organisation, Map of disputes between WTO Members <https://www.wto.org/english/tratop_e/dispu_e/dispu_maps_e.htm?country_selected=CHN&sense=e>.

June 2015	9,687.8	41,145.1	-31,457.3
July 2015	9,500.7	41,077.2	-31,576.6
August 2015	9,166.7	44,117.2	-34,950.5
September 2015	9,423.7	45,700.6	-36,277.0
October 2015	11,384.3	44,358.0	-32,973.7
November 2015	10,681.0	41,940.5	-31,259.5
December 2015	10,127.4	38,015.3	-27,887.9
TOTAL 2015	**116,186.3**	**481,880.8**	**-365,694.5**

NOTE: All figures are in millions of U.S. dollars on a nominal basis, not seasonally adjusted unless otherwise specified. Details may not equal totals due to rounding.

Source: "Trade in Goods with China," US Census Bureau, <https://www.census.gov/foreign-trade/balance/c5700.html#1985>.

Table 2: U.S. Merchandise Trade with China (1980-2014)

Unit: $ in billions

Year	U.S. Exports	U.S. Imports	U.S. Trade Balance
1980	**3.8**	**1.1**	**2.7**
1990	4.8	15.2	-10.4
2000	**16.3**	**100.1**	**-83.8**
2005	41.8	243.5	-201.6
2006	55.2	287.8	-232.5
2007	65.2	321.5	-256.3
2008	71.5	337.8	-266.3
2009	69.6	296.4	-226.8
2010	91.9	364.9	-273.1
2011	103.9	393.3	-295.5
2012	110.6	425.6	-315.0
2013	121.7	440.4	-318.4
2014	123.7	466.8	-343.1

Source: Wayne M. Morrison, "US-China Trade Issues," Congressional Research Service, December 15, 2015, <https://fas.org/sgp/crs/row/RL33536.pdf>.

Similarly, a closer contact can be demonstrated from the bilateral investment as well. According to Wayne Morrison, in 2014 the flow of Chinese FDI to the United States was $968 million while American FDI in China was $6.3 billion as Figure 1 described. At the end of 2014, the stock of Chinese FDI in the United States reached $9.5 billion estimated by the US Bureau of Economic Analysis (BEA),[12] it grew 12.4% compared with the previous year. It made China the 22nd largest overall source of American FDI inflows through 2014. On the other side, the stock of American investment in China was estimated at $65.8 billion through 2014, it also increased 9.7% compared with 2013, making China the 17th largest

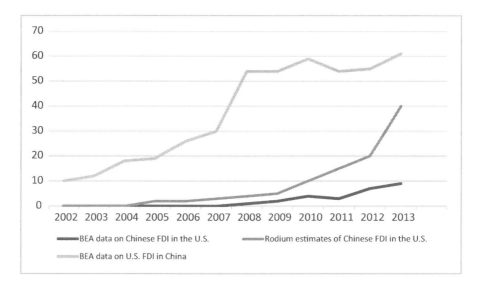

Figure 1: The FDI Flows between the United States and China (2002-2013)
Unit: $ in billions

Notes: As the BEA, the Rhodium Group and Chinese Ministry of Commerce use different methodologies
    to measure China's FDI in the United States, the data on FDI flows are different.
Source: Wayne M. Morrison, "US-China Trade Issues," Congressional Research Service, December 15,
    2015, <https://fas.org/sgp/crs/row/RL33536.pdf>.

---

12   See Wayne M. Morrison, "US-China Trade Issues," *Congressional Research Service*,
    December 15, 2015. <https://fas.org/sgp/crs/row/RL33536.pdf>.

destination of American investment. In addition to their close trade and economic contacts, China now is also the largest foreign holder of American Treasury securities as a share of total foreign holdings of 20.6%, holding $1.26 trillion until September 2015.[13] This number was $118 billion in 2002.

2. Visitors and Students Exchanges

As Figure 2 shows that the numbers of Chinese visitors to the United States have sharply increased from 0.23 million to 2.56 million, it grew over 10 times. There were approximately 2.56 million Chinese visitors to the United States in 2015.Canada, Mexico, Britain, Japan, Brazil, Germany and China now are the top seven origin countries of international travelers to the

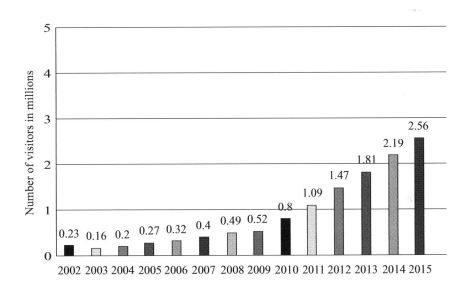

Figure 2: Number of visitors to the United States from China from 2002 to 2015

Unit: in millions

Source: The Statistics Portal, "Number of visitors to the United States from China from 2002 to 2020 ," 2016. <http://www.statista.com/statistics/214813/number-of-visitors-to-the-us-from-china/>.

---

13   Ibid.

Table 3: Top 10 Tourism Source Countries

Order	Country	Number of Tourist Arrivals (Unit in 10,000 persons)	Growth over the same period of 2014(%)
1	South Korea	444.44	6.3
2	Japan	249.77	-8.1
3	Vietnam	216.08	26.4
4	**United States**	**208.58**	**-0.4**
5	Russia	158.23	-22.7
6	Malaysia	107.55	-4.8
7	Mongolia	101.41	-6.3
8	Philippines	100.40	3.7
9	Singapore	90.53	-6.8
10	India	73.05	2.9

Source: "China Inbound Tourism in 2015", Travel China Guide, <https://www.travelchinaguide.com/tourism/2015statistics/inbound.htm>.

nited States.[14] According to the US Department of Commerce, China will become the third largest origin before 2019.[15] In 2014, Chinese visitors spent $21.1 billion in the United States and the amount could be higher in the following years due to the new extended US-China visa agreement signed at the APEC summit in November 2014,[16] which can encourage much more Chinese visitors to the U.S. The new visa program also extends student and exchange visas from one to five years. Similarly, more and more American visitors like to visit China.

---

14   US Travel Association, "Forecast of International Travelers to the United States by Top Origin Countries," <http://travel.trade.gov/research/programs/i94/description.html>.

15   See Megan Willet, "Chinese Tourists Are Flooding Into The US Thanks To A New Visa Rule," *Business Insider*, January 21, 2015, <http://www.businessinsider.com/chinese-tourists-to-us-on-the-rise-2015-1>.

16   The new B-category non-immigrant visa now is cheaper and can be issued for up to 10 years for business or tourist travel for either American visitors to China or Chinese travelers to America. See: Megan Willet, "Chinese Tourists Are Flooding Into The US Thanks To A New Visa Rule," *Business Insider*, January 21, 2015, <http://www.businessinsider.com/chinese-tourists-to-us-on-the-rise-2015-1>.

China ranks third as a tourist destination country in addition to France and the United States. However, if one includes Hong Kong and Macau, China is the most popular tourist destination in the world. Most of the tourists are Chinese people from Hong Kong, Macau and Taiwan. There are 26.36 million visitors from non-Chinese countries and regions to China in 2014 and this number basically was steady from 2007.[17] Americans rank fourth and made up about 11% of the Chinese foreign tourism market in 2014 although it decreased 0.4% in to 2.08 million in 2015 (See Table 3). South Koreans, Japanese, Vietnamese, Americans, Russians, Malaysians, and Mongolians are the major non-Chinese tourist nationality.[18] Beijing, Shanghai, Xian, Guilin and Hong Kong are the most popular Chinese cities for tourists.[19] In the past few years, from to 2007 to 2015, the numbers of American visitors to China have grown steadily from 1.9 million to 2.08 million.[20] These numbers showed that the contacts and exchanges for people of the two countries are closer and intensive.

3. Official Contacts

Moreover, since Chinese President Xi Jinping and U.S. President Barack Obama took office, Xi and Obama have already met 8 times until present in many international occasions, including their state visits to each other. Their updated meeting happened this year in March (2016) on the Nuclear Security Summit in Washington, DC.[21] During the meeting, the

---

17 Travel China Guide, "China Inbound Tourism in 2014", <https://www.travelchinaguide. com/tourism/2014statistics/inbound.htm>.

18 Travel China Guide, "China Inbound Tourism in 2015", <https://www.travelchinaguide. com/tourism/2015statistics/inbound.htm>.

19 See: Gavin Van Hinsbergh, "China Tourism — Current Trends and Facts," *China Highlights*, February 9, 2016, <http://www.chinahighlights.com/travelguide/tourism. htm>.

20 See: Travel China Guide, "China Inbound Tourism in 2015", <https://www. travelchinaguide.com/tourism/2015statistics/inbound.htm>.

21 On the report of this meeting can see: *The US-China Policy Foundation*, "Obama and Xi Meet in DC," April 6, 2016, <http://uscpf.org/v3/2016/04/07/obama-and-xi-meet-in-dc/>. Also, Ministry of Foreign Affairs of the People's Republic of China, "Xi Jinping Meets

two exchanged their views on a series of key issues, including climate change, nuclear security, cyber security, maritime issues, economic access, and human rights, etc. They will likely soon meet again at the G20 Summit being held in Hangzhou, China this September. In fact, in addition to these intensive contacts of the two leaders and high-level officials in the governments, there are many regimes, including dialogues, forums, and foundations, whether official or private, existing in this relationship. For instance, on official regimes, they have "U.S.-China Strategic and Economic Dialogue (S&ED)" established since 2009 and is annually held.[22] In private sector, many organisations and interest groups such as the "U.S. -China Policy Foundation",[23] the "U.S.-China Business Council (USCBC)",[24] and National U.S.-China People's Friendship Association (USCPFA),[25] etc., are all greatly devoted to the improvement and enhancement of mutual understanding and communication of the two states.

---

with President Barack Obama of US," April 1, 2016, <http://www.fmprc.gov.cn/mfa_eng/zxxx_662805/t1353036.shtml>.

22   The S&ED is a high-level dialogue for the United States and China to discuss a wide range of regional and global issues on strategy and economy between the two countries. Its establishment was announced on April 1, 2009 by U.S. President Barack Obama and Chinese President Hu Jintao to replace the former US-China Strategic Economic Dialogue started in 2006 under the George W. Bush administration.

23   The U.S.-China Policy Foundation (USCPF) was founded in 1995 to ensure the continued improvement of U.S.-China relations. On the introduction of the USCPF can see their official website: the U.S.-China Policy Foundation, <http://uscpf.org/v3/about_us/historyactivities/>.

24   The US-China Business Council (USCBC) is a private organisation established in 1973. By means of its offices in Washington, DC; Beijing; and Shanghai, USCBC tries to expand the US-China commercial relationship and the US economy. On its introduction and mission can see: the US-China Business Council, <https://www.uschina.org/about>.

25   The USCPFA is a nonprofit educational organisation whose goal is to build active and lasting friendship based on mutual understanding between the people of the United States and China. It was founded as a national organisation in 1974, working on people-to-people diplomacy between Americans and Chinese. Regarding the introduction of the USCPFA, see: the National U.S.-China People's Friendship Association, <http://www.uscpfa.org/whatis.html>.

IV. Comparison of Power and Competing Issues

After reviewing the highly interdependent US-China relations from many perspectives, in this section, this paper wants to examine the most sensitive and contending issues such as their budget on defense, the gap of military power and the South China Sea territorial disputes in this relationship. Among these competing issues, the most important comparison is their military power.

1. Military Power

On military strength, the United States ranks first and China ranks third, respectively, in 126 countries in the world. In 2013, China spent ¥720.2 billion Chinese Yen (Renminbi) on its national defense. The annual defense budget of China has grown 4 times in the past ten years, 33 times in the past 25 years,[26] hence to reach $155.6 billion in 2015. Being the largest regional power, the United States spent $581 billion on its defense budget in 2015. Table 4 indicates, in 2015, the total population of the United States is 321 million, China has 1.3 billion people. The manpower of the United States is 145 million, and that of China is 750 million; the United States and China have 1.4 million and 2.335 million active military personnel, respectively. From the perspective of land systems, the United States has 8,848 tanks while China has 9,150. On air power, including both fixed-wing and rotary-wing aircraft from all branches of service, the United States now has 2,308 fighter aircrafts, and 957 attack helicopters. China has 1,230 fighters and 200 attack helicopters. On naval power, the United States has 19 aircraft carriers while China only has Liao Ning bought from Ukraine. Now the United States has 62 destroyers and China only has 32. American has 75 submarines compared with 68 Chinese submarines. Americans still spend a huge amount of budget on its defense. Whether one compares their military strength from the land system, air or naval power, the United States apparently has much

---

26   See: Kao Pei-Shan (ed.), *Border Law Enforcement under Globalisation* (Taipei: Wunan, 2016), chapter 3. (forthcoming)

more relative power. China only has the advantage of military personnel.

Table 4: U.S.-China Military Power Comparison

Items	USA	China
Total Population	321,368,864	1,367,485,388
Active Military Personnel	**1,400,000**	**2,335,000**
Aircraft (All Types)	13,444	2,942
Helicopters	6,084	802
Attack Helicopters	957	200
Attack Aircraft (Fixed-Wing)	2,785	1,385
Fighter Aircraft	**2,308**	**1,230**
Trainer Aircraft	2,771	352
Transport Aircraft	5,739	782
Serviceable Airports	13,513	507
Tank Strength	**8,848**	**9,150**
Towed Artillery	1,299	62,46
Merchant Marine Strength	393	2,030
Major Ports	24	15
Fleet Strength	415	714
Aircraft Carriers	**19**	**1**
Submarines	**75**	**68**
Frigates	6	48
Destroyers	62	32
Annual Defense Budget (USD)	**$581,000,000,000**	**$155,600,000,000**

Note: The data was last updated in January 21, 2016,

Source: Global Fire Power, Military power comparison results for United States of America vs. China, <http://www.globalfirepower.com/countries-comparison-detail.asp?form=form&country1=United-States-of-America&country2=China&Submit=Compare+Countries>.

2. Economic Strength and Comprehensive National Power

The military power can only developed under a great economic power; therefore, one can compare their respective economic power. One country's economic power can be evaluated by its economic performance such as its GDP and unemployment rate. According to the International Monetary Fund (IMF), the GDP per capita of the United States and China in 2015 are $56,092 and $6,862, respectively.[27] If one uses the statistics from the US Bureau of Economic Analysis and National Bureau of Statistics of China (See Figure 3), the GDP growth rate of the United States went down to 1.4% in Q4 2015 from 2% in Q3 2015. That of China declined to 1.6% from 1.8% in the same period. Figure 4 showed that the unemployment rate of the United States went up to 5% in March 2016 from 4.9% in February 2016. China's unemployment rate basically has maintained at 4.05%.

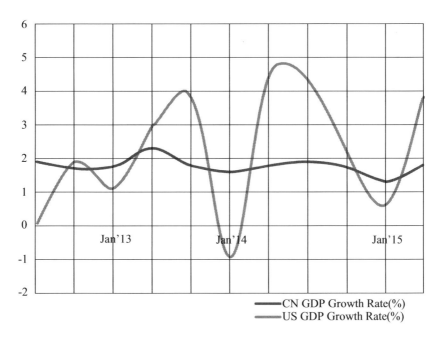

Figure 3: China vs United States on GDP Growth Rate

Source: "United States vs China," *Ieconomics*. <http://ieconomics.com/united-states-vs-china>.

---

27   International Monetary Fund, "International Financial Statistics (IFS)," < http://data.imf.org/?sk=388DFA60-1D26-4ADE-B505-A05A558D9A42&ss=1479331931186>.

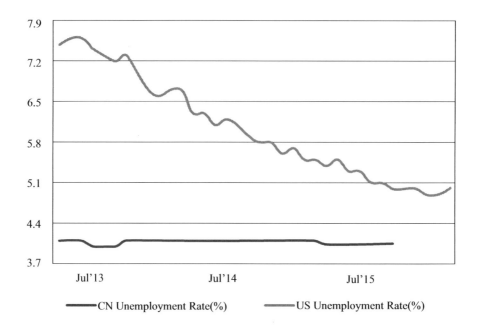

Figure 4: China vs United States on Unemployment Rate

Source: "United States vs China," *Ieconomics*. <http://ieconomics.com/united-states-vs-china>.

On the other hand, comprehensive national power (CNP) is a very important indicator as well. It can be used to evaluate not only the relative power between the United States and China but also their potential and international influence. According to JS Bajwa, "comprehensive national power" is a concept based on contemporary Chinese political thought that refers to the general power of a country.[28] He indicates that the status (or

---

28   There is no unified definition or method of computation on CNP or national power of a country. On the definition and explanations of CNP, can see: JS Bajwa, "Defining Elements of Comprehensive National Power," *CLAWS Journal*, (Summer, 2008), pp. 151.162; Michael Pillsbury, *China Debates the Future Security Environment* (Washington: National Defense University Press, 2000), chapter 5; Wang Songfen (ed.), *Comparative Studies of the Comprehensive National Power of the World'sMajor Nations (Shijie zhuyao guojia zonghe guoli bijiao yanjiu)*(Changsha: Hunan chubanshe, 1996), p. 69; and Huang Shuofeng, *Guojia shengshuai lun (On the rise and fall of nations)*(Changsha: Hunan chubanshe, 1996), p. 337

position) of a country in the international society is mainly related to the rise and fall of its national power and strategic resources.[29] Bajwa explained,

"a nation's strength lies in its harnessing a wide spectrum of its resources — from natural resources to human resources to its economic and military potential. CNP is a realistic broad based assessment of a nation's power and its ability to influence global issues as a significant player- this involves positive participation in multilateral diplomatic activities, big power diplomacy and crucial constructive role in key international and regional affairs."[30]

That is to say, a nation-state's CNP is comprised of military factors, namely, its "hard power", and economic and cultural factors, the "soft power". Based on Michael Porter's research,[31] a nation-state's CNP and competitiveness can be calculated by five critical resources, namely, physical resources, human resources, infrastructure, knowledge resources and capital resources. Table 5 describes the change of American and Chinese economic resources from 1975 to 2010 and their long-term economic growth trend to 2020. It shows that China's CNP has been sharply increasing over the past four decades.

Although the United States remains the largest world power with a stable CNP of 22.71% in the world's total, and 21.64% in 2000, its power decreased to 17.66% in 2010. But it may return to 22.22% in 2020. In 1980, China's CNP only accounted for 3.16% in the world's total. However, until

29　See: JS Bajwa, "Defining Elements of Comprehensive National Power".

30　Ibid.

31　In his book, Michael invented the "diamond model" that is an economic model including factors conditions, demand conditions, related and supporting industries, firm strategy, structure, and rivalry, government, and chance to explain why particular industries become much more competitive in particular locations. This diamond model was explored and expanded by other scholars hence has been used to evaluate a nation-state's comprehensive national power. On the diamond model, see: Michael Porter, *The Competitive Advantage of Nations* (New York: Free Press, 1990).

Table 5: The Economic Resources of the United States and China (1975-2020)

Unit: $ in billions

Country	1975	1980	1985	1990	1995	2000	2020 (projections)
USA	1,730	2,880	3,880	5,620	7,200	9,646	15,329
China	212	414	821	1,520	3,080	4,966	17,057
% of GDP in world's total							
USA	22.71	21.96	21.60	20.85	20.73	21.64	22.22
China	2.78	3.16	4.57	5.63	8.87	11.16	19.96

Note: The GDP is calculated by PPP
Source: JS Bajwa, "Defining Elements of Comprehensive National Power," *CLAWS Journal*, Summer 2008, pp. 151.162; and Hu Angang and Men Honghua, "The Rising of Modern China: Comprehensive National Power and Grand Strategy," *Strategy and Management*, No. 3, 2002, pp. 4-5.

2000, China's CNP has risen to 11.16% in world's total. China now is the second world power with a CNP accounted of 11.16% in the world's total. According to Bawja, the projection of China's CNP in 2020 will be 19.96% in the world's total compared with that of the United States for 22.22%. The relative gap between the United States and China has been narrowed from ten times to two from 1975 to 2000. The rapid rise of China has made it a strategic challenge in the eyes of the United States. Therefore in its domestic politics, many people ask for precautionary and containment strategies against China. However, for Obama's Administration, engagement is still the major policy to China.

In addition, it is interesting to find that not only the statistics and data differ from American and Chinese institutions, the numbers and projections did by Chinese scholars are contrasting as well. Table 6 and 7 indicate the research results did by the Chinese Academy of Social Sciences (CASS) and the Academy of Military Science (AMS). For instance, according to the CASS, by 2020, the United States will be ahead of China by 39% while

Table 6: Projections to 2020 of CASS CNP Statistics

Points and Rank by Year

Country	1990	2000	2010	2020
United States	**279 (1)**	**241 (1)**	**213 (1)**	**192 (2)**
Japan	162 (3)	184 (2)	206 (2)	228 (1)
Germany	161 (4)	162 (3)	163 (3)	164 (3)
France	129 (5)	141 (4)	150 (4)	157 (4)
Italy	115 (7)	125 (6)	137 (5)	151 (5)
England	116 (6)	116 (7)	115 (7)	115 (8)
Canada	100 (8)	92 (9)	86 (10)	81 (10)
Australia	78 (10)	71 (11)	66 (12)	62 (12)
South Africa	36 (15)	34 (16)	32 (16)	30 (16)
USSR	184 (2)	-	-	-
Russia	(139) (4)*	131 (5)	121 (6)	108 (9)
China	**94 (9)**	**102 (8)**	**110 (8)**	**118 (7)**
India	51 (13)	53 (13)	55 (13)	57 13)
Indonesia	34 (16)	37 (15)	39 (15)	40 (15)
South Korea	70 (11)	87 (10)	105 (9)	124 (6)
Brazil	62 (12)	69 (12)	75 (11)	80 (11)
Mexico	46 (14)	49 (14)	51 (14)	52 (14)
Egypt	30 (17)	26 (17)	23 (17)	21 (17)

Source: Wang Songfen, ed., *Shijie zhuyao guojia zonghe guoli bijiao yanjiu* (Comparative studies of the comprehensive national power of the world's major nations)(Changsha: Hunan chubanshe, 1996), p.43; and Michael Pillsbury, *China Debates the Future Security Environment* (Washington: National Defense University Press, 2000), chapter 5.

the AMS showed that the United States will be only 3% ahead of China.[32] Whether which methods of assessment have been used, every country does struggle for power hoping to balance power. However, does this mean

---

32   See: Huang Shuofeng, Guojia shengshuai lun (On the rise and fall of nations)(Changsha: Hunan chubanshe, 1996), p.337; and Wang Songfen (ed.), Shijie zhuyao guojia zonghe guoli bijiao yanjiu (Comparative Studies of the Comprehensive National Power of the World's Major Nations)(Changsha: Hunan chubanshe, 1996), p. 69.

Table 7: Score and Rank Projections to 2020 of AMS CNP Statistics

Country	1989	2000	2010	2020	Yearly Growth Rate
United States	593.33 (1)	816.85 (1)	1066.21 (1)	1391.71 (1)	2.7%
USSR	386.72 (2)	648.34 (2)	-	-	-
Germany	378.10 (3)	558.23 (3)	772.36 (2)	1068.63 (3)	3.3%
Japan	368.04 (4)	537.39 (4)	736.35 (4)	1009 (4)	3.2%
China	222.33 (6)	437.35 (5)	768.57 (3)	1350.63 (2)	5.8%
France	276.35 (5)	384.93 (6)	507.36 (5)	668.73 (6)	2.8%
England	214.08 (7)	281.24 (7)	353.05 (8)	443.19 (8)	2.3%
Brazil	156.05 (8)	267.70 (9)	419.72 (7)	658.09 (7)	4.6%
India	144.16 (9)	274.08 (8)	468.15 (6)	799.67 (5)	5.5%
Canada	136.64 (10)	177.41 (10)	220.56 (9)	274.18 (9)	2.2%
Australia	112.59 (11)	147.91 (11)	185.67 (10)	233.07 (10)	2.3%

Source: Huang Shuofeng, *Zonghe guoli lun* (On comprehensive national power) (Beijing: Zhongguo shehui kexue chubanshe, 1992), pp. 220-221; and Michael Pillsbury, *China Debates the Future Security Environment* (Washington: National Defense University Press, 2000), chapter 5.

that the two great powers eventually will use military force to resolve their disputes? This can be examined and investigated from their model of crisis bargaining.

3. Contending Issues-South China Sea Territorial Disputes

Among the contending issues, the South China Sea territorial dispute can be considered one of the most complicated and sensitive issue between the two great powers.[33] Not just as many countries have been involved into this territorial dispute, including Taiwan (See Table 5), all of them have claimed that they have the sovereignty of the islands. The U.S. intervention in this region has greatly complicated and aggravated the situation. The U.S.

---

33   On the explanations and discussion on the territorial disputes, see: Beina Xu, Council on Foreign Relations, "South China Sea Tension," May 14, 2014. <http://www.cfr.org/china/south-china-sea-tensions/p29790>; and David Rosenberg, "Governing the South China Sea," *Harvard Asia Quarterly*, Vol. 12, No. 3&4, Winter, 2010.

insistence on freedom of navigation, its operations and patrols in the South China Sea, and its military maneuvers with its South East Asian allies, all have provoked China's criticism and anxiety. Since China has built artificial islands in the region, many serious arguments and tense situation frequently appeared. China's action therefore has caused its neighbors' complaints and anxiety. According to Carlyle A. Thayer, there are four reasons for China to construct artificial islands here, including nationalism, fisheries, hydrocarbons and strategic imperatives; strategic imperatives are the most important.[34] Thayer indicated that to counter the Obama Administration's policy of "Rebalancing towards the Asia-Pacific",[35] China wants to control the South China Sea to "protect its sea lines of communications and to secure its southern flank against intervention by the U.S. Navy and Air Force."[36] That is the so-called Chinese version of rebalancing policy. However, just as Mearsheimer argues that it is very difficult and hard to assess and know states' "intensions",[37] it is very reasonable for states to protect its interests and position in the area. Although the situation looks very intense recently, the two have refrained from using force to resolve their disputes. The United States until present has never claimed its support to any related countries and has insisted the peaceful resolution on this issue.

Moreover, from the perspective of the ASEAN countries, on the China-

---

34　Carlyle A. Thayer, "South China Sea: The Strategic Implications of China's Artificial Islands," *Australia Institute of International Affairs*, September 15, 2006. <http://www.internationalaffairs.org.au/events/south-china-sea-the-strategic-implications-of-chinas-artificial-islands/>.

35　On the analysis and discussion on the US police of rebalancing towards the Asia, can see: Kao Pei-Shan, "From Return to Rebalancing to Asia: A Discussion on US Asia-Pacific Policy," *The Chinese Public Administration Review*, Vol. 19, No. 2, June 2013, pp. 157-177.

36　See: Carlyle A. Thayer, "South China Sea: The Strategic Implications of China's Artificial Islands".

37　Regarding the criticism of Mearsheimer's theory, can see: Sverrir Steinsson, "John Mearsheimer's Theory of Offensive Realism and the Rise of China," March 6, 2014, *E-International Relations*. <http://www.e-ir.info/2014/03/06/john-mearsheimers-theory-of-offensive-realism-and-the-rise-of-china/>.

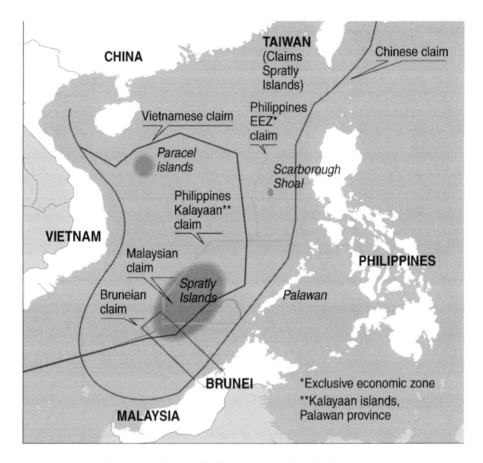

Figure 5: Disputed Claims in the South China Sea

Source:Christopher Willis, "South China Sea Dispute," *Odyssey*, January 9, 2016, <http://
theodysseyonline.com/unf/china-just-did-something-significant-in-the-south-china-sea/270320>.

ASEAN relations, since the 1990s, China has pursued an active diplomatic
strategy, in addition to adopting a "good-neighborly foreign policy" to
Southeast Asian countries.China also promoted its economic and trade
contacts with these countries, and actively participated on regional affairs. In
1996, China became ASEAN's full dialogue partner, and the two established
in 1997 a "good-neighborliness and mutual trust" partnership. In 2003, the

relationship has been enhanced as a "strategic partnership for peace and prosperity". China not only was the first to establish strategic partnership with ASEAN,[38] but also was also the first to join the "Treaty of Amity and Cooperation in Southeast Asia" (TAC). Chinese leaders and high-level officials intensively and frequently visited the ASEAN to strengthen their contacts and exchanges. In 2002, the two signed a framework agreement to establish a Free Trade Area (FTA), that is, the China-ASEAN Free Trade Agreement (CAFTA), with a GDP of $6,000 billion and trade volume of $4,500 billion after the European Union (EU) and the North American Free Trade Agreement (NAFTA).[39] To enhance its relations with ASEAN countries, China proposed in 2013 to establish an upgraded version of the CAFTA, which is the so-called "China-ASEAN Free Trade Area version 2.0". China now is ASEAN's largest trading partner. Table 8 showed the growth of the bilateral trade from 2000 to 2013, ASEAN now is China's third largest trading partner, the fourth largest export market and the 2nd largest source of imports. Under this kind of huge and highly economic and trade interdependence, it is hard to believe that China will go to war with its ASEAN partners. Resolving their territorial disputes by means of international legal principles, bilateral or multilateral regimes by negotiations and consultations should be the best way. ASEAN countries definitely will maintain their position by strategic alliance with the United States, and economic cooperation with China. In sum, the United States and China will keep their competition and maintain their influence in Asia-Pacific region.

---

38 On the discussion of China-ASEAN Economic and Trade relations, can see: Kao Pei-Shan, "Analysis on China's Integration into Asia," paper presented at the 2015 Tamkang School of Strategic Studies Annual Events. (Taipei: Graduate Institute of International Affairs and Strategic Studies, TKU, May, 31, 2015), pp. 145-162.

39 The CAFTA occupies 13.4% of world trade amounts. The average taxes of Chinese products exporting to ASEAN will decrease to 0.6%; and those from ASEAN to China will be 0.1%.-Now the taxes of 93% of all products, about 7,000 items on bilateral trade, have reduced to 0.

Table 8: Data Base Comparison of China-ASEAN Bilateral Trade (2000-2013)

In US$Billions

Year	ASEANstats Database				China Statistical Yearbook				UNCTADstat Database			
	Export	Import	Net Balance	Total Volume	Export	Import	Net Balance	Total Volume	Export	Import	Net Balance	Total Volume
2000	14.2	18.1	-3.9	32.3	22.2	17.3	4.8	39.5	16.5	20.2	-3.7	36.7
2001	14.5	17.4	-2.9	31.9	23.2	18.4	4.8	39.5	16.5	20.2	-3.7	36.7
2002	19.5	23.2	-3.7	42.8	31.2	23.6	7.6	54.8	21.9	28.0	-6.1	49.9
2003	29.1	30.6	-1.5	59.6	47.3	30.9	16.4	78.3	30.9	34.2	-3.3	65.1
2004	41.4	47.7	-6.4	89.1	63.0	42.9	20.1	105.9	41.6	48.4	-6.8	90.0
2005	52.3	61.1	-8.9	113.4	75.0	55.4	19.6	130.4	52.7	63.0	-10.3	115.7
2006	65.0	75.0	-9.9	139.7	89.5	69.5	20.0	159.0	66.7	78.7	-11.9	145.4
2007	77.9	93.2	-15.2	171.1	108.4	94.1	14.2	202.5	79.1	98.0	-18.9	177.1
2008	87.6	109.3	-21.7	196.9	117.0	114.3	2.7	231.3	88.7	113.2	-24.4	201.9
2009	81.6	96.6	-15.0	178.2	106.7	106.3	0.4	213.0	82.4	97.5	-15.1	179.9
2010	118.5	117.7	0.8	236.2	154.7	138.2	16.5	292.9	113.7	127.2	-13.5	240.9
2011	142.5	147.1	-4.6	289.7	193.0	170.1	22.9	363.1	142.5	157.1	-14.6	299.6
2012	141.9	177.6	-35.7	319.5	195.9	204.3	-8.4	400.1	141.9	178.7	-36.8	320.6
2013	-	-	-	-	-	-	-	-	153.2	205.0	-51.8	358.2

Source: Kao Pei-Shan, "Analysis on China's Integration into Asia," paper presented at the 2015 Tamkang School of Strategic Studies Annual Events.

V. Conclusions

Just like Mearsheimer indicates, States' intentions is very difficult to be predicted, that states can never be certain whether other states will refrain from using those offensive military capabilities, it is very reasonable and fair for states to improve and enhance their military power. However, does this mean that a war certainly will happen between two highly interdependent great powers? It is interesting to find that scholars in the field of International Relations have many arguments and debates on this topic. Many scholars, namely, realists in the field of IR have proposed many pessimistic predictions on the rise of China and its relations with the United States. However, their assumptions have been challenged and criticised by liberals, constructivists, Marxists and Chinese scholars in particular. Chinese scholars also have proposed a series of approaches claiming "China's peaceful rise" and "harmonious world",[40] etc. They all have their own arguments and have suggested very insightful viewpoints and have done a series of researches. However, this research agrees that although states will pursue their survival by means of maximizing their power, this does not necessarily be a "zero-sum" game or war. There are still some rooms for states to cooperate with one another. For the United States, many issues such as the North Korea's development on nuclear weapons or protection of global ecosystem, climate change and financial stability all greatly rely on China's cooperation. For China, it is unwise to challenge the dominant power of the United States in Asia-Pacific region, especially when there is still a large gap in power between the United States and China. Although their economic interdependence may be asymmetrical, to quote Bruce Russett and John Oneal, "trade is always to some degree a mutually beneficial interaction; otherwise, it would not be taken."[41] Under the annual huge amounts of two-way trade, a war seems to be unlikely to happen between the United States and China. Why? It is because "if my factory is located in your country, bombing your industry means, in effect, bombing my own property."[42] Since states are "rational", it is unwise for them to use force to resolves problems with their trading partners of highly interdependence.

It is true that it is quite difficult to predict and ascertain states'

---

40 On the discourse of China's foreign policy and the change and adjustment of its strategy see: Shih, Gee-Chong, "From Big-Power Diplomacy to Harmonious World-The Transformation of China's Foreign Strategy," *Prospect & Exploration*, Vol 5, No. 1, pp. 8-12.

41 Bruce Russett and John Oneal, *Triangulating Peace-Democracy, Interdependence, and International Organisations* (New York: W.W.Norton&Company, 2001), p. 129.

42 Ibid.

"intentions", and survival is their principal goal. However, does this mean that states will use so easily military forces to resolve their disputes and problems? This will rely on much more evidence and researches. Just as Mearsheimer claimed that "we have no fact about the future," but doing much more researches can help one to predict the future development on US-China relations. In the past few years, the author has done many researches and has adopted four crises bargaining happened between the two to examine their problem-resolving model and has found that negotiations and consultations are always the useful means for them to resolve problems.[43]Since the 21st century, one can witness the sharp increase of US-China close contacts and exchanges on trade, education, culture, and government officials as this research showed in the previous sections. This research agrees with the offensive realist assumption that states will maximise their power and seek survival. This is fair and reasonable as they are rational. However, do not forget that Mearsheimer also points out that power includes not only military forces but also potential power. That is, states' comprehensive national power. Not just because of their highly interdependent relations, but also when there is still has a widening power gap between the United States and China, China should just wait and not do anything like Mearsheimer reiterated. In addition, according to Mearsheimer, after the rise of China, it will pursue its position as regional hegemon but the premise is China's maintenance on its economic growth. What will it be if China cannot continue the pace of economic growth? This paper therefore believes that in the short term, a stable US-China relationship still can be expected.

---

43   On the process of the four US-China crises bargaining from 1989-2001, can see Kao Pei-Shan, *US-China Great Power Bargaining* (Hsinchu: National Chiao Tung University Press, 2012).

Redefining Culture in Conflict Environment: Shifting from Macro to Micro Level of Analysis

Michał Pawiński[*]

I. Transdisciplinarity of Complex Conflict Environment

War has always been a complex phenomenon. It involves so many elements that it is difficult to follow them all not to mention control or predict their actions and outcomes. One such element is human being along with his irrationality, emotions, and mindsets. Thus, to know the enemy is often perceived as a golden key, a solution that will lead to victory. To gather the knowledge about other societies is not as easy as it seems at the first glance. In particular, it is true when "us" and "them" are separated by the vast sea of otherness and sociocultural differences. It is not surprising that contemporary complex conflict environments require skills and capabilities that go far beyond soldiers' initial missions and trainings. Kinetic operations are often far from satisfying any political and military objectives. Sociocultural understanding of other societies demands extended knowledge and management of large quantity of data. It expects a mindset that is contrary to the traditional military attitudes developed through rigidity military training. It is difficult to achieve sociocultural proficiency in relatively short time span about people who are distinctly alien from "us." Learning facts about culture does not equal to cultural relativism. The worldview gap has been wide-open and well seen in counterinsurgency operations in Iraq and Afghanistan. Thus, through the Human Terrain System (hereafter HTS) the U.S. and allies forces engaged social scientists to build

---

* Ph.D. Candidate, Graduate Institute of International Affairs and Strategic Studies, Tamkang University, Taiwan.

connecting bridges between "us" and "them".[1]

A fundamental element of Human Terrain System was Human Terrain Teams consisting of five to nine members, including Team Leader, Social Scientist, Research Manager and Human Terrain Analyst. The primary objectives of their field research were, to:[2]

1. provide description and analyses of civil considerations for each district, and area of operations.
2. maintain an understanding of local leadership, how they interact with each other, and what their interests and concerns are.
3. provide specialized assistance to brigade combat teams and battalion projects to facilitate completion, efficiency, and social impact.
4. provide guidance to soldiers regarding how to collect human terrain information to improve their intelligence preparation of the battlefield and reporting efforts.
5. respond to requests for information from brigade combat team and battalion.

The HTS project opened a fierce debate among social scientist regarding the ethical side of cooperation with military and intelligence institutions. Among some scholars, there has been a concern that the knowledge gathered by Human Terrain Teams might be used to inflict harm to innocent civilians or targeted killing.[3] The project might have been underdeveloped and poorly

---

1   Hugh Gusterson, "The Cultural Turn in the War on Terror", in *Anthropology and Global Counterinsurgency*, ed. John D. Kelly et all. (Chicago: University of Chicago Press, 2010), pp. 279-297; Montgomery McFate, "Anthropology and Counterinsurgency: The Strange Story of their Curious Relationship," Military Review (March-April, 2006), pp. 24-38; Headquarters Department of the Army, *Counterinsurgency* FM 3-24, 3-33.5 (Washington D.C.: Marine Corps Warfighting Publications, 2006).

2   Marcus B. Griffin, "An Anthropologist among the Soldiers. Notes from the Field," In *Anthropology and Global Counterinsurgency*, ed. John D. Kelly et.all. (Chicago: University of Chicago Press, 2010), pp. 215-231; Nathan Finney, *Human Terrain Team Handbook*, (Fort Leavenworth: HTS Doctrine Development Team, 2008).

3   David H. Price, *Weaponizing Anthropology. Social Science in Service of the Militarized*

designed, it might have been even unethical. However, it also exposed inefficiencies of civilian strategic studies in providing solutions and support in the complexities of conflict environment. The Human Terrain System engaged a variety of disciplines, including but not limited to, anthropology, communication, linguistics, psychology, economics or political science.[4] It was a transdisciplinary approach with the purpose of creating a total system of knowledge that is completely beyond the comprehension by a single discipline.[5] In 1994 Michael Gibbons argued that the older hierarchical and homogeneous mode of knowledge production is being replaced by a new form characterized by complexity, hybridity, non-linearity, reflexivity, heterogeneity, and transdisciplinarity.[6] The methodological rigidity and its sub-disciplinary character of international relations discipline made civilian strategic studies incapable of contributing to ongoing military operations in Iraq and Afghanistan. The problem of strategic studies is well exposed by the theory of strategic culture. Initially designed to understand cultures and behaviors of people in conflict environments, metamorphosed into dangerously oversimplifying, stereotype-producing concept. The Human

---

State (Petrolia: CounterPunch and AK Press, 2011); George R. Lucas Jr., *Anthropologists in Arms. The Ethics of Military Anthropology* (London: Rowman & Littlefield Publishers Inc., 2009); Roberto J. Gonzalez, "Towards mercenary anthropology? The new U.S. Army counterinsurgency manual FM 3-24 and the military-anthropology complex," *Anthropology Today*, Vol. 23, No. 3 (2007), pp. 14-19; Michał Pawiński, "Going Beyond Human Terrain System. Some Thoughts on Ethical Dilemmas," *Journal of Military Ethics*, Vol. 15, Issue 3, (Fall 2016, forthcoming).

4   Christopher A. King, "Academics at War: Anthropologists and Other Social Scientists in Iraq and Afghanistan and in the Framing of Counterinsurgency Doctrine", paper presented at the conference *'The University and National Security after 9/11"*, at Arthur W. Fiske Memorial Lecture, Case Western Reserve University School of Law, Institute for Global Security Law and Policy, September 23, 2011; Yvette Clinton et. all, *Congressionally Directed Assessment of the Human Terrain System*, CNA Analysis and Solution, November 2010.

5   Basarab Nicolescu, "Methodology of Transdisciplinarity – Levels of Reality, Logic of the Included Middle and Complexity," *Transdisciplinary Journal of Engineering & Science* Vol. 1, No. 1 (2010), pp. 19-38.

6   Michael Gibbons, *The New Production of Knowledge: The Dynamics of Science and Research in Contemporary Societies* (London: SAGE Publications Ltd., 1994).

Terrain System suggested a possible escape of out this rigidity. Civilian strategic studies should be reconstructed to live up the demands of modern and future wars. In the first part, this paper will critically evaluate the main theory of strategic studies connecting culture with war, namely, strategic culture. The second part of the paper will consist of three sections, each adding one block of a new framework for the cultural understanding of a complex conflict environment. The first block is knowledge which will focus mainly on the concept of "self;" the second block is awareness, a part discussing the process of cultural shock and acculturation; lastly, the last block of sensitivity is separate into two elements: empathy and trust building capabilities. In all three blocks civilian strategists have a specific role to perform. The conclusive section argues that contemporary strategic studies should focus on finding solutions for practical problems, but such problems rarely can be encapsulated in the terms of a single (sub) discipline.

II. The Simplicity of Macro-level Strategic Studies

A comprehensive review of strategic culture has been done elsewhere.[7] The core of this section will focus on critical evaluation of concept itself. In 1977 Jack Snyder introduced strategic culture in a publication The Soviet Strategic Culture. He argued that the Soviet's leadership perspective on nuclear strategy is distinctively different from the United States approach. The reason behind this difference could have been found in the culture. To be more specific, unique historical experience, distinctive political behavior,

---

7   Lawrence Sondhaus, *Strategic Culture and Ways of War* (London: Routledge, 2006); Rashed Uz Zaman, "Strategic Culture: A 'Cultural' Understanding of War," *Comparative Strategy*, 28:1 (2009), pp. 68-88; Alan Bloomfield, "Time to Move On: Reconceptualizing the Strategic Culture Debate," *Contemporary Security Policy*, Vol. 33, No. 3 (2012), pp. 437-461; Jeffery A. Larson, *Comparative Strategic Cultures Curriculum. Assessing Strategic Culture as a Methodological Approach to Understanding WMD Decision-Making by States and Non-State Actors* (Fort Belvoir: Defense Threat Reduction Agency, Advanced Systems and Concepts Office, U.S. Department of Defense, 2006).

and institutional relationships produced a unique mix of Soviet strategic beliefs and behavior. Hence, strategic culture had been defined as a "sum of total ideas, conditioned emotional responses, and patterns of habitual behavior that members of the national strategic community have acquired through instruction and imitation and share with each other."[8] Two years later, Ken Booth called for a strategy with "human face." Strategists are professionally committed to preserving and promoting a particular national posture, therefore strategists and strategy are ethnocentric driven. To counter ethnocentrism, in-group- and culturally-bounded thinking is to implement cultural relativism, in the meaning that social and cultural phenomena are perceived and described from the perspective of participants or adherents of a given culture. Ultimately, for Booth strategy with "human face" means "peopling of strategic discourse with real nations than stereotypes (…) with groups with national styles and traditions rather than rational strategic black boxes (…) with individuals affected by a distinctive cultural heredity as opposed to individuals supposedly driven by a universal political and strategic logic."[9] Both scholars opened the floor for a diverse and intense debates about the role of culture in warfare and the concept of strategic culture.

In *National Style in Strategy* Colin S. Gray defined American strategic culture as "modes of thought and action with respect to force, derived from the perception of national historical experience, aspirations for self-characterization, and from all the many distinctively American experiences that characterize an American citizen."[10] Strategic culture is, therefore,

---

8   Jack L. Snyder, *The Soviet Strategic Culture: Implications for Limited Nuclear Operations* (Santa Monica: RAND Corporation, R-2154-AF, 1977), p.8.

9   Ken Booth, *Strategy and Ethnocentrism* (New York: Holmes & Meier Publishers, Inc., 1979), p. 135.

10   Colin S. Gray, "National Style in Strategy: The American Experience", *International Security*, Vol. 6, No. 2 (1981), pp. 22; Colin S. Gray, "Out of the Wilderness: Prime Time for Strategic Culture", *Comparative Strategy* 26:1 (2007), pp. 1-20; Colin S. Gray, *Modern Strategy* (Oxford: Oxford University Press, 1999).

distinctively unique and influenced by history, economy and geopolitics. National style provides an enduring explanation of state behaviour (mode of action). Johnston disagreed with this perspective. In 1995 article Thinking about Strategic Culture and in the book Cultural Realism he claimed that the first generation of strategic culture theorists, including Snyder, Booth, and Gray, are at the same time over-determined and under-determine with their concept. Strategic culture is over-determined because, as an independent variable, is the product of a vast range of other independent variables. The question is, which variables are more important or more influential, and how to weight the effects of these various inputs?[11] If strategic culture is a product of all relevant variables, then there is little conceptual space for non-strategic culture explanation of strategic choice; in other words, strategic culture is under-determined, meaning, there is only one possible behaviour due to one existing strategic culture. He observed that strategic culture and strategic behaviour are considered simultaneously as an independent and dependent variables. Therefore, Johnston excluded culture-behaviour linkage from his definition, and focused on habits and traditions. For him strategic culture is an "integrated system of symbols (i.e. languages, analogies, metaphors) that acts to establish pervasive and long-lasting grand strategic preference by formulating concepts of the role and efficacy of military force in interstate political affairs, and by clothing these conceptions with such an aura of factuality that the strategic preferences seem uniquely realistic and efficacious."[12] As a system of symbols strategic culture consists of basic assumptions about the orderliness of the strategic environment, about the nature of the adversary and the threat is poses, and about the efficacy of the use of force. Combined, all three should provide a preference about what strategic options that are the most efficacious for dealing with the threat

---

11   Jeffery S. Lantis and Darryl Howlett, "Strategic Culture," in *Strategy in the Contemporary World*, ed. John Baylis, James K. Wirtz, and Colin S. Gray (Oxford: Oxford University Press, 2013), pp. 76-95.

12   Alastair I. Johnston, *Cultural Realism.* Strategic Culture and Grand Strategy in Chinese History (Princeton: Princeton University Press, 1995), p. 36.

environment. According to Johnson, this is exact moment that strategic culture affects behavioural choices. In his perspective, strategic culture is a limited and ranked set of strategic preferences that is persistent across time.[13]

As this brief recall of the debate between Gray and Johnston has shown, there are many problems associated with strategic culture concept. First of all, there is a persistent issue of continuity. Snyder said that strategic culture evolves relatively slowly. Johnston mentioned that Chinese "parabellum assumptions have persisted across different state systems in Chinese history – from the anarchical Warring States period, to the hierarchical imperial Chinese system, to the increasingly interdependent post-Cold War period."[14] Colin S. Gray as well stated that, although strategic culture can change over time "as new experience is absorbed, coded, and culturally transmitted (…) however, [it] changes slowly (…) if strategic culture is held to be significantly reshapable on a year-by-year, a decade-by-decade, basis, then culture is probably unduly dignified, even pretentious, a term to characterize the phenomena at issue."[15] There is no doubt that history is important element for any society. It is part and parcel of complex mosaic shaping and constituting the identity of social communities. The past experience of the society is otherwise known as a collective memory. Maurice Halbwachs argued that our collective memory is far from comprehensive. Some events are forgotten and others remembered and recorded in a selective way. Sometimes collective memory can be built around fake events in order to support specific political agenda. For example, Benito Mussolini chose as its symbol the ancient Roman Fasces, attempting to associate the 1920s-40s Italy with the Ancient Roman Empire, and Mussolini with the Roman Emperors. Contemporary People's Republic of China leadership promotes

---

13   Alastair I. Johnston, "Thinking about Strategic Culture," *International Security*, Vol. 19, No. 4 (1995), pp. 32-64.

14   Alastair I. Johnston, "Cultural Realism and Strategy in Maoist China", in *The Culture of National Security: Norms and Identity in World Politics*, ed. Peter J. Katzenstein (New York: Columbia University Press, 1996), pp. 216-268.

15   Gray, *Modern*, pp. 131-132.

Sun Tzu and Confucianism as a symbols of defensive mentality, although China in its history have fought wars no less than any other country.[16]

In complex conflict environments collective memories have four negative elements that make intergroup relations much more challenging.[17] First, they are often associated with contempt, hatred and anger directed toward the enemy. Several studies have proven that emotions can have positive or detrimental effect on how the conflict sides interact, and on the chance of successful peace negotiations.[18] Second, there are rituals or current circumstances that maintain or revive the past traumatic event in the present. Third, they are based on chosen traumas that are simultaneously a chosen glory, which makes it difficult to mourn the loss. Lastly, often deny important aspects of the history. Thus, according to Halbwachs it is the needs, problems, and beliefs of the present that determine the memory of the past. The collective memory, then, is constantly renewed and reshaped with each passing generation. Thus, there is no undisturbed continuity. Culture is changing year-by-year, even day-by-day, otherwise change itself wouldn't be possible at all. Because culture is changing constantly, the relationship between culture and conflict is best understood by a multidimensional paradigm that includes both time as experiences of the past with approach of keeping a healthy distance toward its interpretations, present context, and future expectations; and level of relationship (personal, interpersonal, group,

---

16 Maurice Halbwachs, *On Collective Memory* (Chicago: University of Chicago Press, 1992); Barak A. Salmoni, and Paula Holmes Eber, *Operational Culture for the Warfighter. Principles and Applications* (Quantico, Virginia: Marine Corps University Press, 2008).

17 Dario R. Paez, and James Hou-Fu Liu, "Collective Memory of Conflicts," in *Intergroup Conflicts and Their Resolution*, ed. Daniel Bar-Tal (New York: Psychology Press, 2011), pp. 105-124.

18 Eran Halperin, and Ruthie Pliskin, "Emotions and Emotion Regulation in Intractable Conflict: Studying Emotional Processes Within a Unique Context," *Advances in Political Psychology*, Vol. 36 (2015), pp. 119-150; Marija Spanovic, Brian Lickel, Thomas F. Denson, and Nebojsa Petrovic, "Fear and anger as predictors of motivation for intergroup aggression: Evidence from Serbia and Republika Srpska," *Group Processes & Intergroup Relations*, Vol. 13, No. 6 (2010), pp. 725-739.

and intergroup), allowing to focus on minute permutations at the micro-level of society, usually ignored by the macro-level abstract theories like strategic culture.

Another problem is the singularity or totality of strategic culture concept. According to Colin S. Gray all human beings are enculturated, there cannot be a person cultural, or beyond culture. There is no doubt in that statement. However, he goes as far as to saying that "in their strategic behaviour, Germans (or any other nation- added by author) cannot help but behave except under the constraints of Germanic strategic culture."[19] In 1995 Elizabeth Kier argued that the military's culture may reflect some aspects of the civilian society's culture, but this is not always the case. In her case study of French civil-military relations between the two World Wars the political-military subcultures were competing with each other about the future organizational character of the French army.[20] In similar manner, Michael Evans identified two rival traditions or strategic subcultures in Australian strategic culture, namely, political preference for self-reliant defence of the continent vs. military's preference for sending Australian forces overseas to fight in its major allies' wars.[21] Hence, hesitantly, Gray admitted that military culture will vary among the geographically specialized services, and within those services among their separate branches. But, nevertheless, he still argued that countries do have preferred ways of defence preparation and ways of war.[22] On the other hand, for Johnston, security community may have several strategic cultures, however, in this multiplicity there is a dominant one that is interested in preserving the status quo, in other words,

---

19   Gray, *Modern*, p. 132.

20   Elizabeth Kierr, "Culture and Military Doctrine: France between the War", *International Security*, Vol. 19, No. 4 1995), pp. 65-93.

21   Michael Evans "The Tyranny of Dissonance: Australia's Strategic Culture and Way of War 1901-2005", *Land Warfare Studies Center Study Papers*, No. 306, 2005.

22   Gray, "Out of the Wilderness," pp. 1-20.

wants to keep itself in power.[23]

It is easier to live in a defined hierarchy where people are types, and where social groups are not constantly shifting, dissolving or altering. However, wishful thinking of rigid mind rarely ever mirrors the true complexities of existing world, a rigidity that turns multidimensional human beings into mono-dimensional creatures. The inherent danger of labelling other cultures is that the label might turn into a fixed stereotypical image, which annihilates the fact that each cultural group has various sub-groups and that each group is made up of individuals whose actions and norms might not conform with the ideas of an existing unitary concept of culture. According to Binsbergen "culture is not bounded, not tied to a place, not unique but multiply, not impossible to combine, blend and transgress, not tied to a human body, an ethnic group, a birth right. And it suggests that ultimately we are much better off as nomads between a plurality of cultures, then as self-imposed prisoners of a smug Eurocentrism (or any other – centrism – added by author)."[24] Although, some scholars related with strategic culture complied that there can be many subcultures, but if there are many subcultures than there can't be dominant one due to impossibility of finding a cumulative singularity out of existing diversity. It is not true that one's identity with one's community must be the principle or dominant identity a person has. Identity theorists might differ in how to conceptualize how many identities a person is likely to have, but, they agree on its plurality. In other words, how behave, how we act, depends on the context and moment of situation, not on static cultural norms.[25]

In contemporary globalized world the cultural contacts are leading

---

23   Johnston, Cultural Realism., op.cit.

24   Wim M.J. van Binsbergen, *Intercultural encounters: African and anthropological lessons towards a philosophy of interculturality* (Münster: Lit Verlag, 1999), pp. 459-522.

25   Daphna Oyserman, Kristen Elmore, George Smith, "Self, Self-Concept, and Identity," in Handbook of Self and Identity, 2nd Edition, ed. Mark R. Leary, and June P. Tangney (New York: The Guilford Press, 2012), pp. 69-104.

to such a hybridization of behavioural modes across the world that it is difficult to identify any "local culture" as being genuinely indigenous, with a timeless quality.[26] Lisa Wedeen depicted the scale of diversity, by giving example of republicanism and Frenchness: "1. Republican ideas can come to stand for Frenchness because of the ways in which they have been used to objectify what it means to be French; 2. Non-French people may also subscribe to republican ideas; 3. Not all French people adhere to republican ideas; 4. Not all French people interpret republicanism or understand its significance in the same way; 5. Anitrepublican French people may not have the same relationship to republicanism as do antirepublican thinkers and citizens elsewhere; 6. It is not clear who counts as a "French" person."[27] Multiculturalism becomes major influential element in defining "who I am." It is especially true in case of Great Britain, United State or Germany with its large number of subcultural minorities. It is important to recognize that identities are robustly plural, and that the importance of one identity need not obliterate the importance of others. Therefore, strategic culture, in order to be theoretically acceptable, ignored the diversity of culture and identities through the process of categorization, which ultimately can lead to stereotyping and biased thinking about other societies. In a large part, simple categorization denies or severely hinders cultural understanding and intercultural communication between culturally distant societies.

Human existence requires finding one's place in the world, not only one's place in the physical world, but also in the social world. Self and identity are social products. People do not create themselves from the air; all comes from the social context. Categorization facilitates the process of socialization. To be able to categorize within the social system, the first necessary step is psychological identification, the engagement of the self

---

26   Amartya Sen, *Identity and Violence. The Illusion of Destiny* (London: Penguin Books, 2006).

27   Lisa Wedeen, "Conceptualizing Culture: Possibilities for Political Science", *The American Political Science Review*, Vol. 96, No. 4 (2002), p. 721.

in a way that a category is transformed into an in-group. Categorization works to align the person with the realities of the social context, in order "to produce dynamic, context-specific definitions of self and others which both reflect and make possible the almost infinitely variable pattern of human social relations."[28] There are no uncategorized subjects and objects in social context. However, the same process of categorization transforms people's relations into similarities and differences; from perceived similarities and differences flow the perceptions of attraction and dislike, agreement and disagreement, cooperation and conflict. One of the negative outcomes resulting from the categorization, and associated with a strategic culture that simplifies social reality, is outgrouping homogeneity effect. The outgroup homogeneity effect has actually two effects: the first one, the out-group is perceived as less variable than average; the second one, the in-group is viewed as reliably more heterogeneous than average. The outgroup homogeneity is caused by the fact that people know more in-group than out-group members and therefore retrieve more instances when making in-group rather than out-group variability judgments. This greater retrieval leads to the greater perception of in-group heterogeneity. People are motivated to see themselves as unique and special. Classification of oneself as a group member entails a shift from the perception of self as a unique person toward more inclusive social units (groups) that depersonalize the representation of self. It is important to underline that depersonalization refers to contextual change in the level of identity, not to a loss identity.[29] Thus, self-esteem and self-evaluation heavily depend on the distinctiveness of in-group which

---

28   Penelope J. Oakes et. all, "Social Categorization and Social Context: Is Stereotype Change a Matter of Information or of Meaning?" in *Social Identity and Social Cognition*, ed. Dominic Abrams and Michael A. Hogg (Oxford: Blackwell Publishers Ltd, 1999), pp.55-80; Penelope Oakes, "The Root of all Evil in Intergroup Relations? Unearthing the Categorization Process," in *Blackwell Handbook of Social Psychology: Intergroup Process*, ed. Rupert Brown and Samuel L. Gaertner (Oxford: Blackwell Publishers Ltd., 2001), pp. 3-22.

29   Michael A. Hogg, *The Social Psychology of Group Cohesiveness. From Attraction to Social Identity* (New York: Harvester Wheatsheaf, 1992).

we belong. To perceive out-group as homogeneous with negative attributes can generate positive group evaluations and esteem enhancement (through ethnocentrism, in-group bias, and favoritism).[30]

To connect out-group homogeneity effect with strategic culture, we can refer to the example of American Strategic Culture. For someone who is not American, let's say a casual observer, the Americans usually pay a scant regard to the consequences of their military actions; they are culturally ignorant and suffer from a failure to understand the sociocultural complexities of the enemy; they are technologically dependent, and impatient.[31] To add some more negative general attributes, American perceive themselves as exceptional, in the meaning, they have a strong faith in the uniqueness, immutability, and superiority of the country's founding liberal principles with special destiny among nations.[32] To follow the out-group homogeneity effect, in the eyes of an outsider, all Americans and all American military operations had been and will be perceived thought these specific strategic cultural lenses no matter the internal cultural diversity. But, can it be assumed that all Hispanic minorities living on the U.S. soil or serving in the American army are fitting above description, despite the fact that they are from the different sociocultural environment. Categorization assimilates as much as it is possible into one group of the cluster (Asians, Afro-Americans, Hispanic and other minorities are put into category basket

30   Susan T. Fiske, "Stereotyping, Prejudice, and Discrimination," in *The Handbook of Social Psychology*, Vol. II, ed. Daniel T. Gilbert, Susan T. Fiske, and Gardner Lindzey (Boston: The McGraw-Hill Companies, Inc., 4th Edition, 1998),pp. 357-415.; James L. Hilton, and William von Hippel, "Stereotypes," *Annual Review of Psychology*, Vol. 47 (1996),pp. 237-271.

31   Colin S. Gray, "The American Way of War. Critique and Implications," in *Rethinking the Principles of War*, ed. Anthony D. McIvor (Annapolis: U.S. Naval Institute Press, 2005): 13-41; Jeffrey Record, "The American Way of War: Cultural Barriers to Successful Counterinsurgency," *Policy Analysis* No. 577, Cato Institute (September 2006).

32   Caleb Spencer, "American Exceptionalism: Exemplifying Patriotism and Justifying Imperialism," *e-international-relations*, August 1, 2014, <http://www.e-ir.info/2014/08/01/american-exceptionalism-exemplifying-patriotism-and-justifying-imperialism/>.

of "American"). It enables us to quickly identify interconnected subjects. Therefore, strategic culture is often preserved as useful and valid. We hear "American war" we connect it with aforementioned attributes. It's simple and effective. But it is also harmful. When the information is incongruent with the category (for e.g. Americans are cultural sensitive), it will be ignored or intentionally omitted. But the most common way is to make exceptions. In regard to strategic culture, Gray made such exception in the case of maritime British strategic culture, when he admitted that the British had a counter-culture continental military role during World War I. One exception follows another to fit stereotyped conceptualization provided by the theory of strategic culture.

The concept of strategic culture was incapable of any contribution to the understanding of the society in Iraq and Afghanistan. Strategic culture is so abstract theory, so imprecise that it is impossible to make any use of it. In the words of Echevarria "after four generations of effort [in strategic culture theory], it could manage little more than one-sided assertions grounded in vague generalities, stereotypes, and caricatures (…) its problems and flaws make it too risky for policymakers and strategists."[33] National level strategic studies theories cannot reflect the complex reality of any conflict environment. It is so because wars are not fought between nations, but by men. Nations don't behave, people do. Franz Boas once noted that "the forces that bring about the changes are active in the individuals composing the social group (…) it seems hardly necessary to consider culture a mystic entity that exists outside the society of its individuals (…)."[34] What follows is a presentation of an alternative model of cultural understanding of others and the potential role of civilian strategists in contributing to the understanding of complex conflict environment.

---

33   Antulio J. Echevarria, "Strategic Culture: More Problems than Prospects", *Infinity Journal*, Vol. 3, Issue No. 2 (2013), pp. 4-7.

34   Leslie A. White, *The Concept of Cultural Systems* (New York: Columbia University Press, 1975), p. 33.

III. The Three Blocks and the Role of Civilian Strategists

The following section will discuss three blocks of micro-level analysis of cultural complexity in a conflict environment. The purpose is to mitigate the impact of social categorization and improve intercultural relation in complex conflict environments. The first block consists of self-knowledge. A bulk of research has already been done in regard to the knowledge of other societies (intelligence gathering), but little focus was given to the topic of self-knowledge in the field of strategic studies. Through improving self-cultural proficiency one can mitigate existing prejudice in his/her environment. It is especially true in the case of authoritarian military institutions that provide fertile ground for ethnocentrism. The civilian strategists would be responsible for improving self-knowledge that ultimately will lead to reshaping the military mindset. The second block involves an element of cultural awareness. One thing is to possess factual knowledge about self and others, but totally different thing is to apply it into complex social interactions environment. One of the existing challenges is a cultural shock. Due to a different climate, language, social norms and traditions, and even such simple thing as road signs, can impede one's cognitive capabilities and interrupt the communication with other people. It is possible to overcome it through the process of acculturation and by following the prerequisites of social contact theory. There are twofold roles for civilian strategists in the second block: mitigate the cultural shock, and facilitate the process of intercultural contact. In the third block, the most important element is cultural sensitivity. Any conflict environment results in grievances and disappointments on both sides of a conflict. However, cooperation is possible when there is sufficient amount of trust and empathy. Military personal is perceived as the aggressor and distrustful. Thus, civilian strategist could act as a mediator building good conditions for trust.

i. The First Block: Knowledge of Self

The concept of self has a long tradition throughout the history, across cultures and religions. It has been studied and interpreted by various disciplines, from philosophy, sociology to psychology.[35] It is a fundamental idea in social sciences. In its most common form "self" includes both the actor who thinks ("I am thinking") and the object of thinking ("about me"). It is a part that provides individuality, and a unique personality; it contains knowledge of one's attitudes, traits, feelings, and behavior. The self consists of all statements made by a person, overtly or covertly, that include the words "I," "me," and "myself." In other words, a private self, the true self, is a self that belongs to no one else. There is also a public self, that is, the individual self as presented to and perceived by others (for e.g. "people think I am introverted), whether or not it corresponds to the inner, private self. Sometimes we may not be fully aware how others identify us, which may differ from self-perception. Projection is a common tendency to attribute falsely to other people motives or traits that are our own, or that in some way explain or justify our own. It is one of the sources of prejudice. Both forms of self(s) are dynamic concepts under constant interactions, developing and modifying based on past experience, current situation and future expectations. Thus, people constantly evaluate themselves using multiple standards, predict how social interactions will go, and self-regulate by acting in ways that facilitate self-needs and wants.[36] However, there is one more self that is the focus of this section – the collective self.

The collective self corresponds to an assessment of the self by a specific reference group. Individuals are profoundly influenced by their social groups in terms of conformity and belief polarization. As part of a pervasive need

---

35   Roy F. Baumeister, "The Self," in *The Handbook of Social Psychology*, Vol. I, ed. Daniel T. Gilbert, Susan T. Fiske, and Gardner Lindzey (Boston: The McGraw-Hill Companies, Inc., 4th Edition, 1998), pp. 680-740; Susan E. Cross, and Jonathan S. Gore, "Cultural Models of the Self," in *Handbook of Self and Identity*, ed. Mark R. Leary, and June P. Tangney (New York: Guilford Press, 2003), pp. 536-564.

36   Sen, *Identity and Violence*, op.cit.; Gordon W. Allport, *The Nature of Prejudice 25th Anniversary Edition* (New York: Basic Books, 1979); Harry C. Triandis, "The Self and Social Behavior in Differing Cultural Contexts," *Psychological Review*, Vol. 96, No. 3 (1989), pp. 506-520; Daphna Oyserman et.all., "Self," pp. 69-104.

to maintain positive self-regard, people want to view the group which they belong in a positive light. The optimal distinctiveness theory proposes that the collective self may accord the optimal level of self-definition by satisfying two powerful social motives: a need for inclusion, which is satisfied by assimilation of the self into larger collectives; and an opposing need for differentiation, which is satisfied by distinguishing the self from others (out-groups). Tajfel referred to this basic psychological analysis of a motivation for positive social identity, a motivation producing a drive for in-group superiority, favoritism, and distinctiveness, as a sequence of social categorization – social identity - social (intergroup) comparison – positive in-group distinctiveness.[37] Before in-group distinctiveness is articulated, there is a need for a social identity development which is well explained by group prototype theory. A prototype refers to the average or most typical member of a category. The group prototype is the mental image of a group member who embodies characteristics that in particular make in-group members distinct from out-group members. To categorize on the basis of prototypes means to identify a bird as a bird because it looks more like a template for the typical bird than the template for a typical fish. The prototypes have important implications for forming impressions and making judgments about group members. When forming the impressions, the perceiver compares the target individual with a category prototype. If the target individual overlaps sufficiently (or fits) with the prototypical representation, the perceiver assimilate the target into the category. Thus, after forming strong in-group self-identification and following prototype association, the category becomes

---

37 Constantine Sedikides, Lowell Gaertner, Erin M. O'Mara, "Individual Self, Relations Self, Collective Self: Hierarchical Ordering of the Tripartite Self," *Psychological Studies*, Vol. 56, Issue 1 (January-March 2011), pp. 98-107; Marilynn B. Brewer, Rupert J. Brown, "Intergroup Relations," in *The Handbook of Social Psychology*, Vol. II, ed. Daniel T. Gilbert, Susan T. Fiske, Gardner Lindzey (Boston: The McGraw-Hill Companies, Inc., 4th Edition, 1998), pp. 554-595; John C. Turner, Rina S. Onorato, "Social Identity, Personality, and the Self-Concept: A Self-Categorization Perspective," in *The Psychology of the Social Self*, ed. Tom R. Tyler, Roderick M. Kramer, Oliver P. John (Mahwah: Lawrence Erlbaum Associates, Pubslihers, 1999, pp. 11-47.

salient. The perceiver comes to see himself and other category members less as individual and more as interchangeable exemplars of the group prototype. Henceforth, the group identity not only describes what it is to be a group member but also prescribes what kind of attitudes, emotions, and behaviors are appropriate in a given context. The group which a person belongs serves as a primary determinant of self-esteem (and distinctiveness from others). Therefore, the more attributes members the groups share and display of the group prototype, the group members will have positive feelings among group members and be more cohesive.[38] But how does this translates into military institutions and conflict environment?

The military is a specific type of organization that can be described as authoritarian, goal-oriented and ethnocentric. An individual who enters the army has to undergo a process of re-socialization which will de-emphasis individualism (depersonalization)[39] and eliminate traits that might reduce the military performance and group cohesion.[40] One of the most important element in this process is soldier's self-identification at the small group level. Shils and Janowitz defined a small group (or in their case primary

---

38   Vincent Yzerbyt, Muriel Dumont, Daniel Wigboldus, and Ernestine Gordijn, "I feel for us: The impact of categorization and identification on emotions and action tendencies," *British Journal of Social Psychology*, Vol. 42 (2003), pp. 533-549; Don Operario and Susan T. Fiske, "Stereotypes: Content, Structure, Processes, and Context," in *Blackwell Handbook of Social Psychology: Intergroup Process*, ed. Rupert Brown and Samuel L. Gaertner (Oxford: Blackwell Publishers Ltd., 2001), pp. 22-44; Matthew J. Hornsey, "Social Identity Theory and Self-categorization Theory: A Historical Review," *Social and Personality Psychology Compass*, Vol. 2, Issue 2 (2008), pp. 204-222.

39   Joseph L. Soeters, Donna J. Winslow, and Alise Weibull, "Military Culture," in *Handbook of the Sociology of the Military*, ed. Giuseppe Caforio (New York: Springer Science + Business Media, LLC, 2006), pp. 237-255.

40   On the importance of relation between military performance and group cohesion refer to: Darryl Henderson, *Cohesion: The Human Element in Combat* (Washington, DC: National Defense University Press, 1985); James Griffith, Mark Vaitkus, "Relating Cohesion to Stress, Strain, Disintegration, and Performance: An Organizing Framework," *Military Psychology*, Vol. 11, No. 1 (1999), pp. 27-55; Anthony King, "The Word of Command. Communication and Cohesion in the Military," *Armed Forces & Society*, Vol. 32, No. 4 (2006), pp. 493-512.

groups) as intimate face-to-face association and cooperation. It involves "the sort of sympathy and mutual identification for which 'we' is the natural expression. One lives in the feeling of the whole and finds the chief aims of his will in that feeling."[41] However, it is not the interpersonal bonding per se that supports cohesiveness of the small groups of military units. Through the depersonalization and re-socialization at the secondary group level (that is institutional level) the identities and personal traits of individuals are standardized by the establishment of the mental image of group prototype. It is the attraction of individuals to the group as that group is embodied by specific idealized and distinct characteristics of the in-group prototype.

The characteristics of military group prototype toward which an individual is socialized, include discipline that develops (over)conformity among soldiers. According to Kelman the disobedience of authority is not possible due to negative repercussions of punishment by the military court and potential for social stigma among other soldiers. On the other hand, total obedience and loyalty to the authority can have a positive outcome in advancing career or any other form of gratification.[42] Another characteristic refers to what Norman Dixon called a "bull." The aim of the "bull" is to mitigate various anxieties related with military life by preoccupying the mind of a soldier with orderliness or personal pride. In a way, a "bull" is a distractor and time-filler. John Faris described a basic military training as featuring such elements like disparagement of civilian life, unflattering haircuts, glaring uniforms, lack of privacy, emphasis on masculinity and aggressiveness, and physical and psychological stress.[43]

41　Edward A. Shils, Morris Janowitz, "Cohesion and Disintegration in the Wehrmacht in World War II" *The Public Opinion Quarterly*, Vol. 12, No. 2 (Summer 1948), pp. 280-315.

42　Herbert C. Kelman, "Violence without Moral Restraint: Reflections on the Dehumanization of Victims and Victimizers," *Journal of Social Issues*, Vol. 29, No. 4 (1973), pp. 25-61.

43　John H. Faris, "The Impact of Basic Combat Training. The Role of the Drill Sergeant in the All-Volunteer Army," *Armed Forces & Society*, Vol. 2, No. 1 (1975), pp. 115-127.

This form of socialization and depersonalization is leading to frustration among new recruits who were accustomed to civilian life. Frustration and severe emotional repressions are the raw materials for the expression of aggression and violence. In other words, socialization for aggression often leads to interpersonal and in-group violence.[44] Therefore, the "bull" prevents illegitimate outbursts of aggression toward superiors or authority; it's a way of response by the organizations and institutions to the threat of internal disintegration through aggressive impulses of its own members. The "bull" is increasing the feeling of dependency (an organization providing all the needs for daily life), which in turn increase the obedience and loyalty.[45] The negative outcome of this process is the direction of aggressive impulses toward outgroups and limiting the traits of personality that are necessary for successful intercultural interactions.

The military mindset established through to process of socialization along the lines of idealized military group prototype potentially negates and contradicts the essence of cultural awareness and sensitivity that are required in complex conflict environments. Thus, the possible role of civilian strategist would focus on modifying the traditional group prototype into softer version capable of cultural understanding. Robert A. Rubinstein noted a significant difference between two military units in their attachment to symbols that could be considered as symbolic representatives of two possible variances of military group prototypes. In 2001 Rubinstein conducted a practical exercise for two units that were to be deployed as peacekeepers in Kosovo. The training simulated a military checkpoint on a road that joined the Serbian and Albanian parts of Kosovo, during the Albania's National Day. An approaching car is festooned with Albanian flags, the driver, a leader

---

44   Carol R. Ember and Melvin Ember, "War, Socialization and Interpersonal Violence: A Cross-Cultural Study," *Journal of Conflict Resolution*, Vol. 38, No. 4 (1994), pp.620-646. Marc H. Ross, "

45   Norman Dixon, *On the Psychology of Military Incompetence* (London: PIMLICO, 1994), pp. 176-195.

in the Albanian Kosovar community, has been celebrating this event and persistently wants to continue that celebration on the Serb side. This might result in a violent incident, thus he should not be allowed to pass. The soldier from the first unit, after a short but clearly frustrating interaction, exclaimed: "I'm not going to talk to this guy, I'll just tell him what to do. I've got all the weapons!." On the following day, in the same situation, the soldier from the second unit went to great lengths to resolve the situation through negotiation. In order to examine the reasons behind the difference in behavior of both soldiers, Rubinstein visited the hallways of the headquarters of both units. In the first unit, space was decorated with memorabilia of various battles in which the unit had engaged and in which they had particularly distinguished themselves. In general, all were testimonies of the unit's effectiveness in war fighting. The hallways of the second unit were also filled in with a distinguished combat record. But the theme of this unit's display was a sacrifice in peace support operations. It celebrated service in support of peacekeeping missions in Somalia, Bosnia, Haiti, and elsewhere. Rather than celebrating its distinction in war fighting, the second unit chose to honor and display its achievements in humanitarian efforts.[46]

To change existing group prototype might not be an easy task due to the contradiction between the rigidity of authoritarian military institutions and the demands in cross-cultural competencies. Some traits of military group prototype can be changed, others should remain intact in order to sustain the effectiveness and purpose of military units. For instance, the strict obedience of authority should be shifted toward flexible critical thinking. Miller and Tucker in their Intercultural Competence – Situational Judgement Test concluded that a soldier might need to be willing to disobey a direct order from commander if this order will undermine long-term interpersonal relations between the soldier (or military unit) and the host (for

---

46   Robert A. Rubinstein, *Peacekeeping Under Fire. Culture and Intervention* (London: Paradigm Publishers, 2008), pp. 91-92.

an e.g. regional leader in a conflict environment).[47] In other cases, a group prototype that develops war-fighting skills should remain intact, however with the addition of negotiation skills and basic cultural understanding of others.[48] There is still a lot of work to do in developing models, program and academic curriculums that can only be done only by engaged civilian strategist. A future research should tackle the issues of balance between traditional and culture-oriented military training; identify traits that are necessary for military effectiveness, and traits that can be replaced; methods to increase critical and creative thinking among military personnel; as well as a search for a model that would allow to keep the personalized self without necessity of depersonalization and socialization along the strict line of military expectations. As it will be elaborated in the later part of this paper, individualized self is important in developing trust and empathy skills. What is more, from the perspective of military personnel, a civilian strategist is an outsider (an out-group) that does not represent either fit the military group prototype. In a way, such interaction develops interpersonal skills that might be later implemented in a real conflict environment.

ii. The Second Block: Awareness

Building a knowledge about self and another culture is a prerequisite for improvement in any complex conflict environments. In its most basic form, the academic knowledge is an explanation that makes sense out of the complexities of surrounding world through identification of most universal and generally accepted concepts. However, there is often no provision for concrete application, and usually, such knowledge is only providing a "shopping list" of facts that will presumably prevent the most catastrophic cultural indiscretions. Intercultural relations and culture, in general, are

---

47   John W. Miller and Jennifer S. Tucker, "Addressing and assessing critical thinking in intercultural contexts: Investigating the distance learning outcomes of military leaders," *International Journal of Intercultural Relations* 48 (2015), pp. 120-136.

48   Deborah Goodwin, *The Military and Negotiation: The Role of the Soldier-Diplomat* (London: Frank Cass, 2005).

practical endeavors. The discrepancies between academic and practical knowledge had been well depicted in Iraq through cultural smart cards (hereafter CSC) – wallet-sized notes that were aimed to provide a portable orientation to Islam, Iraqi ethnic and cultural groups, and basic examples of phrases or words that might be useful in a daily communication. For instance, CSC advised discretion in interactions with Arab women and warned that Western hand gesture for "stop" mean "hello" in Iraq. In general, CSC was oversimplifying and overgeneralizing sociocultural complexities for the sake of clear and coherent delivery of knowledge to the soldiers. Thus, the cards produced more misunderstanding, cultural oversensitivity, and contributed to the production of stereotypes and prejudice. In the section discussing "don't do this" there were recommendations to "don't use your left hand for contact with others, eating, or gestures. It is considered unclean," or "don't slouch, lean, or appear disinterested when conversing with Iraqi men. Do not expose the soles of feet or shoes." One of the U.S. Army National Guard captain in the battalion intelligence office in Baghdad noted, that "everybody was all freaked out about touching with the left hand and, you know, when you sit down, don't show the bottom of your foot. That's all true, but it's all in context. If it is a friend or someone you've known for a while, they are not going to give a s**t." [49] A cross-cultural or intercultural contact is the only way to verify gathered knowledge and adapt to a new environment.

One of the most common way that attempts to reduce tensions between groups is bringing them into contact with one another. The logic behind contact theory is simple: if separation and unfamiliarity produce stereotypes and prejudice, then these effects should be reversible by promoting contact and increased familiarity between members of different groups and social categories. The central premise of the contact theory is that contact provides

---

49   Federation of American Scientists, "Iraqi Cultural Smart Card," *Marine Corps Intelligence Activity*, 2006, accessed January 4, 2015, <http://www.fas.org/irp/doddir/ usmc/iraqsmart-0506.pdf>; Hugh Guesterson, "The Cultural Turn in the War on Terror," pp.279-296; Rochelle Davis, "Culture as a Weapon," *Middle East Research*, Vol. 40(Summer ,2010).

an opportunity for positive experiences with out-group members that disconfirm or undermine previous negative attitudes and ultimately change into positive perception and beliefs about the groups as a whole.[50] However, the phrase "contact hypothesis" or "intergroup contact theory" is something of a misnomer because it implies that mere contact is sufficient panacea. Actually, the opposite might be true. For instance, a short-term contact between two groups with negative views of each other might only confirm their opinions and existing stereotypes. A long-term, historical relations consisting of clashes and conflicts might lay deep inside the memory of each group, and mere interpersonal or intergroup contact will not obliterate the past experiences.[51] The most conspicuous examples that come to mind are Israeli – Arab world relations, or Chinese – Japanese historical animosities. A lot of contacts had been present between them, but it did little improve or changed their negative attitudes. Therefore, Allport proposed four conditions that could lead to improved intergroup attitudes:[52]

1. Members of each group must have equal status in the situation.

Many stereotypes of outgroups compromise beliefs about the inferior ability of outgroup members to perform various tasks. In the contact situation, such beliefs posit the out-group members in the subordinate role, further reinforcing mutual stereotypes.

---

50 Thomas F. Pettigrew, and Linda R. Tropp, *When Groups Meet: The Dynamic of Intergroup Contact* (New York: Psychology Press, 2011); Marilynn B. Brewer, and Samuel L. Gaertner, "Toward Reduction of Prejudice: Intergroup Contact and Social Categorization," in *Blackwell Handbook of Social Psychology: Intergroup Process*, ed. Rupert Brown and Samuel L. Gaertner (Oxford: Blackwell Publishers Ltd., 2001), pp. 451-472.

51 Daniel Bar-Tal, "Why Does Fear Override Hope in Societies Engulfed by Intractable Conflict, as It Does in the Israeli Society?" *Political Psychology*, Vol. 22, No. 3 (2001), pp. 601-627.

52 Allport, *The Nature*, pp. 261-282; Bernard E. Whitley Jr., and Mary E. Kite, *The Psychology of Prejudice and Discrimination* (Belmont: Wadsworth Cengage Learning, 2nd Edition, 2010), pp. 551-569; Brewer and Brown, "Intergroup Relations," pp. 576-583.

2. The groups must work cooperatively to achieve common goals.

Insofar as members of different groups depend on each other for the achievement of a jointly desired objective, they have instrumental reasons to develop friendlier relationships with each other. There is a sizable body of evidence that demonstrates the effectiveness of cooperative learning groups for increasing attraction and interaction between members of different social groups.[53]

3. The situation must allow participants to get know each other as individuals (acquaintance potential).

The contact has to be of sufficient frequency, duration and closeness to permit the development of meaningful relation between members of two different groups. The optimal condition can be contrasted with touristic contact which lasts for a short time and is of casual character. The optimal contact situation allows acquiring new, more accurate information about outgroup members that would disconfirm negative stereotypes.

4. The intergroup effort must have the support of authorities, law, or custom (institutional support).

Coherent and positive institutional support can help create a new social climate in which more tolerant norms can emerge. In other words, authorities, law or social norms must establish a clear expectation for attitude change in the direction of lower prejudice and behavior change in the direction of less discrimination.

The four presented prerequisites for successful cross-cultural contact are only a half of a story. An individual who is relocated from his/her own, well-known cultural environment into alien societies with a different

---

53   David W. Johnson, Roger T. Johnson, *Learning together and alone : cooperative, competitive, and individualistic learning* (Boston: Allyn and Bacon, 4ᵗʰ Edition, 1994); David W. Johnson, Roger T. Johnson, and Geoffrey Maruyama, "Goal Interdependence and Interpersonal Attraction in Heterogeneous Classrooms: A Metaanalysis," in *Groups in Contact: The Psychology of Desegregation* (Orlando: Academic Press, Inc., 1984), pp. 187-210.

worldviews, norms, beliefs, and languages, is exposed to transition shock, sometimes otherwise referred as a cultural shock. Each experience of change in the cultural environment is inevitably accompanied by stress in the individual's psyche that might impede the development aforementioned four conditions. It's a kind of "identity crisis" rooted in the desire to retain old customs in keeping with original identity; it is a moment when an individual is unable to satisfy a basic need to understand, control, or predict behavior – traits strongly associated with the military institution and mindsets. The failure in overcoming the "identity crisis" results in frustration reactions (an additional layer of frustration to frustration related with socialization process of a soldier) that impede affective, cognitive and behavioral components of individuals. This leads to negative symptoms, like irritation, intense in-group solidarity, grief, depression, apathy (affective symptoms); wish-fulling fantasies, blaming self, inner worldview disintegration, fatalism, resignation (cognitive symptoms); hostility, low productivity, psychosomatic illness, social isolation, do nothing attitude (behavioral symptoms). There are many military examples of cultural shock among soldiers during various military operations. For instance, participating as a part of Unified Task Force in Somalia Canadian units were unprepared to understand gender behavior of Somali men. They were shocked by men holding hands and squatting to urinate like women (even though this is more discreet when one is wearing a sarong). They were further disturbed by the cultural practice of female circumcision and by the way Somali men treated Somali women in general.[54] Normally an individual has a set of choices to deal with cultural shock, like flight (return back to home country), emotional withdrawn from the new environment and focus on self/work, or fight (try to change the host environment).[55] However, the soldier does not have a choice. Thus, the only

---

54 Donna Winslow, Stefan Kammhuber, and Josepth L. Soeters, "Diversity Management and Training in Non-American Forces," in *Handbook of Intercultural Training*, ed. Dan Landis, Janet M. Bennett, and Milton J. Bennett (Thousand Oaks: SAGE Publications, 3rd Edition, 2004), pp. 395-415.

55 Linda E. Anderson, "A New Look at an Old Construct: Cross-Cultural Adaptation,"

option from him/her is to adapt through the process of acculturation.

Adaptation is a recursive and cyclical problem-solving activity. It is a long-term process where ends fade out into new beginnings; it involves both ups and downs and repetitive sequences in dealing with new life's challenges. If the obstacles encountered along the way are perceived as small, they are likely to be surmounted swiftly, and perhaps even imperceptibly. If they are perceived as mountains, their neutralization might demand great effort, generating concomitant risks of impeding our affective, cognitive and behavioral capabilities. To put in other words, adaptation is a human tendency that accompanies the internal struggle of individuals to regain control over their life chances whenever and wherever they find themselves. Acculturation is precisely this type of a great challenge ahead of anyone who endeavors to assimilate, cooperate, coexist or live within alien societies. According to the theory, one of the most important element of a successful process of acculturation is host communication competence. It is an overall capacity to receive and process information and to design and enact plans to initiate a message or respond to others appropriately and effectively in accordance with the host communication system. On affective level of host communication competence, the required abilities are positive attitudes (acceptance of host culture), adaptation motivation (the willingness to learn and participate), and identity flexibility (a socio-psychological orientation with respect to ourselves, our original and the host cultures). Cognitive level involves moderating expectations toward realistic, rather than optimistic, goals; non-judgmental attitude; and perception of reality as it is, than as it should be or along our wishful thinking. Behavioral level involves adaptive personality traits (in some matter it overlaps with adaptive motivation), which consists of such attitudes like openness (tolerance of ambiguity), and

---

International Journal of Intercultural Relations, Vol. 18, No. 3 (1994), pp. 293-329; Janet M. Bennett, "Transition Shock: Putting Culture Shock in Perspective," in *Basic Concepts of Intercultural Communication*, ed. Milton J. Bennett (Yarmouth: Intercultural Press, Inc., 1998), pp. 215-223.

personal strength, defined as internal capacity to absorb "shocks" from the environment and to bounce back without being seriously damaged by them (this includes risk-taking which is related to trust building; elasticity; and persistence). In general, it is important to recognize and remember that in adaptation and in the process acculturation it is "us," the outsiders, not the local people, who are expected to make most of the necessary adaptive self-corrections.[56]

One may ask how all this translates into conflict environment and what is the role of civilian strategists? After shaping the "self" and group prototype of military personnel and units, it is necessary to continue the process of cultural understanding improvement throughout the conflict. Thus, the civilian strategists have twofold purpose:

1. Following the intergroup contact theory, civilian strategists would be responsible for supervising and correcting misbehavior of soldiers. Although equal status is hardly possible to achieve between the invaders and invaded, soldiers can avoid verbal mistreatment of the host society. It is too common and too prevalent to hear words of dehumanization among military units. European colonists called Native Americans savage and beasts; during the Holocaust, Nazis referred to Jews as parasites; in the 70s American soldiers dehumanized the Vietnamese people by calling them "gooks;" in the war in Bosnia and Herzegovina, Serbs called Bosnian Muslims pseudo-humans. The XXI century did not eradicate this phenomenon. The U.S. Armed Forces regularly

---

56   Young Yun Kim, "Long-Term Cross-Cultural Adaptation. Training Implications of an Integrative Theory," in *Handbook of Intercultural Training*, ed. Dan Landis, Janet M. Bennett, and Milton M. Bennett (Thousand Oaks: SAGE Publications, 3rd Edition, 2004),pp. 337-362; Colleen Ward, "Acculturation," in *Handbook of Intercultural Training*, ed. Dan Landis, and Rabi S. Bhagat (Thousand Oaks: SAGE Publications, 2nd Edition, 1996), pp. 124-147; Karmela Liebkind, "Acculturation," in *Blackwell Handbook of Social Psychology: Intergroup Process*, ed. Rupert Brown, and Samuel L. Gaertner (Oxford: Blackwell Publishers Ltd., 2001), pp. 386-406.

referred to Iraqi and Afghan civilians as "hajis" and "towel-heads."[57] Such approach not only set up the negative attitude of military personal but also interrupts intercultural communication. Civilian strategist could also act as a mediator in creating a social climate that respects the norms and law of local communities and actions undertaken by the military units. In general, a civilian strategist could act a facilitator of intercultural communication in all four prerequisites of successful contact theory.

2. Civilian strategist could also act as an ameliorator in a process of adaptation and acculturation. Stress and shock are elements that cannot be avoided in any intercultural contact. How individual copes and deals with those challenges depends on his/her predispositions, which relates to psychology rather than strategy. Thus, so far civilian strategists proposed solutions that deny cultural understanding makes intercultural communication much more difficult to achieve, and foster authoritarian, rigid, and ethnocentric strategies that impede psychological adjustment to cultural shock. According to Ken Booth "strategic practice is always based on a nationalistic view of the world (…) it is only to be expected that negative stereotypes, intense antipathies, and inflated loyalties will reach a pitch," and that "if strategists do not have enemies, they must invent them."[58] It's time to turn around this approach and promote strategies and strategists that include adaptation techniques and acculturation into strategy building process that can contribute to adaptive personality development among military personnel.

Adaptation and acculturation are connected with self-development. It is, therefore, important to remind the existing connectivity between this

---

57 Stephanie Decker and John Paul, "'The Real Terrorist was Me:' An Analysis of Narratives Told by Iraq Veterans Against the War in an Effort to Rehumanize Iraqi Civilians and Soldiers," *Societies Without Borders*, Vol. 8, No. 3 (2013), pp. 317-343; Caleb Spencer, "American Exceptionalism," op.cit.

58 Ken Booth, *Strategy and Ethnocentrism*, pp. 20-31.

and a previous section discussing knowledge about self. It was stated that traditional military mindset depersonalize individual and socialize him/her accordingly to specific group prototype. It was argued that cultural understanding requires the opposite, namely, weaker group mentality and stronger individualization. In this section, it is underlined that adaptation and acculturation expand the definition "self" to include alternative worldviews.[59] This process is only possible if the previous stage of self-knowledge is successful. Therefore civilian strategists who worked on modifying group prototype of a specific unit and in shaping its mindset could further cooperate with this military unit in a complex conflict environment to deal with the application of knowledge into practice and mitigate the negative responses associated with transition shock. In other words, a civilian strategist becomes integrated with the military unit as an intellectual support during military operations.

iii. The Third Block: Sensitivity

Augmenting the "self" and military group prototype, adapting to a new sociocultural environment and follow the prerequisites of successful contact theory, are demanding endeavors for both a soldier and civilian strategists. However, all those processes should not diminish the ultimate role and importance of victims in any conflict environment. It is an independent and free-will decision of political elites with the support of domestic, and preferably international, society, to engage own armed forces in a conflict, nation-building, peace-building or any other military operations. Therefore, the bulk of intercultural understanding is a responsibility of the ones who enter a foreign country. The victims rarely ever ask for such outside intervention. They have their own ways of doing things and solutions, their own norms, beliefs and values which are different, but not worst or

---

59   Janet M. Bennett, and Milton J. Bennett, "Developing Intercultural Sensitivity. An Integrative Approach to Global and Domestic Diversity," in *Handbook of Intercultural Training*, ed. Dan Landis, Janet M. Bennett, and Milton M. Bennett (Thousand Oaks: SAGE Publications, 3rd Edition, 2004), pp. 147-165.

less effective, from "ours." The outside invaders usually brings their own mindsets and worldviews, causing the same challenges among the host society, namely, cultural shock, intercultural contact issues and the need to modify own self to accommodate to the new environment. The difference is that the host society did not ask for those changes. Furthermore, the host society is experiencing threat and fear of unknown that produces distrust of anything that is considered as an alien element to existing and accepted (traditional) sociocultural systems. Hence, to mitigate the negative experiences and pressures on the society, the invader should become sensitive through empathy and trust building processes.

Research on the role of empathy in the field of international relations and, more specifically, strategic or conflict resolution studies, is very limited. It is disturbing fact because the studies on intergroup and intercultural relations point out that empathy can improve that relation, while the lack of it can lead to increased enmity.[60] In general terms, empathy can be defined as "the imaginative intellectual and emotional participation in another person's experience."[61] Thus, empathy is considered by many scholars and practitioners from other fields to be a critical part of the "skill set" of successful negotiators, mediators, and peacebuilders. For example, a conflict resolution workshop had been used by a group of fifteen Turkish Cypriots and fifteen Greek Cypriots to collaborate across sensitive, conflict-prone community lines in developing a strategy for civil society peacebuilding efforts on the island of Cyprus. The workshop explored the needs and fears of each side and ways to resolve the conflict. The participants discussed the forms that new relationships could be shared between them. Evaluation of the workshop indicated that the participants came away with an

---

60 Eran, Halperin, *Emotions in conflict: inhibitors and facilitators of peace making* (Oxon: Routledge, 2016); Evelin G. Lindner, *Emotion and Conflict: How Human Rights Can Dignify Emotion and Help us Wage Good Conflict* (Westport: Praeger, 2009).

61 Milton J. Bennett, "Overcoming the Golden Rule: Sympathy and Empathy," in *Basic Concepts of Intercultural Communication*, ed. Milton J. Bennett (Yarmouth: Intercultural Press, Inc., 1998), pp. 191-214.

increased understanding of one another and a feeling of mutual empathy.[62] Unfortunately, the opposite is true in the case of war, where antipathy-oriented approaches are too often present among military units. It is worth to recall in a full detail a story of the U.S. Air Force Sergeant who described a common procedure of night home raids of both Iraqi and Afghan people as a part of counterinsurgency "heart and minds" strategy:[63]

"The first house we raided, there were no men at home, just half a dozen women with children, and one older gentleman in there. It was a huge fiasco on this one [there was no one useful inside] so why were we there? We needed info. So instead of being a d**k about it, we could have brought them in and said, 'Sorry, we have to do this raid, we're looking for these people,' and if we were smart, we'd bring a woman with them, let the wife get dressed, calm them down and talk to them. When they're getting shot at, bombs are going off, people go into fight or flight. Instead, the interpreter beat the old guy to get information and got nothing. Another problem - the respect for the older guy is gone. So here is the interpreter, who doesn't have to abide by LOAC [Law of Armed Conflict] and is a third country national representing the US [and he's doing the dirty work]. So we go to another house. Here I watched a family get completely mortified. We woke up the family – a husband, son, and wife. The husband is educated but we didn't find this out until later. We are throwing people around, yelling at them. We didn't have any intel on this particular house, just that we were doing an area-wide clearance of homes. The father and son spoke English - therefore they were rolled up and taken to base for interrogation. And we then left a single female alone in the house [with a broken-in door] in the middle of the

---

62 Ronald J. Fisher, "Generic Principles for Resolving Intergroup Conflict," *Journal of Social Issues*, Vol. 50, Issue 1 (1994), pp. 46-66; Benjamin J. Broome, "Building relational empathy through an interactive design process," in *Handbook of Conflict Analysis and Resolution*, ed. Dennis J.D. Sandole et. all (London: Routledge, 2009), pp. 184-200.

63 Rochelle Davis, "Culture, a Weapon System on the Wane," *Middle East Research and Information Project* 264, Vol. 42 (2012), <http://www.merip.org/mer/mer264>.

night after a raid."

It is needless to say that the home raids were a pure example of traditional military mindsets fostered with prejudice, ethnocentrism, and dehumanization – in other words, all the traits that deny any kind of intercultural competence mentioned in this paper. Furthermore, this type of operations, no matter which country, society or culture, activates a common emotion in all human beings – a fear. The arousal of fear is at the roots of many intercultural conflicts and has a negative impact on both relations within and between groups.[64] Within the cultural group perceived threat to identity leads to actions designed to increase in-group cohesiveness and conformity to tradition and norms. Contact, adaptation, or exchange with the out-group members is strongly discouraged. The impact of fear on intergroup relations is even more dramatic. It increases the perception of out-group as more homogeneous and evil, increases tendency to mistrust and misinterpret cues and information received from the out-group as a sign of further threat and danger.[65] While, the lack of empathy is associated with increased aggression among men and antisocial behavior, which corresponds with military mindset. Thus, empathy is an important element in intercultural relations. It does not have to be empathy as in close family-like relationships, it's not possible in a conflict environment. It is empathy that allows perceiving the out-group and its members as human beings with feelings similar to our own. Another problem related to the military institution and empathy teaching methods is what Kelman called "authorization" – a factor that weakens moral restraints against violence and mascaras during

---

64   Elanor Kamans, Sabine Otten, and Ernestine H. Gordijn, "Power and threat in intergroup conflict: How emotional and behavioral responses depend on amount and content of threat," *Groups Processes & Intergroup Relations*, Vol. 14, No. 3 (2010), pp. 293-310; Walter G. Stephan, Oscar Ybarra, and Kimberly R. Morrison, "Intergroup Threat Theory," in *Handbook of Prejudice, Stereotyping, and Discrimination*, ed. Todd D. Nelson (New York, Psychology Press, 1st ed., 2009), pp. 43-55.

65   Stephen Worchel, "Culture's role in conflict and conflict management: Some suggestions, many questions," *International Journal of Intercultural Relations* 29 (2005), pp. 739-757.

the wars. Authorization means explicit orders or implicit encouragement by the authorities for a specific behavior. With permission and diffusion of responsibilities, an individual does not see himself as personally accountable for the consequences of his actions. In a similar manner, techniques designed to active empathy run the risk of creating compassion without simultaneously leading individuals to recognize that they themselves are implicated in the social forces responsible for the suffering with which they are empathizing. Nevertheless, if properly thought empathy can facilitate intergroup relations and help to achieve political and military objectives.[66]

Another related element in the block "sensitivity" is trust. Trust is central, and often unnoticeable, part of human relations of all kinds. We trust our close relatives, that's obvious, but we also trust people from various professions in our daily life. We trust doctors that they have skills and knowledge to cure us; we trust bus drivers that they will follow the schedule and drive safely; we trust any other people because we might have something important in common; we trust more our in-group than out-group members. Russell Hardin said that "with a complete absence of trust, one must be catatonic, one could not even get up in the morning."[67] Trust has been variously defined pending on the discipline. In the wider context trust can be defined as follows: "trust is a relationship between people. It involves having one person thinking that the other person or idea is benevolent, competent/good, or honest/true (...) it makes social life predictable, it creates sense of community, and it makes it easier for people to work together."[68] In social context trust makes complex simple. The opposite is true in a conflict

---

66   Kelman, "Violence without Moral Restraint," pp. 25-61; Walter G. Stephan, and Krystina Finlay, "The Role of Empathy in Improving Intergroup Relations," *Journal of Social Issues*, Vol. 55, No.4 (1999), pp. 729-743.

67   Russell Hardin, "The Street-Level Epistemology of Trust," *Politics & Society*, Vol. 21, No. 4 (1993), pp. 505-529.

68   Gert Jan Hofstede, "The Moral Circle in Intercultural Competence," in *The SAGE Handbook of Intercultural Competence*, ed. Darla K. Deardorff (Thousand Oaks: SAGE Publications, Inc., 2009), pp. 85-99.

environment, where trust is a rare commodity and makes simple complex. In a conflict, both sides are afraid to extend trust to each other because they consider it likely that they will be betrayed, at great cost to their own group. In other words, trust involves risk-taking, which implies some uncertainty about the occurrence of a state of ambiguity in near-term future, as well as the partial impossibility of preventing such an occurrence. Due to low-level acceptance of ambiguity, the military is therefore not comfortable with trust-related efforts. Soldiers are taught to prevent unexpected by gathering intelligence or sending drones for reconnaissance. Furthermore, anxiety and hostility, both products of war environment, deny the establishment of stable trusting relations. However, Pelzmann points out that trust does not presuppose a good will, sympathy, or friendship between people or groups; it can also develop among competitors, adversaries, and even mortal enemies if the proper conditions are put into place.[69]

Personal trust, otherwise known as intrinsic trust, is desirable because it produces strong, long-lasting bonds between people. Such trust can be seen at the primary level of military units as a bonding between soldiers. Although in a conflict such trust is not possible, still trust itself can appear. In December 1914 roughly 100 000 British and German troops were involved in an unofficial cessation of hostilities along the Western Front. Most truces began with carol singing on a Christmas Eve. Graham Williams of the Fifth London Rifle Brigade described the event as follows: "First the Germans would sing one of their carols and then we would sing one of ours, until when we started up 'O Come, All Ye Faithful' the Germans immediately joined in singing the same hymn to the Latin words Adeste Fideles. And I thought, well, this is really a most extraordinary thing - two nations both

---

69   Herbert C. Kelman, "Building trust among enemies: The central challenge for international conflict resolution," *International Journal of Intercultural Relations* 29 (2005), pp. 639-650; Piotr Sztompka, *Trust. A Sociological Theory* (Cambridge: Cambridge University Press, 1999).

singing the same carol in the middle of a war."[70] Amid the bloodshed of war, ordinary soldiers found a glimpse of humanity in the eyes of the opponent whom they should kill. Many of them adopted live-and-let-live arrangements with their adversaries. During the lulls in the fighting, bored men at times engaged in shouting and singing matches, in other cases venturing out to socialize or trade for alcohol or tobacco.[71] This required not only empathy on both sides of trenches, a form of perspective taking that everyone misses home, and everyone would like to feel safe and secure during Christmas, but also the enormous level of trust, that once out of trenches the others side will not start shooting. It is a form of "working trust" that any human being can activate under specific conditions. It allows humanizing the opponent and creating a temporary line of collaborative relationship. Among conditions creating "working trust" are:

1. Knowledge of "self": the perception and evaluation of risk is a highly subjective matter. It differentiates people and promotes a different type of risk-seeking or risk-avoiding, trusting or distrusting individuality. Shaping soldiers along the same group prototype denies individuality and installs a common fear of trust; or rather attitude of distrust. Knowing "self" and developing individual-based intercultural competencies might allow creating environment of "working trust" between soldiers and the host society. Knowledge of "others" can also benefit, because the meaning of trust is different in different cultures.

2. Being capable of applying knowledge into practice (acculturation), development of intercultural competencies, and adaptive personality approach toward new environment.

3. Common goals orientation.[72] The contrary approach is seen in a conflict

---

70   Peter Hart, *Fire and Movement: The British Expeditionary Force and the Campaign of 1914* (Oxford: Oxford University Press, 2014), p. 409.

71   Lawrence Sondhaus, *World War One: The Global Revolution* (Cambridge: Cambridge University Press, 2011), chapter 3.

72   David J. Lewis, and Andrew Weigert, "Trust as a Social Reality," *Social Forces*, Vol. 63, No. 4 (1985), pp. 967-985.

environment, where soldiers serve to fulfill objectives of their home country, rather than objectives of a host society. Iraq and Afghanistan are good examples of implementation of projects that were totally missing the needs of Iraqi and Afghan people, but precisely the same projects supported political argumentations of American and allied forces about progress done in both counterinsurgencies.[73]

A "working trusts" requires two to play, hence, the role of civilian strategists would be to educate and translate to the host society the plans and objectives, as well as explain the general cultural characteristic of the invaders. In other words, civilian strategist would act as independent mediator creating conditions for trust-building between both parties. Optimally, if host society has been properly engaged by the soldiers and "working trust" has been established, members of host population will be able to further assist as cultural instructors and would be able to serve as primary liaisons between the mission objectives of the invader and the host population. It is important to remember that this process is, least to say, a generational change approach. It means that all three building blocks mentioned in the paper have to continue for years and even decades. The changes of mindsets are difficult, in particular when challenged by traditional cultures like in Iraq and Afghanistan. Change for positive is possible, but first of all, it is a change of "self," rather the change of "others."

---

73 There are many ineffective development projects in Iraq and Afghanistan, some examples include: Patrick Cockburn, "Billions Down the Drain in Useless US Afghan Aid," *Counter Punch*, December 13, 2010, <http://www.counterpunch.org/2010/12/13/billions-down-the-drain-in-useless-us-afghan-aid/>; Joel Brinkley, "Money Pit: The Monstrous Failure of US Aid to Afghanistan," *World Affairs Journal*, January/February 2013, <http://www.worldaffairsjournal.org/article/money-pit-monstrous-failure-us-aid-afghanistan>; David Francis, "How the U.S. Lost Billions Over 9 Years in Iraq," *The Fiscal Times*, June 19, 2014, <http://www.thefiscaltimes.com/Articles/2014/06/19/How-US-Lost-Billions-Over-9-Years-Iraq>.

IV. Conclusions: Toward Interdisciplinary Strategic Studies

The theory of strategy culture aimed to combine culture and warfare to produce an approach that would allow to better understanding of the phenomena of war. However, due to the sub-disciplinarity of strategic studies the main approach of strategic culture derived from the field of international relations discipline. Thus, the ideas behind the theory were articulated along the paradigm of the "society at large." The problem of this kind of paradigm is that the groups who have power, namely, whose culture and identity determines the character of major social institutions, tend to be perceived as unitary or in universal terms. It means that the sociocultural traits, ideologies or policies of the dominant group are believed to be applicable to all people, or as being in the interest of all people within their society, and even to those outside of their society. In other words, any concept developed through this paradigm will treat the dominant group equal to the social construct of the nation-state. Hence, there is a strategic culture of United Kingdom because the majority group is English,[74] despite the existence of national identities of Scottish, Welsh or Irish, and despite multicultural society itself consisting of at least 20 minority groups. But, nations do not consist of the single social entity. Around the World, there are a plentitude of "nations" with the whole universe of identities. One researcher has identified 575 ethnic groups as being actual or potential nation-states, another estimated that there are as many as 3000-5000 "nations" in the world.[75] A diversity at large. Hence, any

---

74   Alister Miskimmon, "Continuity in the Face of Upheaval—British Strategic Culture and the Impact of the Blair Government," *European Security*, Vol. 13, Issues 3 (2004), pp. 273-299; Alan Macmillan, "Strategic culture and national ways in warfare: The British case," *The RUSI Journal*, Vol. 140, Issue 5 (1995), pp. 33-38; Lawrence Sondhaus, *Strategic Culture*, pp.14-20.

75   Depending on the country, some ethnic groups accept the governance by the dominant group because status quo fits their interests. Other ethnic groups are suppressed and denied independence. Gunnar P. Nielsson, "States and nation-groups: a global taxonomy," in *New Nationalisms of the Developed West: Towards Explanation*, ed. Edward A. Tiryakian, and Ronald Rogowski (Boston: Allen & Unwin, 1985), pp. 25-56; Wsevolod W. Isajiw, "Approaches to ethnic conflict resolution: paradigms and

complex conflict environment is complex precisely because it deals with the diverse universe of human beings. Single reality theories cannot contribute anything to the understanding of multi-reality of war.

The complex world of humanity can be understood only through constant interactions, relationships, and flow of information in the universe of disciplines. It is a multidimensional universe. Strategy and war cannot be adequately theorized within the limits of disciplinarity, otherwise, interactions are simplified, relationships generalized, and flow of information interrupted. The presented model of knowledge, awareness, and sensitivity attempt to grasp the metauniverse of complex conflict reality. It takes insights from psychology, social psychology, anthropology, intercultural studies, and politology, just to name few of them, to better understand and explain the subject at hand. This is precisely the reason why strategic studies should become interdisciplinary, and through interdisciplinary, a useful tool in the conduct of complex conflict environments. Interdisciplinarians need not become experts in the disciplines they utilize. They merely need sufficient command of its relevant portions to illuminate the specific features of a particular complex system. But interdisciplinary must be understood as a practice or applied social science.[76] The presented three-stage model engages civilian strategists at each level, starting from academic by reshaping traditional mindset of soldiers, to field research by mitigating cultural shocks and facilitating intercultural interactions. Such participation will not only be beneficial for the current rigid methodology of strategic studies but would also show that strategic studies are helpful, applicable and useful tool in dealing with various challenges in a conflict environment. Although it is possible to continue the research and remain within existing

---

principles," *International Journal of Intercultural Relations*, Vol. 24 (2000), pp. 105-124.

76 J. Marshall Beier and Samantha L. Arnold, "Becoming Undisciplined: Toward Supradisciplinary Study of Security," *International Studies Review*, Vol. 7, No. 1 (Mar. 2005), pp. 41-61; Allen F. Repko, *Interdisciplinary Research. Process and Theory* (Los Angeles: SAGE Publications. Inc., 2012).

frameworks of single-reality, and the tyranny of sub-disciplinarity, it is much more insightful, more interesting and more comprehensive if one immerses himself into diverse interdisciplinary reality.

The Importance of the Pacific Alliance for the People's Republic of China: Beyond the Economic Perspective

Idania M. Torrero Perigault[*]

I. Introduction

The Pacific Alliance is a regional integration mechanism that forms the eighth largest economy in the world, with a market of 216 million people with an average GDP per capita of $ 9,910 (in terms of purchasing power parity). Although the main objective of the PA is the deep integration to further drive the growth, development and the competitiveness of the participants for the free movement of goods, services, capital and people, this mechanism of integration is required to make adjustments that include the institutionalization of some figures in harmony with the globalized era we live in.

The People's Republic of China has become the main partner of Latin America in Asia and its growth has transformed the economic model based on export, industry and domestic investment, towards an economic model that requires placing part of its capital abroad, and promotes domestic consumption and services. This change promotes complementarity with Latin America because it offers the benefit of commercial opportunities for food-exporting economies and products with a degree of transformation. However rather than establishing an economic relationship China seeks to consolidate its relations integrally with the aim of satisfying the interests linked to its domestic policy of "One China;" and that is the key element

---

[*]   Ph.D. Student, Graduate Institute of International Affairs and Strategic Studies, Tamkang University, Taiwan.

of the policy of the Chinese government, and the PA acquires importance due to the appendices that its development implies. For this, first we review China's construction ties in Latin America until the time of China's foreign policy in Latin America which was presented in 2008 by former President Hu Jintao. The next part introduces relevant aspects of the PA which avoids being called as a trading bloc and instead defines itself as a mechanism for deeper integration. The profile and fast positioning are reviewed to clarify their role. Then, a review of the importance of the PA for China and also a list of reasons that make it attractive for China to establish relations with this Alliance will be reviewed; and also, the strategic role that the PA has on plans of China to build the Silk Road. Finally, strengthening the relationship between the two actors is analyzed under the concepts of complex interdependence and complementarity highlighting the strengths and weaknesses of the relationship.

Finally, it is shown that on the one hand the PA is seen by China as a mechanism to consolidate its presence in the region with the main aim to achieve sympathy for its goal of "one China" and on the other the perception the countries of the region, except for members of the PA, which see China in a "balance" role against the U.S., though this is widely denied by China and China distances itself from this.

II. China in Latin America: Building Strategic Ties

China is the second largest trading partner in Latin America as a main source of imports and its third major export destination;[1] unlike other countries, China increased its direct investment in Latin America and gained significant momentum in 2010, when Chinese transnationals invested over

---

[1] "China becomes one of the major trading partners in Latin America and the Caribbean, ECLAC reports," *United Nations News Centre.*, May 25, 2015,<http://www.un.org/spanish/News/story.asp?NewsID=32431#.VtAhi_krLIW>.

US$ 15 billion in the region, the vast majority in natural resource extraction.[2] For 2011, the increase in investment exceeded 245 billion.[3] Although world economic growth slowed from 2.6% in 2014 to 2.4% in 2015, a drop of 0.2 percentage points affecting a slowdown in the growth in China in 2015, this strategic tie grew by less than 7% for the first time since 1990 (6.8% in 2015).[4]

Despite a scenario that predicts a rate of slower growth, not only for China but for the rest of Latin America that there would be stagnation of trade between Latin America and China, the latter still bets on and maintains a firm approach for bilateral trade. Thus, China's president, Xi Jinping, said in January 2015 at the first ministerial meeting of the China-CELAC Forum, China will invest about U.S.$250 billion in Latin America over the next 10 years as part of a strategy of the Asian giant to increase its presence in the region.[5] Previously, China intensified its direct investment in Latin America in 2010 thru 2013 in energy and resource projects by 90%. In 2014, China's investment in Latin America continued to grow and also has an increasing number of M&A deals. China Minmetals Cooperation acquired Las Bambas of Peru for U.S.$7b, and CNPC acquired Petrobras Peru for U.S.$2.6b37.[6] In search for new markets based on Chinese consumer need, it is also a value-

---

2   United Nations, "Foreign Direct Investment in Latin America and the Caribbean 2010," *Unit Investment and Corporate Strategies, ECLAC*, July 7, 2011, p. 18, <http://hdl.handle. net/11362/1142> .

3   Manuel Alcántara and Cristina Rivas, "Are Latin American politicians aware to the importance of China in their countries?," *Latin American Parliamentary Elites*, Salamanca University, No. 49 (April, 2013), p. 1.

4   NU. CEPAL, Economic and Social Panorama of the Community of Latin American and Caribbean States 2015 (Santiago : UN, 2016), p. 11, <http://repositorio.cepal.org/ bitstream/handle/11362/39826/S1501405_en.pdf?sequence=1>.

5   Marcos Salas, "Why is China so interested in doing business in Latin America?," *BBC World*, January 8, 2015, <http://www.bbc.com/mundo/noticias/2014/07/140714_ economia_china_america_latina_msd>.

6   ECLAC, Latin American and the Caribbean and China Towards a New Era in Economic Cooperation, (Santiago: United Nations, May 2015), p. 79, <http://repositorio.cepal.org/ bitstream/handle/11362/38197/S1500388_en.pdf?sequence=1>.

added double benefit derived from the high investment which "was crucial for Latin America to cushion the impact of the 2009 recession"[7] Another motive for this investment partner in Latin America was also because those related infrastructure investments allowed, under the terms of agreement, employment for Chinese labor.

i. China's Foreign Policy in Latin America

A brief look at history allows us to see changes in relations between China and Latin America in the twentieth century. Initially, the policy toward Latin America was characterized by strong support from the Chinese government for the national democratic movements and the anti-imperialist struggles of Latin American people.[8] However, due to the recognition of Taiwan as an independent state, immediately after the founding of the China in 1949, China implemented a policy toward Latin America that was to "deploy a non-governmental diplomacy and strive to establish bonds of friendship, develop cultural and economic exchanges, and gradually move towards the establishment of diplomatic relations".[9] The consolidation of this policy not only led to changes in the nature of Chinese interests and the current international environment but also the primary economic interest which has been evident since 1960 when Beijing made public its desire for Latin America's "rich industrial raw materials and mineral products particularly nitrate and copper from Chile".[10]

China's interest in Latin America has matured and expanded greatly over time; initially it depended on an ideological approach, commercial and

---

7   "China is the second largest investor in AL 2015," *La Republica.pe*, April 1, 2013, <http://larepublica.pe/01-04-2013/china-sera-el-segundo-inversor-en-al-el-2015>.

8   Shicheng Xu, "The evolution of Chinese policy toward Latin America," *China Today*, January 28, 2013, <http://www.chinatoday.mx/eco/analys/content/2013-01/28/content_514998.htm>.

9   Ibid.

10 Niccolo Locatelli, *China in Latin America: Political and Economic Implications of Beijing's Involvement in the Region*, (the United States: Dissertation.com, 2010), p. 16.

political factors but always focusing on economics, since China's interest in Latin America is mainly economic.[11] This mature interest arising from the process of development of China, which needs more and more raw materials and food items to meet the growing domestic demand for food, goods production and processing. It also needs to consider the China policy responding to a Chinese interest in Latin America in a quest for legitimacy internationally as part its historic quest for global respectability and authority.[12] It has developed from the perspective of a political nature and in a much more active frame toward the region, it is rooted in the development of a systematic long-term strategy to engage with Latin American countries.[13] This process of readjustment of Chinese policy toward Latin America has undergone modifications such as a policy of reform and opening up began after the decade of the 70s, and this was a prelude to new adjustments that led to a comprehensive, healthy and sustainable development and the establishment and development of friendly relations and cooperation with Latin American countries, regardless of ideological differences.[14]

It is from 2001 under the government led by Jiang Zemin that China's interest intensifies in the Latin American territory, and that is the turning point for what would be the future of trade relations in the region. And it is a well-designed strategy because after the 13-day tour by the Chinese president, he continued a kind of "tracking" by senior Chinese officials who traveled the region, which resulted in a reciprocal relationship because

---

11   Jiang Shixue, "China and the EU: Finding "El Dorado" Together,"*Atlantic-Community. Org*, December 20, 2011, <http://www.atlantic-community.org/index.php/Open_Think_Tank_Article/China_and_the_EU%3A_Finding_%22El_Dorado%22_Together>.

12   Pitman B. Potter, *Assessing Treaty Performance in China: Trade and Human Rights*, (Canada: UBC Press, March 24, 2014), p. 129.

13   Jorge I. Domínguez et al., eds., China's Relations With Latin America: Shared Gains, Asymmetric Hopes, (*Inter-American Dialogue*, June 2006), p. 21, <http://archives.thedialogue.org/PublicationFiles/china.pdf>.

14   Shicheng Xu, "The evolution of Chinese policy toward Latin America," *China Today*, January 28, 2013, <http://www.chinatoday.mx/eco/analys/content/2013-01/28/content_514998.htm>.

"Latin American leaders also have been frequent visitors in Beijing."[15] This alignment also generated various explanations that enunciate China's primary interest in the region which appears to be to gain greater access to needed resources through increased trade and investment. Beijing's goal is to isolate Taiwan by luring the 12 Latin American and Caribbean nations still maintaining diplomatic relations with Taiwan to shift their diplomatic recognition to China[16] according to the "One China Policy", under which neither Taiwan nor Tibet nor any other "rebel province" may be recognized as an independent state.

According to the adjustments of China's policy toward Latin America, it can be clearly understood in three axes of common interest expressed by former Chinese President Hu Jintao to the Brazilian Parliament which were aimed at: the political level, on the support of being trustworthy friends and constancy by deepening the strategic consensus and strengthening mutual political trust; the economic level, promoting mutual complementarity with the respective advantages to be partners of mutually beneficial cooperation based on a new starting point, taking a pragmatic and innovative approach to exploit the potential of cooperation; and the cultural level, strengthening exchanges to be exemplary in the dynamic dialogue between different civilizations, greater attention to cultural exchanges to enhance mutual understanding.[17]

Despite these objectives China maintains a foreign policy that serves criteria of a very clear and specific classification according to the type of relationship between each country. Once China applies the criteria then it

---

15   Congressional Research Service Library of Congress, U.S. China's Foreign Policy and "Soft Power" in South America, *Asia and Africa*, April, 2008, p. 16, < https://fas.org/irp/congress/2008_rpt/crs-china.pdf>.

16   Ibid.

17   Hu Jintao, Ministry of Foreign Affairs of the People's Republic of China, *What we believe together a new perspective of friendship between China and Latin America and the Caribbean*, November 13, 2004, <http://www.fmprc.gov.cn/esp/wjdt/zyjh/t170379.shtml>.

tags its counterpart either as a strategic partner, which is the most important category, cooperative partner, or friendly cooperative relations[18] under the availability and willingness of China to go in depth with the counterpart identified in this classification system.

ii. First policy paper on Latin America and the Caribbean

In November 2008 and with the goal of expressing more clearly China's objectives the Chinese policy paper toward Latin America and the Caribbean[19] was promulgated. In it the policy objectives that reinforce an open strategy based on mutual benefit and win-win are established, and also a provision to continue the development of friendship and cooperation with all countries is announced on the basis of the Five Principles of Peaceful Coexistence.

The paper is also clear in stating that the political base that establishes and develops its relations in Latin America are based upon a "One China principle" according to this, the Chinese government "appreciates the adherence by the absolute majority of countries in the region the policy of One China and its abstention to develop relations and contacts with Taiwan officials, supporting the great cause of reunification of China."[20] The paper develops points in the political field, seeking to strengthen friendship ties and cooperation at all levels; in the economic area, China stands ready to maintain trade ties under the principle of equality, mutual benefit and win-win. In the cultural and social area, the Chinese government will provide assistance and cooperation in education, sports, medical technology and healthcare; it will help in the fight against poverty and exchange experiences in disaster relief. In the field of peace, security and justice, China promotes collaboration for the maintenance of peace, mutual legal assistance in

---

18   Jorge I. Domínguez et al., China's Relations With Latin America: Shared Gains, Asymmetric Hopes, p. 23.

19   "Policy Paper on China to Latin America and the Caribbean," *People online*, November 5, 2008, <http://spanish.peopledaily.com.cn/31621/6527840.html>.

20   Ibid.

criminal and civil matters and extradition, as well as a military exchange and cooperation, where defense cooperation prevails, and responsiveness in the field of non-traditional security and combating terrorism.[21]

Although in general, this is China's foreign policy in Latin America, the strategy has a different operation according to each region. In South America mineral resources and some alimentary ones take precedence. In Mexico, Central America, and the Caribbean the interest is focused on manufacturing goods and raw materials particularly in Central America. Therefore, the study of the PA as a mechanism of deep integration formed with three South American countries and Mexico, that currently seeking to enroll countries of Central America. The success of China's foreign policy has aroused interest attracting various countries to become a trading partner, and the experience has become a positive opportunity for the region as demonstrated by the support it represented for Latin America to escape the worst of the global economic crisis and; in parallel, China consolidated its commercial presence in the region.

III. Pacific Alliance: A Deep Integration Mechanism

The PA is an initiative of deeper regional integration,[22] newly formed, which seems to threaten the hegemony maintained so far by the Mercosur and is shaping up to be the second largest economy in the Americas. It was established by the Declaration of Lima on April 28, 2011, signed by the Presidents of Peru, Chile, Colombia and Mexico. Its official start was verified with the signing on June 6, 2012, of the Framework Agreement, in Antofagasta, Chile.[23] Ranked as the eighth largest economy in the world,

---

21   Ibid., p. 3.

22   Arévalo Luna, Guillermo Alexander, "Geopolitical and Economic Integration: the Pacific Alliance," *Revista VIA IURIS*, No.16 (2014), p. 171.

23   Information System Foreign Trade, Organization of American States, <http://www.sice. oas.org/TPD/Pacific_Alliance/Pacific_Alliance_s.asp>.

the four member countries of the PA totaling a population of 214.1 million, and a GDP per capita of U.S. $ 16.500 (measured in "purchasing power parity" or "PPP"), accumulated a GDP of U.S. $2.164 billion (over 38% of GDP in Latin America and the Caribbean) and a GDP growth rate of 3.8% on average for 2015, higher than the global average.[24] The PA currently has thirty-two observer countries: Uruguay, Canada, Spain, Australia, New Zealand, Japan, Guatemala, Paraguay, Portugal, Honduras, El Salvador, Ecuador, France, Dominican Republic, South Korea, United States, Turkey, China, Singapore, Finland, UK, Germany, Netherlands, Italy, India, Switzerland, Israel, Morocco, Trinidad and Tobago and Belgium, along with Costa Rica and Panama that are a step in negotiations to become country members.

i. Objectives and Structure

The main purpose of the PA is to strengthen cooperation among members of the organization and its integration with the rest of the world in order to help maintain and strengthen mutual cooperation to achieve economic growth. From there, there are three objectives: the first is to build in a participatory and consensual way an area of deep integration towards the free movement of goods, services, resources and people; the second objective is to drive further growth, development and competitiveness of members' economies; and the third objective is to become a platform of political articulation, economic and commercial integration and projection to the world, with emphasis on the Asia-Pacific region.[25]

The structure of the PA is comprised of the presidents of the four countries who constitute the highest decision-making body. The highest organ performs its powers during the Presidential Summits. The Pro-tempore Presidency is exercised in annual periods successively by the members. The

---

24 "Ey, México y Centroamérica. Pacific Alliance, Pacific Alliance Business and Investment Guide 2015/2016 (Maxico: EY, February 2015), p. 10.

25 "Who We Are," *The Pacific Alliance*, <https://alianzapacifico.net/en/what-is-the-pacific-alliance/#what-is-the-pacific-alliance>.

structure consists of the Council of Ministers, the High-Level Group and Technical Groups and subgroups that aim to promote guidelines related to the topics of main interest to the PA.[26]

ii. Profile Pacific Alliance

Although the PA is framed in a predominantly economic-commercial profile,[27] --yet as it deepens its international relevance that will demand immersion in politics--, its antagonistic neoliberal nature[28] separates it from the Mercosur conception bloc which responded to ideological and political similarity lived at the time of its creation, but that has been losing strength over the last decade. There seems to be a glimpse of discrepancy in the Alliance's Presidential Statement which sets down that through economic, commercial and political articulation[29] a new expectation would be created in order to project a leadership perspective competitive among member countries of the bloc. This has been a disputed point that must be adjusted in order to achieve the leadership objectives through inclusion to refine its worldwide projection for the benefit of growth, development and competitiveness of these economies. And it is that while Mercosur looked to the Atlantic, the PA focuses on the effectiveness of the Asia-Pacific region becoming from a geopolitical and geostrategic perspective a turning point when looking for greater participation, progress and modernization in the global economy as well as diversification of political relations with Asia, which is considered one of its objectives in the future, because as stated above, the PA is a trade and economic association which currently has not

---

26 Ibid.

27 "Ey, Méxicoy Centroamérica. Pacific Alliance, Pacific Alliance Business and Investment Guide 2015/2016 (Maxico: EY, February 2015), p. 9.

28 Pablo Arconada, "The Latin American Fracture: Mercosur and the Pacific Alliance," *Dipublico.org* , September 9, 2015, <http://elordenmundial.com/regiones/latinoamerica/la-fractura-latinoamericana-el-mercosur-y-la-alianza-del-pacifico>.

29 Ministry of Economy, Federal Public Administration 2006 – 2012, *Presidential Declaration on the Pacific Alliance, Lima, April 11, 2011*, (Proceedings Documentary, México 2012).

subscribed to some political merger.[30] This mechanism of the Pacific aims to address the hegemony of Brazil,[31] --one of the major trading partners of China--, and Mercosur in Latin America and counter its influence, since PA wants to establish itself as the strongest and most successful integration agreement in the region.

The economic and trade mechanism not only provides for the free movement of goods, it is designed to innovate, facilitating trade through tariff reduction, lowering barriers, dispute settlement, streamlining of operations for import and export,[32] with free movement not only of goods and services but of capital and movement of people. Thereby the PA constitutes an attractive economic mechanism to countries such as China: firstly for its sustained growth in the last ten years demonstrated by its members (with the exception of Mexico), which according to the International Monetary Fund (IMF), are economies with growth in all cases above the average growth in Latin America;[33] secondly because its members occupy the first places in the ranking to do business easily--Colombia (1st), Peru (2nd), Mexico (3rd) and Chile (4th), according to Doing Business 2015;[34] and thirdly, because all its members have trade agreements within the region having as one of their main achievements tariff reductions for 100% of trade in goods (92% immediately and the remaining 8% within a maximum period of 17 years).[35]

---

30 Pablo Arconada, "The Latin American Fracture: Mercosur and the Pacific Alliance," op. cit.

31 Arévalo Luna, Guillermo Alexander, "Geopolitical and Economic Integration," p. 161.

32 Abecé, Pacific Alliance, <https://alianzapacifico.net/wp-content/uploads/2015/06/abc_AP.pdf>

33 Nicolás Marticorena, "IMF Projects that Latin America will Continue to Slow in 2014", *Economy and Business*, April 9, 2014, <http://www.economiaynegocios.cl/noticias/noticias.asp?id=118662>.

34 World Bank Group, "Economy Rankings," 2015, <http://www.doingbusiness.org/rankings>.

35 "The Pacific Alliance," *Journal A new era for Latin America,* First edition, (New York: Pricewaterhouse CooperFirm, October, 2014), p. 7.

IV. Importance of the Pacific Alliance for China

In the past century the trade was focused in the Atlantic region; however, reality has led to a resurgence in the Pacific Ocean glimpsing a fundamental importance of the economic aspect for the overall future of the region. In the case of the Pacific zone, the mechanism of integration is strengthening its relations with Japan, South Korea, Indonesia, Thailand, Australia, New Zealand, and China, the latter with other Asian countries are all observers of the PA and in a dual parallel role are forum members of the Asia-Pacific Economic Cooperation (APEC).

This dual role of being a member country and/or an observer facilitates trade because according to the Framework Agreement a product made in country A with material from country B can be introduced freely to country C if all are members of the Alliance or have entered as a nonmember or have agreements with at least one of the members, such as China or Japan. This will allow a lot of activity in terms of production chains, so, surely, this mechanism of regional integration will become a worldwide reference.[36] The ratio of market liberalization promoted under the formation of the trade mechanism would not only facilitate negotiations with better conditions for Latin American countries planning a business relationship but at the same time are at a disadvantageous geographical position in relation to their peers who lie in Asia, and also helps position itself more competitively for the China market. China has become the first commercial export partner of Chile and Peru, representing 23% and 20% of total exports respectively (from 2012), and is the third most important partner for Colombia and Mexico,[37] Additionally the Asia-Pacific region offers a wide and growing market,

---

36   Gabriela Munguía Vázquez, Osvaldo U. Becerril Torres, Sara Quiroz Cuenca, "The competitiveness of Mexican textile products under the Pacific Alliance, 1980-2014," *RECAI*, Year 4, No.10, (2015), pp. 43-67, <http://revistarecai.mx/index.php/recai/article/view/115/82>.

37   "The Pacific Alliance," *Journal A new era for Latin America*, op. cit. p. 55.

bigger than NAFTA and the PA. If we take into account only China, whose purchasing power is increasing, who has more than one billion inhabitants, whose working class exceeds the total number of the inhabitants of all the previously mentioned blocs, plus added this is the fact that the Alliance's GDP is near \$2 trillion with a market of 208 million people, and a projection of Latin American exports of 55%,[38] then the whole picture indicates the obviousness of the projected benefits and the opportunity of wide benefits and advantages especially in the area of energy and consumption for the Asian giant.

i. The reasons for China's interest in Pacific Alliance

The reasons for China's interest in the PA can be consolidated in the interest that China has for most of the entrepreneurial countries of Latin America; however, a wider view addresses the major factors:

1. The natural intent or spirit of the PA space tends to free trade and tariffs among its members. Its relations open up a space in which the multiple agreements signed between its members and the global economies are in a bloc of an open economy and are more prepared than the preceding blocs in Latin America. This open economy that provides the PA fits China's economic aim and according to Professor Yuan, this goal is driven largely by China's concern in maintaining social stability through continued economic growth. However, this approach has generated diverse opinions that respond to different possible interests in a posteriori examination, so that Yuan wonders if global activism in China, including its growing presence in Latin America, is driven by these economic needs.[39] China has been very clear about the cost involved in leadership and, despite being in an open position, seems to focus its strategy on abstaining from challenging the reign of the U.S.-

---

38 Juan Antonio Fernández, Javier Cuñat, María Puyuelo, *Latin America In China* (Lid Publishing Incorporated, 2014), prologue.

39 Chris Ogden. (New York: Routledge, 2013), p. 99, 351.

- who looks at China suspiciously --, for it seems that although China is betting on diversification for ensuring access to resources and raw materials to meet demand and new markets, China's role as an emerging power or its strategy is not very clear although China's approach has been to develop a managed great power relationship with the United States and other key players, rather than seeking regional dominance.[40]

According to Yuan's opinion, there is little evidence to demonstrate that China's grand strategy is aimed at surpassing the U.S. as the world's new reigning power and, according to Yuan many analysts suggest that if anything, China is more or less a status power with limited but clearly defined goals. However, Chinese policy goals of branching out into the world to secure raw materials and resources and new markets do raise a number of questions about its perspectives on good governance and its own responsibility as a rising power.[41]

2. China has increased interest towards the most dynamic countries in Latin America, which are basically the members of the PA because their formation as a bloc develops the adoption of policies to promote the free flow of goods, services, capital and people. This initiative raises China's interest because it allows for better fluidity and therefore more likely to benefit from the synallagmatic relations between the different states with China, which will also contribute to the progressive acquisition of continuous development in the international arena, as well as stimulating domestic prerogatives (in the case of China) increasing its dominance in the aspects of integration, such as economic, political and cultural ties in the international environment. With the growth maintained for years, China has also revealed vulnerabilities in self-sufficiency strategy to promote socioeconomic development. Thus, the need for economic activism in the Latin America region is explained by its current economic needs in order to have access to natural resources

---

40   Ibid.
41   Ibid., p. 100.

and new markets for its exports.[42]

China's objective seems to be an expansion process to mitigate potential strategic difficulties and shorten the period of time to obtain supplies of raw materials and energy sources required by China.

3. Stability and sustained growth of economic and trade indicators show in respect of the PA that it is becoming a worry to the Mercosur whose economy contracted 0.5% in the previous year while the Pacific Alliance grew 2.8%[43] which places it as a stable economic mechanism with an optimum business climate where prevailing trust facilitates trade between two historically diverse cultures and where there is worthwhile investing going on. Although China has explained its general strategy for Latin America, this tends to readjustments according to regional axes, without it there would be a significant change in the opening strategy approach based on mutual benefit and win-win principles that have characterized its global strategy as already stated. Maintaining ties with PA members, in its Observer role, China encourages the balanced and sustained growth of the economy through cooperation and support to developing countries to increase their capacity for autonomous progress. In general terms, it may indicate that the principal explanation for improved Sino-Latin American relations was due to the extraordinary growth of China's international trade; this commerce between both parties improved as a function of that worldwide trend, not because China preferred to develop its Latin American relations. Moreover, these relations are characterized by a pragmatic and non-ideological environment where the several countries apply a foreign policy to China beyond their own desire or policy belief of shift leader.

4. It is important for China and its expansion project that the PA considers among its objectives diversification in political relations with Asia,

---

42 Yuan, Jingdong, "The Panda in the Eagle's Backyard: What Drives China's Global Activism," paper presented at the Workshop, "China in the Western Hemisphere," The Munk School of Global Affairs, University of Toronto, March 4-5, 2011.

43 Pablo Arconada, "The Latin American Fracture: Mercosur and the Pacific Alliance,"

being their target market, in order to maintain greater harmony due to the ease of interchange and the ensuing benefits to the parties. The field of political relations that China has been advancing has aroused suspicions due to the deployment of aid to the region from financial assistance to arms sales and international diplomatic support, though the support offered by China is not really enough for a continuous development of those recipient countries. The four member countries of the PA, along with other Latin American countries in the region, bear similarities that are valued by China and that facilitates a rapprochement between States. From the ideological struggles that were experienced both in China and in countries of the Latin American region to conflicts of a historical order that have been deposed, both regions gambled on the immersion in economic and political transformations for the benefit of the people through diversification of their international economic and political relations.[44] This is a highly appreciated similarity by China when observing how the process of the conflicts in both regions performed impelled them to find their own interests.

5. The MILA or Integrated Latin American Market initiative is composed of the Colombian Stock Exchange, the Santiago Stock Exchange, the Mexican Stock Exchange and the Lima Stock Exchange; it aims to promote cross-border investment. MILA is one of the most significant agreements of the members of PA and is the first initiative of Market Integration transnationally without the fusion or corporate integration at the global level, and by October 2015 had become the most important market in Latin America in terms of market capitalization (US$836,120 million in October 2015) surpassing Brazil.[45] This integration of the market has had a prolific success with 12 investment funds and with amounts managing over US$45 million; in addition there are more

---

44   Jorge I. Domínguez et al., *China's Relations With Latin America: Shared Gains, Asymmetric Hopes*, p. 25.

45   Pricewaterhouse Coopers , "Economic GPS," No. 8 (December 2015), p. 8, <http://www.pwc.com.ar/es/publicaciones/assets/economic-gps-diciembre.pdf>.

than 60 brokers which generates the possibility that if a member wants to buy shares it has options for about 750 listings in the region.[46] The success and confidence responds to its dynamism and ability to amplify the investment opportunities: investors can measure the performance of markets with a regional perspective through indicators that stock indices deliver to investors; they can know clearly the market rules according to reality and local characteristics of each member, stability and confidence climate are paramount in investment decisions.[47]

6. Closer political ties allow China a greater realization of the objectives set in its domestic politics. China's presence in the region has been widely interpreted as an attempt by China to displace the hegemonic power of the US. Chinese scholars have expressed their perception that some Latin American states want the presence of China to help balance American power but this is not the intention of China.[48] Although some Latin American countries have a desire that relations and presence of China will materialize as a force that achieves a "balance" to the U.S. domination, not all have the same perspective. Brazil and Argentina hope that China will be a "soft balancer" of the U.S. in Latin America by providing new political-economic options, but without expecting it to confront the U.S., while Cuba and Venezuela eagerly search for a political alliance with China to provide a "hard balance" to U.S. power.[49] However, neither Chile nor Mexico, Alliance members, has considered relations with China as a possible means of "balance" of American power in the region. The CASS's expert Jiang Shixue believes that both China and Latin America share interests in helping establish a new economic order and an opposition to the hegemonic

---

46   MILA Official website, <www.mercadomila.com> .

47   Nicolás Almazán, "MILA, achievements and challenges of an integrated regional market," June 17, 2015, <http://www.ictsd.org/bridges-news/puentes/news/mila-logros-y-desaf%C3%ADos-de-un-mercado-integrado-regional>.

48   Jorge I. Domínguez, et al., *China's Relations with Latin America: Shared Gains*, p. 26.

49   Ibid., p. 38.

idea.[50] According to the expert's opinion and by peering into China's strategy in Latin America specifically the rapprochements to the members of the PA, of which both China and the U.S. are members Observers, it can be deduced and understood that China's strategy is not poised to become the hegemon of the region, primarily because China has stressed such in its foreign policy towards the region, and secondly because, although gaining strength, it still lacks the potential to address and reduce the U.S. supremacy; in addition the achievements China has made in relations with the Alliance members has not needed the implementation of such a strategy. Then the question is: What is China pursuing in Latin America?

China has used both material and intellectual resources through its administration not only for pragmatic support but by giving an important address to the major leaders who have an influence in changing its political strategy in the region Asian. This has been interpreted as a paradigm shift in some parts of Latin America. Without this increasingly close relationship, it would have been considered as a threat to U.S. hegemony by members of the PA. Besides China has manifested reluctance (which has generated some ostracism) in supporting that rising trend. Some opinions do not discard possible difficulties in the future since China can present through its relations with the PA, or those generated by other actors to its passivity in the face of this hegemonistic issue, but safely pundits affirm their belief that all stakeholders perceive China's role in America and in respect of the U.S. as non-intimidating and quiet.[51]

ii. The Silk Road And The Role Of The Pacific Alliance

President Xi Jinping proposed in 2013 when visiting the four countries of central Asia, the project of jointly building the Silk Road economic belt

---

50   Jiang Shixue, "New Developments in China-Latin American Relations [Zhongla Guanxi de Xin Fazhan]," in Jorge I. Domínguez, p. 26.

51   Jorge I. Domínguez, et al., *China's Relations with Latin America: Shared Gains*, p. 48.

and the 21st-Century maritime Silk Road.

According to the Chinese government the project seeks to promote the economic prosperity of the countries along the Belt and Road and regional economic cooperation, strengthen exchanges and mutual learning between different civilizations, and promote world peace and development embracing the trend towards a multipolar world, economic globalization, cultural diversity and greater IT application. It is a positive endeavor to seek new models of international cooperation and global governance, and to uphold the global free trade regime and the open world economy in the spirit of open regionalism.[52]

This macro program to consolidate China-Eurasia raises an interesting point that allows an expansion plan beyond the continent. The expansion of the wider space through Siberia and the Pacific Ocean, and extending to Latin America, is not affecting the enthusiasm of Chinese investors,[53] and on the other side, China has also set up plans. It should be noted that China has with three of the four members of the PA, established agreements to boost the "One Belt One Road" initiative. China Development Bank (CDB) signed Memorandums of Understanding on Infrastructure Cooperation with Brazil, Colombia, and Chile, encouraging the machinery manufacturing industry to "go out".

Following this strategy, China, Brazil and Peru started a feasibility study on the construction of a railroad linking the Atlantic and Pacific Oceans;[54]

---

52 Ministry of Foreign Affairs, and Ministry of Commerce of the People's Republic of China, National Development and Reform Commission, March 28, 2015, <http://en.ndrc.gov.cn/newsrelease/201503/t20150330_669367.html>.

53 "Navigating the Belt and Road Financial sector paves the way for infrastructure,"August 2015, p. 1, <http://www.ey.com/Publication/vwLUAssets/EY-navigating-the-belt-and-road-en/$FILE/EY-navigating-the-belt-and-road-en.pdf> .

54 More than 12 countries responding to the "One Belt, One Road", project promotion is the main method", June 10, 2015, <http://finance.people.com.cn/n/2015/0610/c1004-27128806.html>.

all projects under the umbrella of a "special fund of Sino-Latin American production capacity cooperation" of US$30 billion will be set up by China to support cooperation projects in capacity and machinery manufacturing fields. With increasing economic and commercial activity in China, the Latin American economies along the Pacific coast are a business opportunity. If this is added to the trade agreements developed by the PA with Asian economies, the picture shows the constitution of previous steps towards an expansion to generate global interdependence. From the strengthening the Maritime Silk Road as the gateway to transpacific trade, the PA has played a preponderant role because it focused from the start exclusively as the supplier of natural resources then emerging as a supplier and building administrative and logistical operations. On the basis of the justification of International Trade and International Relations, the PA is the best way for a new phase in the China-Latin America relationship exerting interdependence through economic growth and stability increased through expansion of capitalism and trade.[55]

To the extent that the railway project materializes, it will contribute to achieving several key targets for domestic and foreign policy. China retains its interest in achieving support for its policy of "one China"; as well the implementation of the project would generate greater economic integration of China which would gain a privileged position and consolidate its international influence, because having projects on both sides of the globe would facilitate the creation of free trade areas intensifying trade and financial flows between countries in these regions, not to mention the impact on the streamlining and harmonization of administrative processes such as customs clearance and general freight movement. The question that arises from this successful planning is whether, over time and the positioning generated with the participation of China in the region, will China also dilute

---

55   Amitav Acharya, "Theoretical Perspectives on International Relations in Asia" in David Shambaugh and Michael Yahudaeds. (the United States: Rowman & Littlefield Publishers, 2008), p. 67.

the non-interventionist rhetoric[56] that the Chinese government professes? Although the Silk Road is a macro project which has started talking about the desirability of establishing monitoring mechanisms for investment and coordinate economic policies to ensure the success of the project, will it be applied using the same methodology for the construction of the railway? And how will this interventionist concept be assimilated in the region?

V. Strengthening Relations between the Pacific Alliance and China

i. A complex interdependence and a complementarity relationship

In relation to the PA, the interdependence is based on the structure composed of national companies that produce in their own countries of origin and export to the regional market. PA members such as Colombia and Mexico have increased interdependence with China equivalent to 44.8% and 13.9% of the total trade in Colombia and Mexico;[57] however, an interaction through this mechanism of integration constitutes a win-win stable relationship. The PA and China relationship is a complex interdependence because is the best one that defines that relationship and fits the concept of Keohane and Nye that characterizes complex interdependence as the multiplicity of channels connecting societies from government elites to NGOs, banks, corporations. In this case multinational companies influence internal and external relationships: "internal policies of different countries

---

56   Mario Esteban and Miguel Otero-Iglesias, "What are the prospects for the new Chinese-led Silk Road and Asian Infrastructure Investment Bank," April 17, 2015, <http://www.realinstitutoelcano.org/wps/portal/web/rielcano_en/contenido?WCM_GLOBAL_CONTEXT=/elcano/elcano_in/zonas_in/ari23-2015-esteban-oteroiglesias-what-are-prospects-for-new-chinese-led-silk-road-and-asian-infrastructure-investment-bank>.

57   José Luis León Manríquez and Juan José Ramírez Bonilla, "The Pacific Alliance. Scopes, competitiveness and Implications for Latin America," Friedrich Ebert Stiftung(2014), p. 21, <http://library.fes.de/pdf-files/bueros/mexiko/11062.pdf>.

interfere with each other more and more",[58] so there is an absence of a hierarchy in the interstate agenda; in this sense, the agendas of the foreign affairs of States are wide and diversified.[59]

Currently, the interrelationships between states are defined by the principle of cooperation. International agendas contain countless topics such as economic, ecological, energy and cultural, that have replaced those traditional ones, giving rise to new dynamics between actors to create procedures, rules or institutions according to the operations required for performance and allowing governments to regulate and control (domestically and internationally) transnational and interstate relations.[60] The PA leans towards open regionalism determined in practice by interdependence and economic cooperation; in this regard the mechanism of integration has undertaken various initiatives such as specific rules of origin in customs matters to generating broader convergences; it has made possible the integration of financial markets Bogota, Lima and Santiago[61] and recently Mexico; another initiative at the diplomatic level was consolidated with the opening of a joint embassy by the four members of the Alliance in Ghana, and the consequent interest in opening joint embassies, Colombia and Peru in Vietnam and Colombia and Chile in Algeria and Morocco responding to the concept of mutual dependence.[62]

Regarding the complementarity China has open fronts where it is developing slowly but effectively its strategy. One is through the China-CELAC; China is promoting a five-year plan to boost trade and pledging financial support in order to capitalize on the wealth of the region in

---

58   Robert Keohane & Joseph Nye, , (Buenos Aires: Latin American Publishing Group, 1988), p. 41.

59   Ibid., p. 42.

60   Ibid., p. 41.

61   Silva, María Cristina, "Implications of Latin American regional integration beginning of this century," Paper prepared for presentation at the , (Santiago de Chile, October, 2012).

62   Robert Keohane & Joseph Nye, Power and interdependence, p. 22.

raw materials, energy, and food. Another is aimed at promoting bilateral cooperation with the major economies of the region, which has high complementarity, such as Venezuela, Brazil, Mexico, and Argentina. And finally China is oriented toward countries identified by the PA and focuses on the expansion of trade through a Free Trade Agreements strategy.

The development of the interaction of these actors framed the strategic principle of complementarity, as defined by Borón promoting the harmonious development of the production forces of each part that is integrated through active and countervailing political forces by States.[63] This is relevant because of the opportunity to take advantage of exchange that promotes stability and stimulates the development of the regional economic structure. The complementarity perspective is to accomplish a structured relationship that allows the provision of inputs that contribute to the equitable, harmonious and systemic development of all acting parts[64] based on the greater interconnection and greater dynamics of the relationships. This challenge of complementarity itself generates profits given in terms of the benefits arising from the relationship in addition to the proper exercise by States to overcome barriers and achieve complementarity itself that generates the development and strengthening of the structures.

Despite the benefits that doctrine and practice show about the relationship of complementarity, this seems to respond chronologically to the approaches of China, and also to the apparent requirements to achieve the Chinese expansion project. The Alliance is made up of the four countries with greater economic dynamism and together they have generated growth that exceeds the South bloc; this mechanism is open and aims at the Asian market, and guidelines are established to connect the Silk Road from the ports of the members of the Alliance. Members keep the exchange of

---

63   Atilio Borón, (London: Zed Books, 2005), p. 169.

64   Roberto Muñoz González, Zulma Ramírez Cruz, "Theoretical considerations in regard to a new model of integration and development in Latin America and the Caribbean," , Year 5, No. 2(2012), p. 9.

materials needed by China and the spirit of competition drives them to grow. It seems that is a model that fits the paradigm of development. However, there is not a positive consensus on the benefits of complementarity.

Detractors believe that because Latin America depends much more on China than the contrary and that although China develops a relationship with countries as a bloc, China is still stronger and therefore, according to detractors China has a growing influence on Latin America.[65]

Against this background, the PA seems to be the most viable alternative to achieve the transformation that is required to continue the pace of win-win relationships with China and brings a new model of integration which should be a complementary means that contributes to the structural transformation of underdevelopment which requires the Latin-Caribbean countries to take the "form [of] unsubordinated competitive and committed integration with national and regional long-term development"[66] which in turn affects additional benefits in terms of safety and respect in the international community given the operational ability. Dr. John Chipman, Director-General and Chief Executive, IISS refers to the Pacific Alliance "... reminding us that the security dimension is, in fact, very important and that without holding security, there can be no prosperity".[67] All the items listed require adjustments in policy matters; in the case of the PA they must be realized in order to achieve successful integration, but this does not mean that political unity is the only aspect to induce the integration process.[68] The

---

65 Marcos Salas, "Why is China so interested in doing business in Latin America," BBC World, January 8, 2015, <http://www.bbc.com/mundo/noticias/2014/07/140714_economia_china_america_latina_msd>.

66 Olga Pérez Soto, (Cuba: Ed Félix Varela, 2009), p. 216, 235.

67 John Chipman, "The Trans-Pacific Summit. IISS Cartagena Dialogue. Second Plenary Session. Asian Perspectives on the Pacific Alliance: Q&A," March 7, 2015, p. 6. <http://www.iiss.org/en/events/cartagena%20dialogue/archive/2015-8d0d/plenary2-b370/qa-5a0b>.

68 Roberto Muñoz González, Zulma Ramírez Cruz, "Theoretical considerations in regard to a new model of integration," p. 11.

matter has been discussed so widely that in regards to the benefits that the PA involves if it were the "only game in town, all of us will, no doubt, speak of its importance, on how we need to move forward the cooperation."[69] But the demand is "to have a more pragmatic snapshot of where we are in all the different forums and to see where the Pacific Alliance Cooperation with ASEAN and others can be adding value".[70]

In general terms, it can be concluded that there is a willingness of countries from both Asia and Latin America to establish links to develop a complementarity to the benefit of both parties based on existing and future advantages, geographic location of resources, the priorities of regional development, and the strategic and sustainable projection. These factors fit the case treated and this interaction is modified according to development needs. As it was explained at the beginning, Latin America is evolving from being a provider to new stages of the relationship with purchase, participation, and new investments, so currently and based on theory, complementarity so far is beneficial for both actors.

VI. From Threat to Stakeholder?

There are conflicting positions regarding the Chinese presence in Latin America. Previously it has been verified that the welcome to China from Latin America has generated three different connotations: those who see China as a chance to exercise "hard balance" as Cuba and Venezuela;[71] those who see the exercise of a "Soft Balancer", as is the case of Argentina

---

69   Natalegawa, Marty, "The Trans-Pacific Summit. IISS Cartagena Dialogue. Second Plenary Session. Asian Perspectives on the Pacific Alliance: Q&A," March 7, 2015, p. 5. <http://www.iiss.org/en/events/cartagena%20dialogue/archive/2015-8d0d/plenary2-b370/qa-5a0b>.

70   Ibid.

71   Jorge I. Domínguez et al., *China's Relations With Latin America: Shared Gains, Asymmetric Hopes*, p. 26.

and Brazil; and those who in no way see to China as a possible "balance" of power in the region and who are members of the PA like Mexico and Chile. In addition, there are the views of scholars who differ in regard to the Chinese approach, and those who discard any concern on the other hand. There are many voices that warn of the true intentions of China in the Latin American region as a response to the U.S. presence in Asian territories. Ibid.

Increased Chinese presence seems to have coincided with the detachment of the U.S.; but the U.S. administration seemed to try to correct the past in April 2015 on the occasion of the celebration of the Summit of the Americas in Panama City, and urged the so-called Trans-Pacific Agreement, which would involve some Latin American and Asian countries, such as Chile and Japan. Precisely as a result of the presence of the U.S. President Barack Obama, the administration of Beijing was consulted about a possible dispute over the influence of both countries in the Latin American region; however, as has been the position of China, it highlighted China's interest in mutual respect and non-intervention in internal affairs of each country. China emphasized the benefits of the China-Latin America relationship and categorically denied the possibility, stating that "does not affect, does not exclude and is not directed against relations with other countries".[72]

Among the critics of the approach of China to Latin America emphasizes Dr. R. Evan Ellis, Professor of Latin American Studies at the U.S. Army War College Strategic Studies Institute, who says that China's presence is oriented to undermine the U.S. efforts to advance Western-style democracy and capitalistic free trade in the region,[73] and he further argues that the U.S. security is affected by the financing, investment and trade in China with regimes seeking the independence of Western penal systems and

---

72   Hua Chunying, "Chinese Presence in Latin America," Diario de Cuyo, April 11, 2015, <http://diariodecuyo.com.ar/home/new_noticia.php?noticia_id=664108>.

73   R. Evan Ellis, "The Emergence of China in the Americas," Military Review the Professional Journal of US Army, January-February, 2015, p. 73.

contractual liability.[74] In the same vein, Ellis recognizes that the presence of China in Latin America "is transforming the region, including the reformulation of the agenda of their leaders, businessmen, public," and also "hits U.S. interests in the region and globally, and how China complements and sometimes competes with other external actors in the region".[75] Faced with these alarming positions, clear-minded Western-Asian scholars such as CASS's expert Jiang Shixue believe that both China and Latin America share interests in how to help establish a new economic order and to oppose the hegemonic idea,[76] and also discards the possibility that China defies the dominance of the U.S. in that "the rapid development of China-Latin America relations has not yet posed a security threat to the United States, but China is currently in the process of becoming a political competitor in America's own backyard."[77]

Although critics against China seem inflexible, the rapprochements to the members of the PA, where both China and the U.S. are members Observers, should be taken into account. Thus it seems the picture of China's strategy is not poised to defy the hegemon of the region, primarily because as China has stressed in its foreign policy towards the region, and secondly because, although gaining strength, China still lacks the potential to address and reduce the U.S. supremacy. In addition, the achievements China has made in relations with the Alliance members has not needed the implementation of such a strategy.

Trying to keep an impartial stance on the issue, as there still is not a consolidation of power in the region, the scenario emerges that China is gaining more presence, with opinions for and detractors against, and the U.S.

---

74 Ibid., 3.

75 Ibid., p. 66.

76 Jiang Shixue, "New Developments in China-Latin American Relations [Zhongla Guanxi de Xin Fazhan]," in Jorge I. Domínguez, et al., China's Relations with Latin America: Shared Gains, p. 26.

77 Ibid.

is losing ground. In this condition, the following are some considerations about China and the U.S. in Latin America:

1. China has said its strategy towards Latin America seeks to consolidate friendship in a peaceful environment. China also has expressed respect for the relations between countries and does not practice a policy of intervention.

2. The PA is the integration mechanism which currently offers the highest levels of development and maintains a dynamic growth in the region. The PA is developing business with China, and its members are among the main suppliers of raw materials to China without mentioning that the PA is an initiative that has the broad and open support of America.

3. In relation to the previous point, the PA members are maintaining an increasing inter-exchange with China in terms of the resources they are able to provide; and also the Pacific represents strong advantages for China in terms of future connections for the purposes of infrastructure and creating Silk Road.

4. The largest group of the U.S.' critics who see China's presence as a "support" to their cause is diverse: some people support a balanced and smooth equilibrium or a presence that contravenes any American presence. Alliance members, which have been criticized as responding to the U.S. interests do not see China as a potential balance or threat either.

5. China, despite increasing its armament, does not have enough power to raise a confrontation with the U.S. and has focused its strategy specifically on meeting its diverse demands; in that sense, experts have stated that "for its growth, China depends on exports to the U.S., and the U.S. trade benevolence, far more than it could benefit from contesting the U.S. power and presence in Latin America."[78]

6. Related to the previous point, China has maintained a policy of

---

78 U.S., Department of State, (with Foreign Minister Ignacio Walker of Chile, Santiago, Chile, 20 November 2004.)

cooperation instead confrontation in order to get sympathy in the international community to achieve its main objectives.

7. The main objective of China is to maintain a foreign policy consonant with its internal policy and to strengthen international respect and recognition of its "One China" policy.

In the past, it has been questioned the U.S. government staff members have responded in various ways that feed the suggestion of China as a threat. Already in 2008 in a document called "The New Challenge: China And The Western Hemisphere" the Senior Associate, U.S. Policy Director, Caribbean Programs Inter-American Dialogue, Daniel P. Erikson, gave "Testimony before the House Committee on Foreign Affairs, Subcommittee on the Western Hemisphere" related to China's challenge; he collected some US positions in relation to the presence of China in Latin America. A partial transcription from the last page is reproduced below.

June 11, 2008

...Clearly, the United States does not enjoy the same comfort level with China that it has with the European Union, but nor should China's presence in Latin America be interpreted as a de facto "threat" to U.S. interests. Rather, China's evolving role in Latin America reflects the increasingly complex mosaic of international relationships that is a product of a more globalized world. China is poised to be a major player in the Western Hemisphere for the foreseeable future, irrespective of what actions the U.S. does or does not take in reaction to Beijing's growing influence. The proper U.S. response will be to strengthen its ties with Latin America and the Caribbean, maintain an open dialogue with China on issues of U.S. concern in the hemisphere, and carefully monitor the evolution of China's ties with Latin America and the Caribbean in consultation with countries of the region. The primary

goal of U.S. policy as its relates to China in the Western Hemisphere should focus on ensuring that China acts as a responsible stakeholder that contributes to the region's economic prosperity while respecting the democratic principles that are the guiding values of the Inter-American system.[79]

In the year 2013, the same government official was asked about the benefits that the development of trade represents especially in relation to China's growth. Daniel P. Erikson, also a Senior Associate in regional programs, said in relation to the commercial activities of China in that: "[T]he growing economy of China [has] forced [her] to seek new markets, a need which Latin America also shares for the same reasons. That's good for the region and, therefore, is also good for America."[80] He was discarding concern and discomfort towards the steps that have led China into Latin America.

VII. Conclusions

1. The approach and further consolidation of relations with the most dynamic and fastest growing countries in Latin America and coincidentally are members of the PA are not limited to a purely economic strategy for China. This is the gateway to the Latin American region to establish itself as a partner and develop different binding aspects to the region in order to meet its interests linked to its domestic policy. China in this way tries to achieve sympathizers and international support for its one China policy; with this known tactic, China hopes to

---

79   Daniel P. Erikson, "The New Challenge: China and the Western Hemisphere," Testimony before the House Committee on Foreign Affairs, Subcommittee on the Western Hemisphere, June 11, 2008.

80   Eva Saiz, "Latin America, the new field of economic battle between China and the US," El País, March 30, 2013, <http://internacional.elpais.com/internacional/2013/03/30/actualidad/1364601531_428554.html>.

achieve the total ignorance of Taiwan, anticipating the latent possibility that the Republic of China can increase its international participation to achieve more diplomatic allies. The opening of relations with the PA, primarily commercial, is an interactive bridge with other states and for various purposes.

2. The policy of opening relations with the most dynamic countries in the Latin American region, generating stability and sustained growth, willingness to diversify political relations and closer ties are just some of the features that promote a climate of mutual benefit and have propitiated the approach of China to the PA as part of its foreign policy towards Latin America.

3. The Silk Road is an ambitious project for which China is advancing initiatives showing its leadership in the international community with an inclusive and participatory but apart from the logic of blocs speech practiced in the past. In that sense, the PA outlines a future performance highly preferred because China's initiatives to connect South America by railway and the use of Pacific ports for connections to the Silk Road. With this in mind, the members of the PA generate greater participation initially as suppliers of natural resources and emerging as a supplier along with administrative and logistical operations. All of this consecrates the PA as the most viable initiative for a new phase in the relationship between China and Latin America exerting interdependence through economic growth and stability.

4. The PA emerged as a mechanism of deep integration with many expectations and so far, with increasing performance. Members of this integration mechanism maintain a strong and increasingly growing trade with China. However, the PA was born as a commercial and business mechanism of integration, which contrarily instead of rejection has raised expectations internationally. To meet the expectations, the Alliance requires establishing positions on peace and security, which must establish some changes in the political order to achieve the institutionalization of formal and informal relationships and thereby

generate greater confidence, which is currently supported by the economic area, to achieve greater integration with its target market: The Asia-Pacific region. Similarly, and because of U.S. support for this initiative, the Alliance can serve as a bridge in relations with China.

5. Complementarity is based on existing and future benefits, the geographical location of resources in relation to the priorities of regional development, and strategic and sustainable projections; these factors and their interaction are modified according to the needs of development and the result in intention of the actors to achieve common interests. In this light and based on reasons of economic and geopolitical strategy, China has signed three FTAs in Latin America, two of them with members of the Pacific Alliance and a third, Costa Rica, which is on track to become a member of the Pacific Alliance too. The Latin American side is evolving from being a supplier to new stages in the relationship as a purchaser, participant, and providing new investments, so today and on the basis of the theory, complementarity so far is beneficial for both actors.

6. China has denied its role as the "balance" in Latin America disappointing the expectations of most non-Alliance members. Besides speech that promotes peace and turns away from any possible conflict, China develops international relations aware that the relationship maintained with the U.S. is more beneficial in terms of cooperation than confrontation, and as well not to mention the weaknesses that China has. Meanwhile, although there is a degree of discomfort, the U.S. has expressed its pleasure in the China-Latin American relations so that the possibility of a confrontation is not immediate.